D0857713

A History
of Information Science
1945–1985

Library and Information Science

Consulting Editor: *Harold Borko*
Graduate School of Library and Information Science
University of California
Los Angeles, California

A list of books in this series is available from the publisher on request.

A History
of Information Science
1945–1985

Dorothy B. Lilley
East Texas State University
Commerce, Texas

Ronald W. Trice
Georgia College
Milledgeville, Georgia

Academic Press, Inc.
Harcourt Brace Jovanovich, Publishers
San Diego   New York   Berkeley   Boston
London   Sydney   Tokyo   Toronto

Academic Press, Inc.
San Diego, California 92101

United Kingdom Edition published by
Academic Press Limited
24–28 Oval Road, London NW1 7DX

Library of Congress Cataloging in Publication Data

Lilley, Dorothy B.
    A history of information science, 1945-1985 / by Dorothy B. Lilley
and Ronald W. Trice.
        p.   cm. -- (Library and information science)
    Bibliography: p.
    Includes index.
    ISBN 0-12-450060-9   (alk. paper)
    1. Information science--History--20th century.   I. Trice, Ronald
W. II. Title. III. Series.
Z721.L643   1989
020'.9--dc19   88-34856
                                                      CIP

Printed in the United States of America
89 90 91 92   9 8 7 6 5 4 3 2 1

*Our duty is not only towards things; it is also towards men,
and the message must be passed on from generation to generation.*

MIGUEL SERRANO
C.G. Jung and Hermann Hesse

Contents

Tables

Chapter 5

Chapter 6

Preface

In this history our efforts have been directed toward what a British scholar has called ''the attempt to discover the significant things about the past'' for the enhancement of the present. It was Geoffrey Barraclough who wrote that history ''should be relevant to our needs, and provide answers for questions which concern us'' (Barraclough, 1960). With these thoughts in mind, we have identified and examined three facets of information science: activities that have become trends, people who have contributed to these trends, and environments in which these trends have occurred. The projected audience for this book is students, faculty, and other potential and practicing information professionals who can benefit from a look backward to the beginnings of information science. In the first five chapters we explain five trends: (1) information science, (2) nonconventional information systems, (3) information science applied to libraries, (4) online activity, and (5) networks. Over the forty-year period 1945–1985 these trends have been cumulative. Information science has emerged as a discipline; nonconventional information systems have permitted such advantages as postcoordination of terms at the time of retrieval; information science methods and technologies have been applied to libraries; the first bibliographic utility has been created; bibliographic database vendor services have been developed and expanded; and computer and telecommunications networks have opened possibilities for new management techniques and coordination methods.

Although our emphasis is on trends, it is also on people, a selection of twenty-four of them who to us seemed to be specialists. They are among those individuals who have been instrumental in moving information science from the dreams of five visionaries through the creation of nonconventional information systems, the development of the machine-readable record, the services of online bibliographic utilities, and database services to the further development of networks. These several applications had the effect of increasing the kinds and number of computer and telecommunications networks, the kinds and number of databases, and the number of locations where services could be directed and received. Our apologies are extended to readers who do not find their favorite representatives among our selected specialists. Future historians may make other choices, but the major trends they will identify over the same period will probably be the same.

Besides the principal trends as indicated by the titles of the first five chapters and by the backgrounds and contributions of the twenty-four selected specialists, we also consider a third factor: activity from the information environments, that is, responses and concerns of other than the featured individuals, the activities of related groups such as those attending conferences on salient topics, the effect of technologies, the beginnings of large-scale evaluation of information systems, and other similar phenomena. We bring such items into the history of information science because they have had major influence on the specialists' work and on future trends. Throughout the chapters, we have reported on pertinent conferences—those that led, for example, to important decisions on new methods of information storage and retrieval or on mission-oriented information services. Conference proceedings can answer the following questions. What types of people were in attendance and why? What types of criticism and ideas were expounded? What plans were announced? How were these plans received? What key issues were presented?

We begin Chapter 1 with the establishment of the fact of information science as a discipline, then move to its already recorded history and to the backgrounds and contributions of five selected visionaries: Vannevar Bush, Norbert Wiener, S. C. Bradford, Arthur C. Clarke, and Claude E. Shannon.

In Chapter 2 we feature contributions of three creators of nonconventional information systems: Mortimer Taube, creator of the UNITERM system with its accompanying capability of postcoordination of terms along Boolean lines and coorganizer of *Science and Technical Aerospace Reports (STAR);* Hans Peter Luhn, whose KWIC index was applied to the field of chemistry in *Chemical Titles;* and Eugene Garfield and his application of *Science Citation Index* to control the periodical literature of several of the sciences.

We also consider environmental factors in Chapter 2, among them the 1948 Royal Society Scientific Conference held in London, which catalyzed the development in the United States of mission-oriented services for sciences, and a 1950 Chicago conference at which Taube introduced to librarians the idea of organizing materials along mission-oriented lines. We discuss informal and formal evaluation of information systems, and ERIC, the first nonconventional information system to be used in a soft science.

In Chapter 3 we report the transfer of information science methods and techniques to the creation of machine-readable records (MARC I and MARC II). These records combine with transmission of information online—Library of Congress (LC) with the Ohio College Library Center (OCLC)—to furnish online cataloging to libraries. This Library of Congress involvement succeeded the National Library of Medicine's MEDLARS system and preceded the National Agricultural Library's AGRICOLA. Machine-readable cataloging revolutionized the control of library holdings in widely separated locations as well as contributed to the development of the first bibliographic utility, for which Frederick G. Kilgour received the American Society for Information Science Award of Merit. In these activities "economy of scale" was obvious: a book could be cataloged once instead of the thousands of times that it previously had to be cataloged. Kilgour, Henriette D. Avram, and Richard De Gennaro are the specialists featured here. In this third chapter we also report on the beginnings of information science techniques in the development of computer-based information systems and transmission activities from the National Library of Medicine and the National Agricultural Library. We note the magnificent and key positions of each of the three national libraries for further expanding services.

Chapter 4 emphasizes database services but also examines the online public access catalog (OPAC), where focus is on the user–computer interface. The selected specialists here are Christine L. Borgman, Carlos A. Cuadra, Ruth M. Davis, Donald T. Hawkins, Charles R. Hildreth, J. C. R. Licklider, Roger K. Summit, Carol Tenopir, and Martha E. Williams. In Chapter 4 the concept of the cumulation of trends is gloriously visible. The online activity embraces the techniques and methods of information science from the machine-readable record—databases from which intermediary and end users retrieve according to Boolean logic—and researchers continue to demystify the user–computer interface.

Our study of networks, Chapter 5, incorporates bibliographic utilities, vendor database services, and library networks. It also includes ARPANET, TYMNET, and TELENET as the computer and telecommunication networks in this history that is also theirs. We here add Joseph Becker, Glyn T. Evans, Barbara E. Markuson, and Susan K. Martin to our list of specialists.

Significant summaries appear in Chapter 6. Table 17 is a review of the principal contribution of each of our twenty-four specialists; Table 18 is a summary of the conferences that we consider part of the information science environment. We also give a brief review of the trends that emerged from 1945 to 1985 and take a quick look to the future.

The following five points define this history.

1. This is a conceptual history. Information science emerges, nonconventional information systems are created, information science is applied to national and other libraries, online bibliographic retrieval systems are manned by entrepreneurial giants, and networks that incorporate advanced technology are developed.

2. This is an interpretative history. Tensions between information science and library science personnel are related; tensions exist between indexers, catalogers, and public service personnel as well; librarians fear the intrusion of outsiders into the realm of information services; an information technology expert threatens librarians with the menial task of dusting books if they fail to adjust to the new communications complex.

3. This is a history of the principal contributions of twenty-four representative specialists to the development and expansion of information science.

4. Writing this history has been an exercise in deciding the level of abstraction that would provide the necessary perspective to encompass and embrace the forty years of activity and related literature, without becoming entangled in the details.

5. This is a history that, while containing irony, humor, and, most

of all, well-documented facts, is meant to convey the magnitude of the change that has occurred in the past forty years.

This history of information science is largely reflected in the influence or spread of the basic concepts of information science. We judge this influence by the extent to which there has been a visible break from traditional methods of preparing and extending information services. We have reported mainly the successes. The one exception is the lack at the Library of Congress, at OCLC, and elsewhere of a subject system with the capability of providing in-depth indexing and Boolean operative flexibility at the time of retrieval. The major trade-offs are the massive collections that have come under bibliographic control, awareness, and access through MARC II and RECON and the many libraries both at home and abroad that have benefited from the influence of information science even when it has not been complete.

There have been many contributions to the cumulative success of information science. Technological advances have played important roles as have the people—visionaries, creative individuals, promoters, and others with entrepreneurial spirit in both for-profit and not-for-profit institutions. A mature and sophisticated literature and strong professional organizations have been significant contributing assets. Extraordinary growth and expansion is due somewhat to peripheral activities in the information environment; many aspects working at one time have accelerated expansion of services to a phenomenal degree.

The future is as much a mystery in 1989 as it must have been in 1945. Research, further technological advances, continuing and diverse sets of creative individuals, education at all levels, continued funding, and pertinent legislation are expected to determine the direction and force of information science. The electronic network still would seem to have fantastic potential.

We have been guided in chronology and in confirmation of our selection of trends by the evidence in the reviews in the chapters of the *Annual Review of Information Science and Technology (ARIST)* and their references. Besides *ARIST,* upon which this history is based, we have had access to several full-length histories of segments of the information environment that have been published within the past decade. Even with so much help, only a small part of the rich history of information science could be covered. Others, several of whom have already expressed a desire to write the history, may want to build on our beginnings.

One prominent information scientist remarked that in today's libraries and library schools everyone knows about MARC, about online information retrieval, about networks. However, the British information scientist and critic also noted correctly, when assessing Taube's breakthrough, that "it is difficult now to convey to relative newcomers in the field the tense and bitter argument, the absolute rage, which this system provoked," and that, "regrettable as this may have seemed at the time, it was this public argument which was largely responsible for shaking at least one section of the library world out of its lethargy and bringing it face to face with the new problems which were arising" (C. W. Cleverdon, 1970). The history of information science is a history of growth and expansion, of the insights and initiatives of many people, of the frustrations and excitements of fruitful communications, and of the achievement of a new level of information service for many users, a level that will forever be demanded now that it has been experienced.

If this effort is flawed in any way, only we are responsible. We welcome suggestions, either through the regular review channels or through personal correspondence. We have been helped immeasurably by many people, whom we respectfully acknowledge. We are grateful to the two editors of the *ARIST*, Carlos A. Cuadra (Volumes 1–10) and Martha E. Williams (Volumes 11–20), to the reviewers, and to the authors whose works are reviewed. We especially thank our series editor, Harold Borko, who by exercising the rare combination of noncommittal stance and positive attitude kept us writing. We express our heartfelt thanks to the editors at Academic Press. We appreciate the services of the principal libraries at the University of Georgia and at East Texas State University, especially those people therein who answered our questions, searched the databases, and filled our requests for materials. We want to recognize C. Hugh Gardner of the Instructional Technology faculty at the University of Georgia and Patricia M. Trice for their technical support in preparing the manuscript. We are grateful for the services rendered to us by information specialists at the University of Georgia, John L. Campbell, Mary Ellen Brooks, and Susan Field; and at East Texas State University, Diane Saucier, Carolyn Trezevant, Scott Downing, Marsha Blair, Frank Neuhouse, Marilyn Hoye, and Sue Weatherbee and staff. Associate Director of East Texas State University Library Donald R. Kerr, who has been deeply involved with computer applications to library processes, favored us by reading and commenting upon relevant sections in this book. James H. Conrad, historian and archivist at the library, advised on technical points of historiography. We have been fortunate in obtaining high-level guidance in all aspects of our work.

Dorothy B. Lilley
Ronald W. Trice

---

[1]Barraclough, G. (1960). The relevance of history. *Books,* **VI,** 41–46.

[2]Cleverdon, C. W. (1970). Review of the origins and development of research. 2. Information and its retrieval. *Aslib Proc.* **22(11),** 538–549.

CHAPTER 1

Information Science
1945–1968

Introduction

In the United States, information science (Heilprin, 1963) officially replaced documentation (Bradford, 1948) in the late 1960s (Borko, 1968a). The architects of information science in the United States wanted to be sure that it would no longer be mistaken either for the microfilm-oriented discipline that documentation had become or for the document-oriented discipline that was library science. This new discipline would be free of real or imagined appendages.

In much of the free world, documentation and library science exist side by side and are sometimes merged in their professional associations and in their publications, as is the case in England. But in the United States there has been no such merger of associations nor of the journals and indexes.

In 1909 the Special Library Association broke with the American Library Association and refused, somewhat later, to join with the American Documentation Institute, even as the latter was about to become the American Society for Information Science. Information science journals and indexes, in fact most of the literature, are clearly separate from the literature of library science, but both are beginning to cross over. Eventually they may merge, under another name, or one may consume the other, as has been the case with information science and documentation in the United States. The relationship between information science and library science in the United States has been and still is a spurious, uneasy one.

The factions involved in information science have walked a tightrope for a long time because, to a certain extent, researchers were forced to prove to financial backers such as the National Science Foundation that information science qualified for basic research funds (not as a basic science, because as one insightful researcher has pointed out, a science cannot be "basic" and interdisciplinary at the same time) and because library schools were better prepared than other branches of higher education to initiate curricula.

Information science advocates did not want to be identified with librarians (they even changed the traditional vocabulary), nor did librarians, for the most part, want to be won over by "the high tech advocates." As Shera and Cleveland (1977, p. 251) pointed out, one librarian, "whose name is happily forgotten, has defined documentation as 'librarianship performed by amateurs.' "

To understand the history of information science, one must first acknowledge the following phenomena: (1) Its terminology may differ markedly from that of library science or documentation; for example, information retrieval, descriptor or term, relevance, precision, recall, Boolean logic, and even indexing and abstracting. (2) To a certain extent, the discipline of information science has developed from interdisciplinary principles, that is, principles brought to the field by some of its new members, although Pratt (1975) has observed that in the past few decades much of the activity was carried out in libraries. (3) Whereas documentation in the United States yielded long ago to information science, library science may still be in limbo. Several of the library schools with information science programs have not been concerned with sharing new concepts with their library science graduates. Also, from the beginning, information science projects and research were almost certain to have personnel in the wings with library science backgrounds, if for no other reason than to keep the new breed from reinventing the wheel.

To the credit of the information science professionals, the literature of information science is amply developed. There are dissertations, research reports, conference proceedings, a variety of abstracting and indexing services, an outstanding annual review plus other significant annuals, and new periodicals that reflect changes in the discipline of information science. All these sources contribute to the foundation from which a graduate-level curriculum in information science is developed. Research has shown that the structure of a discipline's literature is a reflection of the maturity of that discipline.

The documentation movement began in Europe in the 1890s as an attempt to capture and record information for the improvement of science. This concept was transported to the United States in the late 1930s, where it flourished but gradually was either incorporated into or abandoned to the newer discipline of information science. The former died here; the latter was born.

Plan of the Book

Some of the people, events, and activities that brought information science to fruition are featured in this history. The only criteria imposed on our selection of what to report were that the people, events, and activities be within the authors' ken and that in some way they contributed to positive trends that affect us today.

Two working hypotheses have directed the inquiry: (1) The emergence of the field of information science can be traced to the following outside forces: a backlog of scientific and technical reports that had stockpiled as a result of research conducted during and shortly after World War II; a continuing increase in funds for scientific research and development, including the documentation and information science field; the availability of the computer; inspiration from several visionaries; and the forceful ideas and temperaments of those who actually initiated change. (2) Further developments are attributable to some of the same factors, but principally to increased and improved user services and to continuing emergence of new technologies.

The objectives of this history are to identify selected creative people from various disciplines; to describe their contributions to successful trends; to tabulate chronologically some of the events and activities that have led to the current state of the discipline of information science in the United States and in the world; and to clarify some of the terminology. We include a list of acronymns and abbreviations in Appendix A and a chronology in Appendix B. The six chapters in this book discuss the following subjects: (1) an introduction to information science, brief reviews of the evolution of information science and of existing histories, reviews of other historical works, a discussion of the availability of research funds and technology at the discipline's beginning, and an introduction to five visionaries whose writings between 1945 and 1950 inspired further changes; (2) nonconventional information systems; (3) information science applied to libraries; (4) online activity; (5) networks; and (6) conclusions.

As early as 1945–1948 there was evidence that information science was beginning to form (Harmon, 1971). By 1958, the International Conference on Scientific Information was held in Washington, D.C., and by 1968, in the United States, information science had become a discipline apart from that of documentation. By 1978 it was a mature and sophisticated discipline, not, however, without some problems. The most obvious problems were that research funds had virtually dried up and educational programs were still searching for identity. Meanwhile, technology continued to develop. Information appeared to be even more important than it was previously.

This short history spans forty years, 1945–1985, during which information science has germinated, matured, absorbed documentation, threatened library science, and now seems ready, according to some experts, to join forces with library science in a new, cooperative effort to provide information by utilizing the latest and most dependable knowledge and technology. This history emphasizes the principal creative people who were instrumental in initiating or influencing several trends. These trends are examined in the chapters that follow.

The Discipline of Information Science

Dr. Glynn Harmon, currently a faculty member at the University of Texas at Austin, is a graduate in library science from Case Western Reserve University, where Jesse Shera was then the Dean. One of Harmon's long-time research interests has been the study of the nature and content of the paradigm, or model, of the discipline of information science. Harmon's "Opinion Paper on the Evolution of Information Science" (1971) discusses the many people who have contributed to information science as a discipline.

Harmon has postulated that information science, as a mature discipline, would probably have nine divisions, just as documentation had the following nine at its maturity in 1966 (Harmon, 1973, p. 90): "1. Information needs and uses; 2. Documentation creation and copying; 3. Language analysis; 4. Translation; 5. Abstracting and classification; 6. System design; 7. Analysis and evaluation of systems; 8. Pattern recognition; and 9. Adaptive systems: artificial intelligence." Harmon (1969, 1970) has found that discipline paradigms tend to develop about this number of divisions.

Harmon considers the years 1945 and 1948 to be significant in the history or, as he calls it, the evolution of information science. He believes that the combination of Bush's concern in 1945 with providing the human mind with artificial memory together with Bradford's refinement and expansion of the scope of documentation in 1948 formed the beginning of the transition from documentation to information science.

The year 1957 was another significant turning point. By 1957, Cherry declared the unity in the diversity of communications studies and activities. 1957 also saw the shift from manual to computer-based retrieval systems as well as the appearance of three distinct categories of the documentation field in "Current Research and Development in Scientific Documentation": (1) Organization of Information; (2) Equipment for Storage and Retrieval; and (3) Mechanical Translation, and various emergent concerns such as information needs of scientists and potential contributions of other fields to documentation. (Note the vagueness of these headings; that may be attributable to the fact that they were the topics funded for research) (U.S. National Science Foundation, Office of Scientific Information, 1957). In 1959, a fourth area, Information Needs of Scientists, was added, and by 1966 there were the nine listed earlier, "at which time the documentation paradigm began to be challenged by the information science paradigm" (Harmon, 1971, p. 239). Harmon stated at that time that the information science paradigm may itself be challenged in a similar manner by some discipline with a newer or different scope.

Many researchers contributed to this discussion of organization, including Mohrhardt (1964), Fairthorne (1969), Vickery (1973), Becker (1976), Hayes (1969), and Borko and Doyle (1964), all of whom recognized Mooer's (1960) "information retrieval" appellation as a road sign pointing to the future. Harmon (1971) noted that general systems theory (Boulding, 1956; von Bertalanffy, 1968) and cybernetics (Wiener, 1948) were two other disciplines that influenced the full development and definition of information science.

Between 1967 and 1969, Weisman (1967), Gorn (1967), Slamecka (1967), Kochen (1969), and Kitagawa (1968) contributed to the information science paradigm. Harmon made three predictions: "an end to the era of the generalist in information science, that two more stable disciplinary subsystems should emerge in the early 1970s and that the information science paradigm could experience further changes" (1971, p. 239). In 1972, Wellisch addressed the new terminology.

Thus during the late 1960s and the early 1970s the discipline of information science emerged as a mature but still-growing discipline. In 1968 the name of the field was changed from documentation to information science. Next the professional association, the American Documentation Institute (ADI), was changed to the American Society for Information Science (ASIS) and Volume 21 of *American Documentation* became Volume 21 of the *American Society for Information Science Journal*. The information science paradigm has continued to evolve. These changes are reflected annually with the publication of the *Annual Review of Information Science and Technology* (1966–present).

Review of Existing Histories

In a speech to the American Association for the Advancement of Science (AAAS), Foster E. Mohrhardt (1964), then Director of the National Agriculture Library (NAL) and Vice President of AAAS, identified Ralph Shaw, Jesse Shera, and Mortimer Taube as the three pioneer librarian documentalists. Jesse Shera (1903–1982) was the principal author of the next work we review in which Ralph Shaw (1907–1972) and Mortimer Taube (1910–1965) are mentioned. These pioneers, as Mohrhardt called them, were intellectuals. Each was innovative in his own way. They often held opposing views. Shaw and Shera were both graduates of the University of Chicago with doctorates in library science, while Taube was a graduate of the University of California at Berkeley with a doctorate in philosophy and some previous education in library science. While many of the giants in information science were from outside the library science field, the history of information science rests firmly on a background of library science and documentation activities, particularly in England and the United States.

In the following we discuss three histories published in the United States during 1976 and 1977: Shera and Cleveland (1977), the March 1976 issue of the *Bulletin of the American Society of Information Science,* and Hammer (1976). Shera and Cleveland wrote a chapter in *ARIST* entitled ''History and Foundations of Information Science'' (1977). The ''Foundations'' section has been updated by Pranas Zunde and John Gehl (1979) of the Georgia Institute of Technology, who conclude that ''no sufficiently general principles have been discovered, and theories of information science are in the early stages of development. Most of the proposed laws and hypotheses have limited applicability'' (p. 80).

Shera and Cleveland consider the emergence of the International Federation of Documentation (FID) to be a culminating activity in 1908 after Paul Otlet and Henri LaFontaine, in 1892, had met in Brussels and decided to form the International Institute of Bibliography. Bradford, in ''Documentation'' (1948), explained in detail not only the origin of the term ''documentation'' but also the unfolding of the ideas of Otlet and LaFontaine.

Shera and Cleveland note that in the United States, by 1937, Watson Davis (1896–1967) had held a meeting to organize the American Documentation Institute. Among the persuasive points in favor of ADI were that it promised a microfilmed index to the world's scientific knowledge, a comprehensive abstract service to be established at the Library of Congress, and the use of microfilm to satisfy interlibrary loan requests. In 1938 the ADI began a journal titled *Journal of Documentary Reproduction*. Because of the pressures of World War II, the journal was discontinued in 1943, but reemerged after the war as *American Documentation,* with Vernon Tate as its first editor and Mortimer Taube its second.

Taube and Luther Evans (who later became Director General of UNES-CO) are considered to have steered the ADI toward the documentation functions tions and away from microphotography. Some of the technological innovations related to the microfilm era had been Kodak's Recordax camera in 1928 that made possible the microcopying of documentary material on a large scale, and Ralph Shaw's Rapid Selector. But it was Vannevar Bush's seminal paper "As We May Think," which appeared in 1945 in the *Atlantic Monthly,* that ushered in the new era (Bush, 1945a).

This new era was confirmed in London by the 1948 Royal Society-sponsored Conference on Scientific Information. By 1958 the International Conference on Scientific Information (1959) was held in Washington, D.C. Substantial practical foundations were now in place. Shortly thereafter the "search for theoretical foundations" began. Shera and Cleveland cite a moderately long list of contributions, among them Shannon and Weaver's "The Mathematical Theory of Communication" (1949), Schramm's "The Information Theory and Mass Communication" (1955), and Kochen's "Stability in the Growth of Knowledge" (1969), as well as works by Brillouin (1962), Fairthorne (1969), Artandi (1975), Bar-Hillel (1957), Verhoeff and Belzer (1961), Berry (1965), Weisman (1967), Otten and Debons (1970), Foskett (1973), and Vickery (1973).

Among those cited as contributing to the discussion of terminology are the well-known names Mohrhardt, Heilprin, Borko, Brookes, Hayes, and Wellisch. Credited with aiding the movement from documentation to information science are Mooers, Taube, Perry, Luhn, and Garfield. These latter are especially interesting because they had all developed nonconventional information systems. Other histories are those by Shera (1972), Borko and Doyle (1964), Gilbert (1966), Harmon (1971), and Becker (1976). Shera reviewed the movement from documentation to information science and published it in a library journal; Borko and Doyle evaluated nonconventional information retrieval systems and published in a humanities journal; Gilbert discussed the Shannon theory of communication in *Science;* Harmon reported data on the evolution of the discipline of information science (reported earlier); and Becker, as Shera and Cleveland point out, went back to the "Coonskin Library and frontier days" in his two-page history that appears in the bicentennial edition (1976) of the *Bulletin of the American Society of Information Science.*

The Shera and Cleveland history, with its 122 references, is well written and well documented. There are some obvious omissions, principally regarding education and practical application of research to "soft" subject areas for ERIC [Educational Research (now Resources) Information Center] at the Center for Documentation and Communications Research.

The second general history (as opposed to histories of a specific aspect only) to be reviewed is the full March 1976 issue of the *Bulletin of the American Society of Information Science.* These articles were written by 22 information scientists and cover 55 pages. Most segments of the information-handling community were represented. It was well planned and executed by its then editor Lois Lunin.

There are obviously too many articles in this issue to be reviewed individually, especially since each is only about two pages long. The main idea is that many individuals and groups in many institutions participated in the field and made the United States the stronghold of information science (or documentation) in the world. Although this is chauvinistic, it is, no doubt, true.

Among those involved, for example, were representatives of the Federal government from institutions such as the National Science Foundation, the three national libraries, and the many federal libraries and information centers, as well as individuals from the American Society for Information Science, many universities, and commercial and industrial institutions. The March 1976 issue of the *Bulletin of the American Society for Information Science* discusses the history of information science from its beginning through 1975. Much of its treatment concerns libraries, but not many traditional librarians are among the authors.

The only book format to date (1989) that relates the history of information science was edited by Donald P. Hammer, then a representative of the American Library Association. The book's title is ''The Information Age: Its Development, Its Impact'' (1976). It contains nine topic chapters covered by twelve authors.

Review of Reviews

There are five reviews of ''The Information Age'' that warrant our attention. One appeared in each of the following journals. Note the two to three ratio of information science to library science titles: *Information Processing and Management* **13**(4):260, 1977; *Journal of Library History* **12**:299–301, Summer 1977; *American Society for Information Science Journal* **28**:373–374, November 1977; *Library Journal* **102**:82, January 1, 1977; and *College and Research Libraries* **38**:342–343, July 1977.

Although four of the five reviewers comment both positively and negatively, one review was entirely positive. There is, in fact, much to recommend the book once consideration is given to the affiliation of the editor and his criteria. The editor was affiliated with the American Library Association (ALA). His criteria were that the book be readable and that ''the bibliographic trappings of academia be minimized.'' The reviewers were four educators; Professor Harold Borko of the Graduate School of Library and Information Science, University of California at Los Angeles; Robert S. Taylor, Dean of the School of Information Studies, Syracuse University; Professor Susan Artandi of the Graduate School of Library and Information Studies, Rutgers University; Professor A. J. Goldwyn of the Matthew A. Baxter School of Information and Library Science, Case Western Reserve University, Cleveland; and one university librarian, Fay Zipkowitz, University Library, University of Massachusetts. Taylor found the title ''pretentious''; Goldwyn regretted that the ''innovative and creative persons'' and their contributions did not come through; Zipkowitz did not find the expected drama; Artandi thought that an individual who did not know the field might not find a proper introduction; and Borko declared the ''editors and authors were successful in meeting their criteria.'' Their criteria were clear. But at least one reviewer, Artandi, said that ''despite the last instruction, most of the authors did provide extensive bibliographies, a valuable feature of their articles.'' Information scientists expect scholarly documentation. Of course, they also expect readable material.

There were several disagreements among the reviewers. Taylor thought that the chapter on professional education was "disappointing," while Artandi found it "interesting and well-thought-out." Zipkowitz declared that "the most irritating reading is Kraft and McDonald on library operations research which I am not entirely convinced even belongs in the book." Taylor, on the other hand, said that "Donald Kraft and Dennis McDonald on 'Library Operations Research' have written a good presentation of various OR methods from decision theory to stochastic methods." There are other differences of opinion, but it is difficult to get a critical consensus, even among top-level information scientists such as these individuals. Whatever the Hammer book may lack in excitement, it is only fair to say that all the topics are important and the chapters are replete with facts.

While the Shera and Cleveland chapter covered basically four main topics—the development of documentation as a profession through the emergence of information science that replaced it, the search for theoretical foundations, terminology, and histories, all general topics—the Hammer book covers nine more or less special topics: information retrieval by computer; library networks; the commercial sector; the federal sector; library operations research; standards in the world of information science; professional education in information science; the lessons of problems and failures; and historical development of library computerization. Some of these treatments are cited in this book at the appropriate place.

Other Historical Works

There are, of course, other works with historical information of value, for example, Herman Skolnik's "Milestones in Chemical Information Science" (1976). Certainly no one would quarrel with the fact that "Key Papers in Information Science," edited by Arthur W. Elias (1971), is a history. The latter is a collection of selected papers from journals that were published between 1958 and 1970. The *Annual Review of Information Science and Technology (ARIST),* Volumes 1–20 (1966–1985), serves history by annually presenting the priority subjects and their bibliographies.

We should also mention two excellent, specialized books. The first is Burton W. Adkinson's "Two Centuries of Federal Information" (1978), followed three years later by Scott Adams' "Medical Bibliography in an Age of Discontinuity" (1981). These works are written with care and authority. Adkinson, by his own account, filled numerous positions at the Library of Congress and was, in 1948, Chief of the Maps Division. In 1957, he transferred to the National Science Foundation as head of the Office of Scientific Information. When the Office of Science Information Service was established in 1958, he became its first director (Adkinson, p. 156).

Adkinson's book emphasizes "the Federal story," mainly the scientific and technical policies and programs from 1942 to 1972. He stresses the cooperative efforts between the United States government and other governments, as was the case with the UNISIST program, and with "profit organizations," professional societies, universities, and other institutions in the United States.

The book is well organized. It begins with "Federal Information Services, 1790–1942," and continues in chronological order through 1972. The remainder of the book is devoted to research and development (R&D) programs and studies, and relationships with other federal agencies and nonfederal organizations. The last chapter is "Trends, Persons, and Future Directions." Throughout Adkinson's book one is aware of a cautious air in the reporting but also of the authority of his point of view in light of his many years of experience in key positions, especially as Director of the Office of Science Information Service, National Science Foundation, one of the most prestigious and responsible positions in the United States during the years that he served. His is a truly great contribution to the literature of library and information science and to a specific segment of the history of the development of services through research.

Equally important is Scott Adams' contribution in "Medical Bibliography in an Age of Discontinuity," published by the Medical Library Association. The design and appearance of the book are beautiful yet effective; it is a welcome change in comparison with the many pragmatic-appearing formats that we have come to tolerate.

Adams brings sincerity but no particular caution to the book, gives credit where he thinks credit is due, and expresses apprehension when "things" start to go wrong. It is a book about mission-oriented versus traditional blanket services as well as the major figures in the field, but more particularly, as the title indicates, about information services in turbulent times—in this "Age of Discontinuity."

Research Funds Available

Adams (1981) pointed out how increased funds for research and for mission-oriented information services were characteristic of the post-World War II years and that Vannevar Bush was largely responsible for the new funding from the United States government agencies. Although much of the money was earmarked for science bibliography, biomedical research was not among the responsibilities of the National Science Foundation.

According to Adams, the 1947 federal budget for research and development was 58.9% of the national expenditure, an increase of 300% over the 1940 level. Even though the government expenditure had increased 800%, and university and industry spending had increased 45% and 84%, respectively, John Steelman, Chairman of the President's Scientific Research Board, recommended that federal expenditures for basic research be quadrupled, that expenditures for research in health and medicine be tripled, and that overall government commitment to scientific research and development be doubled (Adams, 1981, pp. 18–19). All types of information science benefited, in libraries and elsewhere. The distribution is reported by Adkinson (1978) (see Chapter 2).

Similar information was reported by Fry (1953), who noted that research and development expenditures in the United States rose from $800 million in 1941 to $2,930 million in 1952 (Source: Research and Development Board, Department of Defense, Table 1, p. 22). A parallel expansion occurred in England: $120 million in 1952 compared with $22 million before World War II (Fry, note 6, Chapter 1).

In an article that is inspiring for its frankness, Cleverdon (1970) asks: "From this mass of activity, what is there that can be selected as significant?" He refers to the research funds allocated to scientific documentation, specifically on the subject of storage and retrieval—10 projects were listed early on by the National Science Foundation in "Current Research and Development in Scientific Documentation." By 1960 there were 44 projects listed, and in 1966 there were 288 projects. Cleverdon's comments will be further reported in Chapter 2, "Nonconventional Information Systems."

Technology Available

"We are pleased to submit herewith 50 copies of our report." This statement is a common one from a principal investigator to his funding agency upon completion of a study. How could this be? The publisher, the Library of Congress, and the library are all bypassed. Is not the publisher the party responsible for submitting copies of an item to the Library of Congress to assure its bibliographic control? Does a publisher not also sell or contribute the item to libraries? And do these libraries not lend the item to library users? This is the dissemination problem that troubled the President's Science Advisory Committee in 1963. We all know that long before the 1950s there were electric typewriters that could deliver "near-print," and there were xerography copiers that could make 50 acceptable copies in a few minutes. Because of such technology, every writer became his or her own publisher.

Next came the computers. "The pre-1950 era was the pioneering era, when basic concepts were developed by a few people and computer feasibility was proven by very few machines such as Mark I and ENIAC" (Hobbs, 1976). Mark I was assembled at Harvard between 1939 and 1944 under the direction of IBM's Howard Aiken. ENIAC appeared in 1946, "a splendid example of the first generation, electronic digital computer." It was assembled at the University of Pennsylvania by J. W. Mauchley and P. F. Eckert, according to the specifications of John von Neumann (Davis and McCormack, 1979; Nilles, 1984). The ENIAC weighed 30 tons, utilized vacuum tubes, and required a cooling system when in operation. "Today's microcomputer, at a cost of 1/10,000, has more computing capacity, is twenty times faster, has a larger memory, is thousands of times more reliable, consumes the power of a light bulb rather than of a locomotive, and occupies 1/30,000 the volume" (Noyce, 1977, p. 65).

Before 1951 there were no commercially available electronic digital computers. Then, in 1951 Remington Rand introduced UNIVAC I and others soon followed. This kicked off a revolution by utilizing the transistor that had been invented in 1947 by researchers at AT&T (who, incidentally, had never considered that the digital computer would be its biggest consumer). The growth of the number of transistors that could fit into a silicon chip is as follows: 1960, one; 1970, one thousand; 1980, one million; and, projected for 1990, one billion (Renmore, 1980, p. 12). This second-generation computer experienced phenomenal growth for about 15 years, but in the late 1960s and early 1970s a third generation appeared that utilized integrated circuits, which allowed the powerful mainframes such as the IBM 360 and 370 as well as comparable computers by

Honeywell, Sperry Rand (UNIVAC), and National Cash Register (to name just a few) to be built (Nilles, 1984).

The fourth generation, for those who are willing to call it that, appeared in 1971 with the Intel 4004, the first microcomputer. Many others rapidly followed. The battle for the personal computer market is fierce—in 1983 more than two million units were sold in the United States.

At the beginning of this history, that is, 1945–1955, there were mainly second-generation computers. Their sheer bulk was frustrating and at the same time fascinating. Many of the operations that are now performed so quickly by the much smaller and more efficient versions had their beginning with those original monsters.

The use of computers in information centers and in libraries is now well established. So far we have spoken only of hardware, but there has been a parallel growth in storage media, though not of such large proportions. The advent of the video disk may soon result in another major change.

Five Visionaries: Bush, Wiener, Shannon, Bradford, and Clarke

Next we introduce five scientists whose work and vision have influenced information science. The first four are important to us mainly because they are so often cited in the information science literature. The fifth individual will be introduced separately. Harmon (1971) believes the influence of some of them sparked a change from documentation toward the information science era in the United States. These four are Vannevar Bush (1890–1974), Norbert Wiener (1894–1964), Claude E. Shannon (1916–), and S. C. Bradford (1878–1948).

These men enter our history between 1945 and 1950. Their academic backgrounds are diverse: Wiener and Shannon were mathematicians; Bush was an engineer; and Bradford, who was British, was a scientist and documentalist. Three of them, Bush, Wiener, and Shannon, were once affiliated with the Massachusetts Institute of Technology (MIT), Bush and Wiener on the faculty and Shannon as a doctoral student. They each published seminal work during the period 1945–1950.

Their principal publications during this period are the following: Vannevar Bush: "As We May Think" (1945a), "Science, The Endless Frontier" (1945b), and "Endless Horizons" (1946); Norbert Wiener: "Cybernetics: Or Control and Communication in the Animal and the Machine" (1948) and "Human Use of Human Beings, Cybernetics and Society" (1950); Claude E. Shannon and Warren Weaver: "The Mathematical Theory of Communication" (1949); and S. C. Bradford: "Documentation" (1948).

Of these publications, Vannevar Bush's "As We May Think" appears to be the most cited in information science literature. "Science, The Endless Frontier" was the key work in inspiring the increased funding that the United States government spent for research and development in the post-World War II period. It is also the one work that indirectly led to the establishment of the

National Science Foundation (NSF) in 1950. The book was reprinted by the NSF in 1960 on its 10th anniversary, in honor of Bush for his extraordinary vision. The book also had significant influence on the government and its attitude toward resources for the Library of Congress and other large libraries, especially for obtaining the literature of other countries so that at least one copy would be available in the United States (Bush, 1945b, pp. 118–119). This was also the beginning of an increased effort to foster international interaction to improved science bibliography. "Endless Horizons" (1946) contains a reprint of Bush's original "As We May Think." For information specialists it sets forth a visionary, imaginative description of an ideal information system, the "Memex," for the individual science researcher. In a later work, "Science Is Not Enough" (1967), Bush has a chapter entitled "Memex Revisited" (pp. 75–101) in which he admits that Memex had not yet been realized but that the technology (then) was making it a possibility.

When Bush wrote "Science, The Endless Frontier" in response to President Roosevelt's request for Bush's recommendations for post-war control and utilization of science research results, he held the position of Director of the U.S. Office of Scientific Research and Development. Before that, during the war, he was the initial Chairman of the National Defense Research Committee, during which time he had earned the respect of his colleagues for his unfailing "human characteristics which command the respect, admiration and loyalty of men who are themselves able, respected and admired" (Bush, 1945b, p. iii in comments by Frank B. Jewett, then President of the National Academy of Sciences).

Jewett gives the details and achievements of Dr. Bush's life (from "Who's Who in America" and "American Men of Science"). Bush was born in Everett, Massachusetts, earned a B.S. and M.S. from Tufts College, and earned an engineering doctorate from Harvard and the Massachusetts Institute of Technology simultaneously. He joined the MIT faculty in 1919, became Professor of Electrical Engineering in 1923, and was elevated to Vice President and Dean of Engineering in 1932. In 1939 he was elected President of the Carnegie Institute of Washington (Bush, 1945b, p. vi) and from there he succeeded to the positions previously noted. Wiener knew and consulted frequently with Bush at the Massachusetts Institute of Technology. Much of their concern was for a successful computer. The Charles Babbage (1792–1971) idea and design submitted to the British government in 1812 as a difference and analytical engine (Belzer, 1969) had progressed dramatically to Bush's differential analyzer machine of the late 1940s. Bush's machine was beginning to fill the gap by being "able to do effectively the sort of thing which Babbage had only dreamed of theoretically" (Wiener, 1950, p. 177). But Wiener dreamed of something different. He proposed ideas for Bush and the whole East Coast Group, including von Neumann, to consider in advancing the computer design. There is a suspicion but no sure indication that any of them heeded his advice:

1. That the central adding and multiplying apparatus of the computing machine should be numerical . . . rather than on a basis of measurement, as in the Bush differential analyzer.
2. That these mechanisms, which are essentially switching devices,

should depend on electronic tubes rather than on gears or mechanical relays, in order to secure quicker action.

3. . . . it would probably be more economical in apparatus to adopt the scale of two for addition and manipulation, rather than the scale of ten.

4. That the entire sequence of operations be laid out on the machine itself so that there should be no human intervention from the time the data were entered until the final results should be taken off, and that all logical decisions necessary for this should be built into the machine itself.

5. That the machine contain an apparatus for the storage of data which should record them quickly, hold them firmly until erasure, read them quickly, erase them quickly, and then be immediately available for future work and related to the study of the human nervous system (Wiener, 1948, p. 4).

It must be understood that Wiener was a modest and shy man. He preferred to remain in the background, although he was confident in his discussions as a researcher and in his forecasting. His self-proclaimed researches were in the fields of partial differential equations, during which, incidentally, he had "become convinced that the process of scanning, as employed in television, was destined to be more useful to engineering by the introduction of such new techniques than as an independent industry" (Wiener, 1948, p. 3).

Wiener did not hear immediately from Bush regarding these recommendations, mainly because the computer was not originally thought to have a very important place in the war strategies. But later on, when the computer became exceedingly important, among the several institutions that were already constructing computers (these probably included Harvard and the University of Pennsylvania) there was a "gradual progress from the mechanical to the electrical assembly, from the scale of ten to the scale of two, from the mechanical relay to the electrical relay, from humanly directed operation to automatically directed operation; and in short, each new machine more than the last," Wiener wrote, "was in conformity with the memorandum I had sent to Dr. Bush" (Wiener, 1948, pp. 14–15). His recommendations to Bush are, in effect, a systems design for the computer that was developed, that is, the von Neumann version. Although Wiener was working with a team of scientists throughout the war effort, and this team seems to have included von Neumann, it is obvious that Wiener's recommendations, if they were truly his, were influential.

Wiener's "Human Use of Human Beings" (1950) was, as the title indicates, a plea to let the computer do its work and release man for other pursuits. Eventually the computer may be able to do all that we want it to, but that is largely dependent on our efforts and some improvements in computers.

Wiener received his doctorate from Harvard University in the field of mathematics. He spent more than 30 years of university research, writing, and teaching at the Massachusetts Institute of Technology, where most of his colleagues and students came to revere his eccentric habits and profound abilities (Heims, 1980, pp. 330–346).

Claude Shannon's treatise on "The Mathematical Theory of Communication" (1949) and S. C. Bradford's "Documentation" (1948) probably run a close second to Bush's "As We May Think" (1945a) in terms of the prevalence of citations in the literature of information science. Shannon earned his doctorate at MIT in 1940 and shortly thereafter was employed at AT&T as a principal researcher.

Bradford, as previously noted, was both a scientist and a documentalist, and was a good choice to present the English-speaking world with this first general treatise on documentation since Paul Otlet's "Traite de documentation: le livre sur le livre" (sounds rather like Watson Davis' request for "documentation of documentation" that resulted in the initiation of the *Annual Review of Information Science and Technology*). In Bradford's preface to "Documentation" (1948) he described the book as a "fairly comprehensive text-book on the subject." In a way it still is, but so much has changed that it has become dated, although it was and is a landmark work. It communicates how the subject system evolved, sets forth the advantages of the Universal Decimal System of organization, points out its advantage on a continent with so many languages, and confirms to the reader how it is almost impossible to form a consensus on anything in a democracy.

According to Shera (1966, p. vii), Bradford was "the father of documentation in the English-speaking world." Shannon has been called the father of information theory (Gilbert, 1966). Wiener is surely the father of cybernetics; he even named his offspring. Bush might be called the father of the National Science Foundation, although he didn't get exactly what he asked for. Now that the first four visionaries have been identified, the mystery man, also a father, will be introduced.

Our fifth visionary is a giant, a man who most readers may know as a forecaster or a science fiction writer. He knew Claude E. Shannon for several years and met him again in 1976 during a celebration held at MIT on the 100th anniversary of Alexander Graham Bell's invention. This British gentleman, who had written more than 50 books, had been invited to deliver the concluding address for the occasion (Clarke, 1967–1977). In 1945 he wrote a seminal paper that was published in the October 1945 issue of *Wireless World*. The article went unnoticed except in California, where a group from the Rand Corporation realized its implication, a fact which was reported in the *Los Angeles Times* of February 3, 1946. The article proposed that we position communication satellites in space around the earth to facilitate radio and television transmission and ultimately, according to his plan, the reading of library catalogs and indexes, perhaps even books and articles. This visionary is Arthur C. Clarke. Forty years later, these communications satellites are in place.

Born in 1917 in Somerset, England, Clarke attended King's College, London, where he obtained First Class Honors in Physics and Mathematics. He predicted that "the communications network of which the satellites will be nodal points, will enable the consciousness of our grandchildren to flicker like lightning across the face of the planet. . . .They will be able to go anywhere and meet anyone, at any time, without stirring from their homes. All knowledge will be open to them, all museums and libraries of the world will be extensions of their living rooms" (Clarke, 1962, p. 21).

Summary

In Chapter 1 we have (1) documented the existence by the late 1960s of a formal discipline of information science with a projected paradigm of from eight to ten separate facets; (2) reviewed the recorded histories of information science, including reviews of one of these histories by several information scientists; (3) explained the objectives of this history, that is, the identification of five successful trends, the importance of a group of visionaries, and the influence of new journals and professional societies on the maturing discipline; and (4) discussed the problems of uncontrolled technical and research reports, a plethora of available research funds, and the need to integrate new technologies.

Lest we forget, information science had its European beginnings as "documentation" in the 1890s. Its purpose then was to better serve the documentation needs of scientific investigators. The discipline of documentation was transported to the United States in the 1930s, where it developed along the lines of utilization of film and its reproduction. Information science was to turn that tide since Americans, during the war, had become expert at storing items inexpensively so that they could be reproduced as needed.

CHAPTER 2

Nonconventional Information Systems 1948–1968

Introduction

Beginning in the mid-1940s following World War II, when research funds were abundant and the pent-up need for new information services was growing, creative workers began to emerge from a variety of disciplines. In 1945, as already noted, Vannevar Bush, by profession an engineer, published his projection of an ideal information system, the "Memex" (Bush, 1945a). Bush envisioned that the individual scientist could use this system in the laboratory or office to review research that had been accomplished in any given scientific field. The system could include all the articles, reports, personal correspondence, clippings, and laboratory reports that the individual scientist needed: a dream, perhaps, but one that galvanized others to action. New nonconventional information systems were to be a major trend for the next two decades.

The decades from 1948 to 1968 were a period of exciting activity for the people involved in information science, or documentation, as it was then called. At this time many different operating nonconventional information systems were developed (Bohnert, 1977). There was competition for research funds and for the unique and prestigious information system ideas that could utilize the computer, which had recently arrived on the scene. There was also feverish activity to invent and to utilize the various types of peripheral equipment and storage media. Information businesses emerged as did "many hundreds" of largely government-sponsored information analysis centers (Henderson, 1976). These centers mainly processed technical reports and disseminated either the items or the secondary documents announcing them.

Three Creators: Taube, Luhn, and Garfield

Three pivotal creative people, who designed nonconventional information systems that still exist, will be studied in some depth. First, Mortimer Taube (1910–1965) developed the Uniterm System, but he is particularly known for his ideas on coordinate indexing. Second, Hans Peter Luhn (1896–1964) designed various systems and products using computer applications; these include SDI (Selective Dissemination of Information) and KWIC/KWOC (i.e., Keyword-in-Context and Keyword-out-of-Context) indexes, and as a result of his researches with KWIC, *Chemical Titles 1960–* became the first commercial application and the first computer-based publication in the world (Troan, 1963, p. 19). Third, Eugene Garfield (1925–), famous for his many information systems, developed the *Science Citation Index* that established his Institute for Scientific Information (ISI) as an international information industry.

When these three creative people began to break the librarians' rules and traditions, some librarians were shocked and others became accomplices. Co-workers (documentalists and information scientists) in the various institutions reacted with jealousy, or cast disparaging remarks; legitimate and serious critics and evaluators of information systems had emerged for the first time. The three creators did not, of course, exist in a vacuum. The activities of other people in the information environment both influenced and were influenced by them.

Information Environments

Four types of information environments are discussed in this chapter: conferences, evaluations, the development of the first nonconventional information system in a soft science, and research into nonconventional information systems. Conferences, both national and international, provided opportunity for face-to-face communication in this rapidly changing field. Conference programs and their list of participants and observers proved useful and interesting.

In the following sections we discuss the informal criticism of the creations of Taube, Luhn, and Garfield. The new evaluation terminology and two specialists in evaluation are introduced. They are Wilfred Lancaster, a critic and evaluator who gained a reputation through his evaluation experiences and his written communication on a variety of aspects of evaluation, and Tefko Saracevic, who was particularly interested in the concept of relevance as it pertains to information retrieval. The relevance concept, as well as the concepts of recall and precision, developed mainly through the process of testing and evaluating the nonconventional information systems against traditional ones.

We then discuss the development of ERIC (Educational Research, later Resources, Information Center), the first nonconventional information system in a soft science, as a prime example of the rapid influence of information science methods and strategies, including the pattern of preceding the development of an information system with relevant research and of conducting evaluation studies after the system is operational.

Reports of the research conducted during this period and Wooster's modification of the statistics involved are important in determining the extent of research into information storage and retrieval systems (Wooster, 1971). Taube was the first to break with tradition on a major scale, but not before carefully listening, communicating, and forecasting.

Taube: His Break from Tradition

In 1948: Taube at the Royal Society Scientific Information Conference

We have already noted how drastically scientific research and development increased after World War II. As a result there was not only a backlog but also increased current research reports from scientists who were utilizing the new funds to advance their scientific endeavors and at least theoretically to improve the economic and social conditions of their various countries. Acting on this and the accompanying problems, the Royal Society Empire Conference of 1946 (London) ended with a mandate to convene a conference of personnel from libraries, societies, and institutions responsible for publishing abstracting and information services for the purpose of solving the increasingly difficult questions of the collection, organization, promotion, distribution, and use of scientific literature. The Royal Society recommended that this conference be limited to consideration of the problems of use by and service to the scientific community, that the conference embrace all sciences, and that appropriate authorities from several locations, including the United States, be invited. The conference was carefully planned and convened, and the proceedings were published (Royal Society, 1948).

Among the papers presented was one of particular significance delivered by Jason Farradane, a British information officer who was well known in the United States. He spoke on ''The Scientific Approach to Documentation'' (Farradane, 1948), during which he covered such topics as the need to have a list of journals that publish original work and the need for improvement in the abstracting and indexing services. Perhaps his most important recommendation was that the conference reject the UDC (Universal Decimal Classification) as a system for organizing scientific information.

One may speculate that Farradane's decision influenced Mortimer Taube, the invited guest of the U.S. Library of Congress, who, just two years later in 1950 at the University of Chicago, was the sole advocate of mission-oriented bibliography and service, as opposed to the general, traditional library classification. It should be noted that Farradane's recommendation was not included in the final recommendations of the 1948 conference (pp. 203–204). Among other salient points brought out at the conference were that computers were useful in the designing of new information systems (pp. 158–159) and that there are times when scientists need to be able to coordinate terms at the time of the search (pp. 680–685).

In 1950: Taube at the Chicago Conference

On July 24–29, 1950, the 15th Annual Conference of the Graduate Library School of the University of Chicago was held with Jesse H. Shera and

Margaret E. Eagan as directors. This was two years after the London conference. At the time of the 1948 conference, Taube had been at the Library of Congress as Head of the Science and Technology Project. By 1950 he had transferred to the Atomic Energy Commission as Deputy Director of the Technical Information Section, and by 1952 he had left the Commission to form his own company (Adkinson, 1978, p. 161). At the conference Taube (1951) proposed that science bibliography should organize along mission-oriented lines. Adams reported that "in his paper for the Chicago Conference, Dr. Taube effectively ridicules both the concept of a complete national bibliography and the proposal that subject bibliographies be constructed from it" (Adams, 1981, pp. 10–11). In making his plea for specialized separation to facilitate individual disciplines, Taube was asking, in effect: Do those who need and use *Chemical Abstracts* or *Nuclear Science Abstracts* need the complete national bibliography? Taube's Documentation, Inc., was to receive the first contract to provide information services on an international basis to the National Aeronautics and Space Administration (NASA), which was established in 1958 (Adkinson, 1978, p. 175).

Needless to say, even after the Chicago conference, librarians held to their ingrained preference for Universal Bibliographic Control (UBC), both at the Library of Congress level and at the international level as represented by the International Federation of Library Associations (IFLA) (Adams, 1981, p. 11). But, according to Adams, "the information scientists have dedicated their abilities to the creation of sectorial science information systems at the national level and to UNESCO's UNISIST program at the international level" (1981, p. 11). Adams paid the ultimate compliment: "In a real sense, Taube was a prophet of things to come" (p. 12). After Taube's death, Shera wrote: "He was, in many ways, the Melvil Dewey of the mid-20th century" (Shera, 1978, pp. 512–513).

It is easy to see how librarians and information scientists came to take different routes. The precedents are numerous. At Chicago, Taube had strengthened his case by recalling for his audience how the Library of Congress had rejected the Army Medical Library's "W" classification schedule for medicine and how the medical library had responded to this rejection. Taube, of course, stated that "the specialist saw no point in sacrificing his special interests to an alien unity" (Taube, quoted in Adams, 1981, p. 11).

It is understandable that there is a mutual wariness regarding close alliances for any but the most temporary time periods. At this stage of development, it is clear that librarians, at least the majority of those at Chicago, would not change. Most of us who passed through the library schools in the 1960s understood the consequences if any of us had suggested a major change in the classification scheme. Information scientists had no such qualms. Taube's students can attest to the fact that he had absolutely no respect for consistency, especially since it might mean consistently wrong. As Herb White has noted, "Mort Taube had strong convictions. . . . His ideas were frequently controversial, but that was largely because he was so often well ahead of contemporary thinking" (White, 1965, p. 603).

Wilfred Lancaster (1968b, p. 32) has noted that "there is little doubt that the real impetus to modern methods of information retrieval was given by Mortimer Taube, founder of Documentation, Incorporated." The significant contribution was the breaking with traditional information systems such as the

Universal Decimal System and the Library of Congress Classification System and not necessarily the tremendous value of the Uniterm System and the capability of coordinating terms at the time of the search. It is the capability of bringing terms together *at the time of the searching* that is significantly different, not the coordinate indexing system itself, for all subject systems can bring terms together. Also important is the capability of fully exploiting the Boolean operations of intersection, alternation, and complementation that Lancaster found to be amazing (Lancaster, 1968b, p. 33). Taube's critics counter that he was not original. Taube never said that he had original thoughts in this regard. He merely applied the best thoughts of others in decision making, with perhaps some confirmation from the Royal Society Conference in 1948 and elsewhere. Adams summarized Taube's contributions as follows: "Much credit must be given to Dr. Mortimer Taube and his concept of coordinate indexing, which involved the posting of items to subject terms, for establishing the principle of the inverted file and for introducing the Booleian [*sic*] operatives 'and', 'or', and 'not' as basic elements of search strategies for computer files" (Adams, 1981, p. 60).

Cleverdon noted in his critique of research in information storage and retrieval during this period that Taube was in the enviable position of having formed his own company (Taube was now the boss) and while "coordinate indexing was not a new concept . . . combined with commercial exploitation of the technique, the new element was the emphasis on what virtually amounted to an uncontrolled vocabulary" (Cleverdon, 1970, p. 539).

Reaction to Taube's move was, in some instances, extreme. Cleverdon recalled that "it is difficult now to convey to relative newcomers in the field the tense and bitter argument, the absolute rage, which this system provoked." He further remarked that "regrettable as this may have seemed at the time, it was this public argument which was largely responsible for shaking at least one section of the library world out of its lethargy and bringing it face to face with the new problems which were arising" (Cleverdon, 1970, p. 539). The reason Taube insisted on his unique system appears to be that he worked at the Library of Congress long enough to have experienced the bulkiness, the slowness, and the inappropriateness of the Library of Congress Classification System (LCCS) for organizing the scientific literature in this emergency. Our national medical library had rejected it long ago.

The inefficient LCCS would eventually yield to those who were committed to improving it. Taube had been told by his good friend at the Atomic Energy Commission, Bernard Fry, librarian and public administrator, how at that agency and elsewhere, he and others had observed the lack of organization of the multitude of technical reports being generated largely from U.S. Government-sponsored research (Fry, 1953). Many of these reports lay uncataloged and therefore unavailable to such an extent that the same research could be refunded for lack of evidence of its prior acceptance and funding.

Taube realized that the computer could help organize the report literature and what was needed in conjunction with the computer was the technology for utilizing some form of logic, which turned out to be Boolean. At the time there were only second-generation computers with which to work on mechanizing his already manually operative Uniterm System. Although his was not the first coordinate system, it probably was the first computer-based, postcoordinate, subject retrieval system. Lancaster (1968b) considered this to be Taube's great contribution to computer-based retrieval. Taube's was apparently the first such system to be widely used. Kilgour (1976) noted that the first computer-based systems were used in engineering libraries, where the simplicity of the Uniterm System was very appealing.

A reading of Taube's five volumes, ''Studies in Coordinate Indexing'' (1953–1959), will explain his views on many issues as well as the views of others. For example, he reveals (1954, Vol. 2) that he probably was inspired by Bush and also by his colleagues and contemporaries who designed or reviewed systems such as Mooer's Zatocoding System and any number of the punched-card and peek-a-boo systems.

Not revealed in these volumes is the fact that he surely was inspired by the prospect of receiving the contract from NASA that Documentation, Incorporated fulfilled with *Scientific and Technical Aerospace Reports (STAR)* beginning with Volume 1, January 8, 1963, and continuing through 1968 when the contract, as is customary in government operations, was awarded elsewhere. *STAR* was devoted entirely to the report literature. The contract also included *International Aerospace Abstracts,* which covered books, periodicals, and other published literature. The two secondary periodicals functioned as one system in terms of utilizing identical subject categories. The two information services were intended to provide comprehensive service.

In 1958: The Taube–Wooster Conference—The Search for Agreement on Principles for a New Information Storage and Retrieval System

On March 17–18, 1958, Taube and Wooster (1958) were hosts to an Information Storage and Retrieval conference in Washington, D.C., that clarified for both participants and observers some of the ideas that were developing in the area of nonconventional information systems. By this date, Taube was President of the Board of his own company and Wooster was affiliated with the Air Force Office of Scientific Research (AFOSR). Besides Taube and Wooster there were 15 invited participants as well as 150 additional observers. Of the 15 participants, several were to exert influence on further development toward the field of information science. These included Charles Bernier, then of *Chemical Abstracts;* Robert M. Hayes, then of Magnavox and since 1975 Dean of the Graduate School of Library and Information Science at the University of California at Los Angeles; Laurence B. Heilprin, then of the Council on Library Resources and later on the faculty of the University of Maryland; Hans Peter Luhn of International Business Machines (IBM), now deceased, but not before making his substantial contributions to the information science field; and Calvin N. Mooers, then of the Zator Company. Equally well-known names appear on the list of observers: Jesse H. Shera, then Dean of the Library School at Western Reserve University; Foster Mohrhardt, Director, National Agricultural Library; Frank B. Rogers, Director, National Library of Medicine; Richard Angell, Henry Dubester, Charles Gottschalk, David Haykin, Williard Hess, Robert Newhall, and John Sherrod of the Library of Congress, and Lea Bohnert, Marshall C. Yovits, and Gerald Jahoda, all well known in the information science field today.

It is apparent that the guest and participant list at this conference (this one was actually called a symposium) is a telltale document. Present were both the enthusiasts for and some of the critics of the new trends in the field. The criticisms expressed were a healthy sign of the increasing vitality and maturity of the field.

The following are lists of papers presented at the symposium. Part I contains the working papers that Taube prepared and sent to the participants before the symposium. The papers appear in Part I of "Information Storage and Retrieval" (Taube and Wooster, 1958). Also in Part I is a list of Terminological Standards and a list of participants with their affiliations (not shown here). Part II contains the papers presented at the symposium by the participants. The published version includes a record of the discussions that took place following the presentations, as well as opening remarks by Colonel Frank Moyers, Vice Commander, Air Force Office of Scientific Research, and Harold Wooster, Symposium Chairman. A list of observers and their affiliations completes the report.

Part I: Taube Working Papers

1. The Scope and Limits of the Problem
2. Historical Solutions
3. The Present State of Theory with an Addendum on Indexing, Language, and Meaning
4. The Present State of Devices and Systems
5. Future Research in Theory
6. Future Development of Devices and Systems

Part II: Participant Working Papers

- The Relation of Storage to Retrieval, by Alexander Kreithen from Documentation, Inc.
- The Relation of Physical to Symbolic Systems, by Ralph Shaw, Rutgers University
- The Logic of Retrieval Devices, by Mortimer Taube
- Digital Coding for Information Retrieval, by Calvin Mooers of Zator Co.
- The Grouping and Arranging of Terms, Items, and Their Codes, by Eugene Wall of Dupont
- The Environment and the Requirements of a System, by Charles Bernier of *Chemical Abstracts*
- Indexing, Language, and Meaning, by H. P. Luhn of IBM

(Taube and Wooster, 1958, pp. v–x)

Luhn: His Computer-Based Creations

Among the foregoing working papers by Taube, the papers presented for discussion by 6 of the 17 participants, and the carefully considered discussions that followed, the paper by H. P. Luhn presented a potent concept that was new to most librarians and documentalists. It was Luhn's answer to an age-old question that had been confronting librarians and documentalists for some time: Who is responsible for indexing and abstracting documents? His answer: the computer.

Shera has gone to some pains to explain how librarians lost that prerogative and how indexing (and presumably abstracting) had become the responsibility of documentalists:

> The abandonment of an important and previously well-recognized part of professional responsibility not only weakened the prestige of the library profession in relation to other professional groups but, more important, immeasurably weakened and stultified the growth of the intellectual discipline of librarianship. The segment of librarianship which has thus been sloughed off was picked up and developed by the growing group of documentalists. (Shera, 1966, p. 27)

Although librarians in special libraries were more likely to accept the responsibility, the problem was universal. The documentalists apparently were no more accustomed to the new information systems than were the librarians. With the advent of new systems, library schools began to make proposals, plan curricula, and receive funds, as happened at the University of Maryland (1966).

At least partially because of Luhn's work, continuing attention has been paid to automatic indexing and abstracting as a research area by investigators such as Salton (1970, 1971a,b), Bookstein and Swanson (1974, 1975), and others. Textbooks by Borko and Bernier (1975, pp. 161–186; 1978, pp. 113–137) and by Cleveland and Cleveland (1983) dedicate a considerable portion of their texts if not, in the case of Borko and Bernier, to completely constructing the index and the abstract by computer as Luhn had foreseen (Luhn, 1957, 1958a, 1968a,b), at least to employing the computer in an "assisting capacity." The Clevelands refer to Luhn's work and include a chapter in their book entitled "Automatic Methods." Library school dissertations from Jahoda (1960) to Svenonius (1971), to name only two, have devoted considerable effort to research on indexing, much of it reflecting the concerns of future information scientists.

Hans Peter Luhn was an engineer by education and an IBM inventor when we first heard of him. In the 1940s, at his beginning with IBM, he was given his own enclave in New York City. He later moved around the IBM environs until 1956/1957 when IBM named him their Manager of Information Retrieval. Shortly after this they transferred him to "research" and he moved his headquarters to Yorktown Heights (Schultz, 1968). From the beginning he was revered and supported, not because IBM adopted many of his 80 plus inventions, which they did not, but because he served as a catalyst for other inventors, thereby enlarging the total adoptable output. Moore put it this way: "Although not many of his numerous inventions have been incorporated in IBM product lines, the constant flow of ideas and fresh approaches to engineering problems challenged his associations to develop the solutions that did reach production" (1968, p. 20).

Luhn attributed his interest in the field of information retrieval to the request of James W. Perry and Malcom Dyson, in 1948, to join with them to "develop and test a pioneer electronic information searching system that became known as the 'Luhn Scanner' " (Moore, 1968, p. 19). In 1953, after Luhn had met Perry, who first piqued his interest in the information field, and before IBM crowned him their Manager of Information Retrieval (Schultz, 1968, p. 7), Luhn published his first paper in the new field. This was entitled "A New Method of Recording and Searching Information" (Luhn, 1953).

In 1958: The Luhn Scanner, KWIC, KWOC, and SDI— Topics of Conversation at the International Conference on Scientific Information

It is interesting to note that at the 1958 International Conference, Luhn was demonstrating not only the Luhn Scanner but also Taube's machine, that is, Taube's before IBM modified and built it. Originally this machine was called the COMAC (Continuous Multiple Access Collator). Rogers (1960b, p. 490) considered it "an ingenious idea," though not more ingenious, probably, than the Luhn Scanner. There appeared to be no animosity between the two men. Both machines are explained in detail in Taube's "Studies in Coordinate Indexing" (1953–1959, see Taube, Vol. 5, pp. 72–139, 1959).

Luhn was on the planning committee for the International Conference for Scientific Information that was held in 1958 in Washington, D.C., under the sponsorship of the National Science Foundation, the National Academy of Sciences, and the American Documentation Institute. Two papers were distributed at this conference on the subject of permuted indexes prepared by machine. The first of these was by Luhn (Fischer, 1966, p. 57) and the second by Citron *et al.* (1958). Luhn's classic paper on the subject of the Keyword-in-Context Index for Technical Literature (KWIC index) was issued in 1959 as an IBM technical paper and also published the next year in *American Documentation* (Luhn, 1959a, 1960, 1968c).

Since by this time both the process and the applications are well known, only the aforementioned classic reference and one other, a retrospective review to 1966 are cited here (Fischer, 1966). Fischer noted that Luhn coined the term KWIC in 1958 and the process was accepted by the American Chemical Society, which received a $150,000 grant from the National Science Foundation to produce its publication *Chemical Titles*. Volume 1, Number One is dated April 5, 1960 (Schultz, 1968, p. 12). This publication, conceived as a current awareness tool for the field of chemistry, was announced at the April 1960 meeting of the American Chemical Society held in Cleveland (Fischer, 1966, p. 59). In 1985, from observations in chemistry departments across the country, it was still alive and running smoothly. Hundreds of applications of the KWIC/KWOC indexes have been utilized by prestigious and utilitarian institutions alike with modifications to suit the needs and whims of the users.

KWOC, Keyword-out-of-Context, was designed to compensate for an author's negligence, or inability when faced with the need, to explain a work's content by its title. Some researchers were famous for not disclosing the true contents by the titles. This usually happens in the soft sciences. According to

Fischer (1966, p. 63), KWOC indexes are very popular, for example, the *Annual Review of Information Science and Technology* uses one. Usually the need for a KWOC is sensed when additional keywords are to be assigned; but an obscure title necessitates the use of KWOC.

Selective Dissemination of Information (SDI) was introduced by Luhn shortly after his introduction of the KWIC/KWOC index. In a way it was an application of his KWIC. The need was expressed by Luhn in the following manner: "Effective dissemination of scientific information has of late become the subject of major interest and concern because of the realization that it is apt to play a decisive part in the race for leadership in technological accomplishments, be it among nations or be it among organizations and businesses within a nation" (Luhn, 1959b, 1968d, p. 246).

A good summary of the activity in SDI was presented by a University of Chicago graduate student under a training grant in medical librarianship from the National Library of Medicine (Connor, 1967, 1971). An SDI system consists of matching an individual researcher's interest profile with that of the current literature in all formats. The system can be modified in different ways by different institutions. A group profile has been one of the successful modifications. Other current awareness tools were to be forthcoming.

In 1963: Luhn Revealed New Use for the Computer

At the 1963 annual meeting of the American Documentation Institute, where Luhn was Program Director by virtue of being the incoming President, he chalked up another exciting first: he earned the distinction of having published (through an Oklahoma firm) the first set of technical articles ever composed by computer. Luhn seemed to think that the computer could do almost anything and he did make it do unusual tasks. Inventions, papers, demonstrations, travel, and the honor of being the President of the American Documentation Institute characterized his last years.

Garfield: His Obsession

A third creative genius in the realm of nonconventional information systems is Eugene Garfield (1925–). Garfield's contribution is similar to Taube's in that neither invented anything totally new—their genius was in adapting and fitting pieces together. Garfield has kept adapting and fitting until his scientist-users have all they need to keep ahead, each in his or her own field. Garfield, an entrepreneur since 1957, not only provides, he promotes, educates, and explores how to improve his services. Would that the noncompetitive institutions behaved similarly.

Garfield is a chemist by education, but he calls himself an information scientist. He fell into information science (documentation) in much the same way that Luhn had: through a meeting with James W. Perry. After earning a bachelor's degree in chemistry from Columbia University, out of curiosity he attended a documentation meeting at the Diamond Jubilee of the American Chemical Society in 1951 in New York City, which Perry was conducting. To

Garfield's question of where could one get a job in the field, Perry's answer was: at the Army Medical Library Project at Johns Hopkins University. The project involved the application of machines to medical literature indexes. Garfield (1975, p. 153) did in fact work on the project from 1951 until 1953 when it ended.

At the same time Garfield was working at Johns Hopkins University in Baltimore, he was attending the Columbia University School of Library Service in New York City, where he earned a master's degree in 1954. He was stymied there at the doctoral level when he could not locate an advisor nor even a department or school to approve doctoral work in machine methods in scientific information (Garfield, 1975), but he persisted.

During his period at Johns Hopkins he came to know *Shepard's Citations,* a legal reference tool of long standing. Later, he focused on a conception of a science index modeled along similar lines. This idea became his obsession. As he has admitted, "when the discovery is a novel one, the task of going from a general to a specific conceptual model and then from the concept to reality can be done only by someone obsessed with an idea" (Garfield, 1979, p. xiv). About this time he wrote "Citation Indexes for Science" (Garfield, 1955). In 1956 he formed his own information business, DocuMation, Inc. (Garfield, 1978a, p. 6).

In 1958: Garfield Publicized His Intentions

In 1958, Garfield unveiled the philosophy underlying his dream of a multidisciplinary science index when, at the International Conference on Scientific Information, he presented a paper entitled "A Unified Index to Science" (Garfield, 1959). In presenting the various papers whether in print or in an oral presentation, Garfield was setting a pattern that he continued through the years— that of sharing his research with others.

Referring to the fact that he did not get a faculty position at the Rutgers University Graduate School of Library Services, Garfield said it was "the best thing that ever happened to me" (1978b, p. 5). Dean Lowell Martin had told him that if Ralph Shaw did not accept the faculty position, it would be open to him. Shaw accepted and Garfield pushed forward in his own direction. For years Garfield had been producing *Current Contents* or its precursors. In 1960 he introduced *Index Chemicus,* which is a registry of new chemical compounds that provides chemists with the only current weekly guide to published reports on new compounds and new reactions. In 1970, *Index Chemicus* became *Current Abstracts of Chemistry,* with published abstracts for all articles in more than 100 core journals as well as for articles from some 2500 other journals that report new compounds (Garfield, 1977, Vol. 1, p. 63).

In 1956, Garfield had named his business DocuMation, Inc. He admitted that "this caused some consternation to Mortimer Taube who had formed Documentation, Inc. in 1953" (Garfield, 1978a, p. 6). Later, on the advice of a public relations expert, he renamed it Eugene Garfield Associates—Information Engineers. He subsequently discovered that to use the word "engineers" without the credential was illegal (Garfield, 1978a).

In 1960 he renamed it again, calling it the Institute for Scientific Information (ISI), inspired by the USSR All Union Institute for Scientific and Technological Information (VINITI), which was appropriate until he added services in the social sciences and humanities.

In 1961, the year Garfield earned a doctoral degree in the field of structural linguistics from Johns Hopkins University (Garfield, 1961), he received a grant from the National Institutes of Health, later transferred to the National Science Foundation, to prepare an experimental citation index for the field of genetics. It involved 613 journals and 266,000 citations. At the time the prospects looked good for the multidisciplinary citation index for science, but the NSF rejected the proposal. Garfield, as was his habit, was not deterred and decided to continue alone (Lazerow, 1974, p. R-4).

In 1963: Garfield's Obsession Becomes a Reality

In 1963, Garfield and his colleagues presented papers for the annual conference of the American Documentation Institute held in Chicago. This was the year he produced what was to become a full-fledged *Science Citation Index*. There were approximately 725 people registered for this conference and Hans Peter Luhn had delivered, as mentioned earlier, the first volume of preconference papers ever produced by computer. It was Luhn's big year, as well as Garfield's and Taube's, since on January 8, 1963, the first volume of *STAR(Scientific and Technical Aerospace Reports)* had appeared.

By 1966, Garfield had added a permuted subject index (Garfield, 1976) to his citation index grouping that was constructed by computer from journal titles. In combination with other user-oriented amenities that kept appearing, it came to constitute what may be termed a complete information service for his users. Of course these services were provided for a considerable fee, but that is part of entrepreneurship. There probably will be more entrepreneurs in the information field once the process is clearly understood.

Garfield won several awards in 1977. They included the Information Industry Association Hall of Fame Award (Taube had also won this one), the American Society for Information Science Best Information Science Book Award, and the Division of Information Science, American Chemical Society Award. In addition, he received the American Society for Information Science Award of Merit in 1975.

In 1976 the American Chemical Society established its award for "outstanding contributions in the field of chemical information." This award was entitled "the Herman Skolnik Award" in honor of a man who for many years had contributed extensively to communication of the literature of chemistry. The first year that the award was given, Herman Skolnik was himself the recipient. He delivered a lecture entitled "Milestones in Chemical Information Science" (Skolnik, 1976), which detailed the advances made over the past 20 years in nonconventional information systems. While Skolnik admitted that Taube's Uniterm System, preceded by the influential punched-card systems, had made considerable impact on the field of chemical information, he also noted that because of its tendency to false drops, it had led to concepts of "relevance" and "precision." In his view, Luhn's KWIC index had largely superseded Taube's Uniterm System. Skolnik remarked that while in the early 1950s Taube "popularized the uniterm concept due to his dissatisfaction with library classification and indexing systems and the way documents were filed on the library shelves'' (Skolnik, 1976, p. 190), in 1958 Luhn had rebelled against the necessity of employing indexers and abstractors. Therefore, he developed a system for eliminating the indexers and, in 1959, the abstractors as well (Skolnik, p. 191). In 1969, critical of both, Skolnik introduced his own ''multiterm'' indexing system that, according to him, gave the user the best of all indexing and classification worlds. The reader may have noted that everyone prefers his or her own information system, and if he does not have one, he knows exactly how to design one.

Skolnik said little about the *Science Citation Index* except to state its history and that it was produced commercially by the Institute for Scientific Information. However, he did comment favorably on Garfield's *Index Chemicus* and his own use of the Rotaform Index on which, he said, Garfield published a paper in 1963.

In the following year, 1977, the Skolnik Award was presented to none other than Eugene Garfield (Garfield, 1978c). If in this treatment of Garfield's life it appeared that he was perhaps lacking in judgment, or that some of his decisions seemed inspired more by the aim of annoying his competition than by good logic, one can also recognize his humor, his competence in maneuvering out of a difficult situation, and, not the least, his sincere gratitude at receiving the award in the chambers of his toughest competition. In his usual discursive style he accepted the award with gracious comments and then gently attacked Skolnik by suggesting that Skolnik had never used any of his works, perhaps not even *Current Contents,* the simplest of all his methodologies, so simple in fact that Garfield himself had never been able to get a paper published on the subject. Skolnik probably took these comments in good humor. The year 1977 had indeed been his golden year of awards.

Of Garfield's capable entrepreneurship, Adams (1981, p. 165) pointed out that even with his multidisciplinary science bibliography, he had managed to serve the principal demands of mission orientation: services include speed in delivery through use of *Current Contents,* a weekly alerting service in several fields that was conceived in 1954 and is now much improved and expanded; the personalized services of Automatic Subject Citation Alert (ASCA), ''which announces only the literature that meets the personalized specializations of the subscribers''; and a do-it-yourself service for users based on a selection from *Science Citation Index.* Adams concluded that ''in the opinion of many, this ability constituted a better bibliographic 'mousetrap' than the preselected published specialized bibliographies and made ISI's services highly competitive even against subsidized competition'' (1981, p. 165).

Adams devoted a full chapter to discussing Garfield's endeavors and considered him to be among the top contributors to the new information services. Adams also pointed out the discontinuity in scientific information services over the past few decades and how the old methods were no longer effective. The first big break with tradition was the advent of computer-based services, including coordinate indexing with its postcoordinate merging of subjects for retrieval, and, of course, mission-oriented services. Then came Garfield's citation indexing with its multidisciplinary bibliographies in broad subject areas such as science, then later the social sciences and the arts and humanities. New directions were needed. Adams recognized the ''changing directions,'' the new requirements, and increased funding directed toward the social and economic aspects of research, the environment, and new technology. It became possible with the large mainframe computers, with their power, increased storage capacity, and interactive online search, to perform the specific retrieval from large databases that formerly had required specific databases. Even without computer-based search and retrieval, the manual citation indexes were designed to serve the individual scientist or humanities scholar through Garfield's continuous monitoring of the database in relation to the user and economy.

Garfield's business at ISI continues to expand both in territory covered (it is now international) and in subject coverage (the social sciences and the arts and humanities). The uniqueness of the citation indexes, according to Katz, is that they form "a network of connections between authors." The *Source Index* is then used to establish the full bibliographic reference to the citing author (Katz, 1982a, p. 182).

Garfield has, to a large extent, been his own biographer. The weekly essays that appear in *Current Contents* and that have enticed and informed readers for nearly a quarter of a century are now available in several volumes of "Essays of an Information Scientist" (Garfield, 1977, 1977–1980, 1981–1983, 1983, 1984).

One may now consider whether Garfield had not outwitted the practitioners, the competition, and the theorists, as well as the funding agency, when he developed and funded his own multidisciplinary *Science Citation Index*. In the beginning, searching was simple. One consulted the *Citation Index* then the *Source Index*. There were no worries about postcoordination of terms, false drops, or "relevance." All the sciences were represented and there were no services from competitive sources. The question of "relevance" is perhaps the most interesting. If the citation that the user selected seemed to be relevant, for all practical purposes it was relevant. The responsibility rested with the user. The Clevelands commented:

> In other words, given a particular paper, a citation index shows who cited that paper at a later point in time. In addition to this basic index there may be supplementary indexes arranged by author or keyword subject term, but such approaches, obviously, are not considered to be the primary approach to a citation index. Basically this kind of index implies that a cited paper has no internal subject relationship with the papers that cite it, and we use this relationship to cluster related documents . . . only the author's judgment of relevancy is involved. (Cleveland and Cleveland, 1983, p. 44)

Borko and Bernier, on the other hand, state that "it is important to note that citation indexes are not meant to be a substitute for subject and author indexes" (1978, p. 155). They do not comment on relevance in this context. Regarding the weaknesses of the citation indexes, they mention some problems: "The citations are unedited . . . only the last name and initials are used . . . therefore scattering will occur . . . [and] the document cited may be partially or wholly irrelevant to the citing article; if so, the searcher is led to irrelevant material'' (Borko and Bernier, 1978, pp. 151–152). They do confirm the citation index as a subject index: "The *Citation Index* functions as a subject index by means of which the searcher is able to trace closely related subjects" (p. 153).

Through the 1970s, ISI and other groups were largely concerned with the print version of the citation indexes. But in the 1980s emphasis has shifted to the online versions, not only *SCISEARCH,* the online version of the *Science Citation Index (SCI),* but also *Social SCISEARCH,* the online version of the *Social Sciences Citation Index (SSCI),* as well as the *Arts and Humanities Citation Index* online version. These online versions are said to be easier to use than the print versions (Katz, 1982a, p. 181; Kronick, 1985, pp. 132–133), and online "presents much greater flexibility and capabilities" (Kronick, 1985, p. 133). Another advantage is avoiding the unusually small print of the print versions. Katz (1982a, p. 184) noted that *SSCI* is updated monthly and, therefore, can be used to update ERIC. Garfield (1979, p. 253), in his projections for the future, promised that "access to the ACI/SSCI databases will become more convenient. Microstorage techniques or minicomputers could eventually make it economically practical for individual scientists and departmental groups to have their own copies of the databases."

The Environment: Other People, Other Places

Informal Evaluation of the Information Systems

So far, criticisms, or evaluations if you prefer, of the information systems created by "the big three" have been presented individually. The following papers by Cleverdon (1970) and Borko and Doyle (1964) are criticisms of the work of Taube, Luhn, and Garfield. Each sets forth philosophical points that have significant value to understand the emergence and future of information science. Cleverdon points out the drastic change from tradition. Borko and Doyle identify research as an inherent quality for the advancement of science.

Among the information systems designed by Taube, Luhn, and Garfield, Cleverdon (1970, p. 539) seems to favor Taube's mainly because it represents a clear break from tradition that incited others to further action and change. The shock value of an apparently uncontrolled vocabulary and the capability of the postcoordinate search triggered the rage that Cleverdon identified. One may speculate that Taube's entrepreneurship, which allowed him to be decisive, added fuel to the fire. His credentials and experience were another annoyance to some of lesser academic achievements and experience. The power of his pen in intellectual combat, no doubt, stirred still others.

Cleverdon acknowledged Garfield's important contribution, his realization that the computer could be used to overcome the practical difficulties of the "massive and valuable citation indexes of today." Garfield too had experienced some resistance, if not rage. But he was not the first to deal with the traditional libraries and library schools as they experienced the shock of drastic change, nor ultimately the formal comparison and evaluations of traditional and nonconventional information systems (Gull, 1956). Garfield was apparently prepared both emotionally and eventually academically for what he has called the "initial hostility" as well as the inertia of some in the field.

Borko and Doyle (1964), on the other hand, doubted the value of Taube's Uniterm System because of its false drops and its unstable mechanism for retrieving "relevant" materials. They were also skeptical of Luhn's automatic indexing and abstracting proposals, and considered Garfield's citation indexing along with associative indexing to be a natural progression, the new generation of indexes. Borko and Doyle suggested the use of systems analysis, a quest for constant and stable features in the environment, and that more attention be paid to the needs and habits of the user. Their list of tasks was to consume years of study. They also explained that research is constantly being conducted (and that surely has been the case with automatic indexing and abstracting) with the aim of further improving information retrieval. This last consideration raised information science to the level of other sciences whose researchers know that the final state of a phenomenon is seldom the goal. This improvement differentiates information science from the nineteenth-century librarianship that had unfortunately continued into the twentieth century. In two chapters in the *Annual Review of Information Science and Technology*, the first by Bourne (1966) on testing and evaluation of information systems and the second by Borko (1967) on the design of information systems, information scientists were alerted to the importance of continuing improvement in the methods of information retrieval. In nearly every volume of *ARIST*, from Volume 1 in 1966 through the present Volume 21, there is a focus on the continuing search for improvement.

Formal Testing and Evaluation

A miracle happened in 1966 that influenced the future of information science. This was, of course, the appearance of the *Annual Review of Information Science and Technology*. Volume 1 contained a review of the long list of literature on the subject of testing and evaluation of information systems. Among the chapters was Charles P. Bourne's review entitled "Evaluation of Information Systems" (1966, pp. 171–190). Apparently formal testing had begun in the United States as early as 1953 with the study by Documentation, Inc., and the Library of Congress (Gull, 1956). According to Bourne, this "appeared to be the first large-scale test of an indexing language or system and very quickly pointed out the difficulties of planning, executing, and interpreting the results of such tests" (1966, p. 172).

Bourne recommended the Swanson (1965) article and bibliography as a good overview of the activity up to this point. Bourne explained (1966, p. 172), however, that although there were many involvements in the testing and evaluation of information systems, none had caused more excitement than the Cyril Cleverdon and Cranfield experiments in the United Kingdom (Cleverdon, 1960, 1965, 1967).

Review chapters for the next three years (Rees, 1967; King 1968; Katter, 1969) established the trend of reporting on the testing and evaluation literature reviews by including them with the subject of information systems design. This trend continued through "The Design and Evaluation of File Structures" (Yang, 1978) and "Evaluation of and Feedback in Information Storage and

Retrieval Systems'' (Kantor, 1982), to name several. Online and full-text information systems are covered in separate chapters. Other chapters will no doubt be written as technology develops.

Before we continue this history through 1968, it is worthwhile to reflect on what Volume 1 of *ARIST* revealed. We begin with Fairthorne: "To test is not to evaluate. Tests reveal to what extent a retrieval system performs in some specific way; what value is or should be put upon such performances is another matter altogether. . . . Clearly one should test only such performance as is necessary to the aim of the system . . . then test to find out how well it achieves this aim" (Fairthorne, 1965, quoted by Bourne, 1966, pp. 81–82).

In Volume 1 of the *Annual Review* one outstanding feature appears that succinctly describes the state of the art in 1965/1966. Table 1 presented by Bourne (1966, pp. 176–179), collects the following information: testing orientation, size (i.e., number of items in the file), subject, number of questions used in the analysis, source of questions, degree of request negotiation with user, number of relevance levels used, relevance judges, index languages tested, primary performance measures used as well as the reference numbers that refer to the bibliography, and the date of the first published report of test results. The number of references to each test varies from one to seven. Bourne's table is a masterful example of communication. The only term in the headings that needs explanation is "relevance."

In the 110 references reviewed by Bourne, "relevance" was considered to be one of the measures for evaluation. It and "relative relevance" are among the 31 terms that Bourne gleaned from the literature that were used for measure. In examining the references, he discovered the labels "recall" and "relevance" with "precision ratio" used as a synonym for "relevance." He concluded that the definition of "relevance" in most common use was "that fraction of retrieved material that is actually relevant to the request." The value of this definition seems doubtful in view of the fact that the term is used in its own definition.

Among Bourne's unanswered questions were: Is relevance an adequate measure? How should relevance be measured or described? How many degrees of relevancy are there? After 20 years these questions still persist.

Rees (1967), after reviewing the 52 references for the chapter entitled "Evaluation of Information Systems and Services" in Volume 2 of *ARIST,* had this to say about the Cranfield methodology and about the concept of relevance: "The dialog between those who 'accept' the Cranfield methodology and those who, for a variety of reasons, are critical of it, has not been particularly productive from the point of view of advancing the state of the art" and "relevance cannot be considered as the sole criterion" (Rees, 1967, pp. 81–82).

King (1968), in reviewing the 210 references for the chapter "Design and Evaluation of Information Systems," declared 1967 (the year he reviewed) to be the year of "relevance" (p. 91). It does seem, in fact, to be the year in which the controversy peaked. From then on (Katter, 1969), other topics already mentioned entered the systems design chapters, for example, systems analysis, online retrieval, and interactive systems. The bibliography of the review literature follows roughly the dates of the *Annual Reviews* (Bourne, 1966; Rees, 1967; King, 1968; Katter, 1969; Lancaster and Gillespie, 1970; Cleverdon,

1971; Debons and Montgomery, 1974; R. W. Swanson, 1975; Stern, 1977; Yang, 1978; Kantor, 1982).

The book entitled "Information Retrieval On-line" (Lancaster and Fayen, 1973) contains a chapter entitled "Performance Criteria." In it the authors list six criteria as "the most important ones" and admit that they are basically the same as those Cleverdon used in 1964 (Lancaster and Fayen, 1973, p. 125): (1) coverage; (2) recall; (3) precision; (4) response time; (5) user effort; and (6) form of output. This chapter must be read to understand fully how these various criteria fit into a pattern of testing and evaluation.

In plain English, the definition of recall ratio is the expression of the ability of the system to let through what we want, whereas precision ratio, its companion measure (one is not meaningful without the other), expresses the ability to hold back what we do not want. In other words, the recall ratio equals the number of relevant documents retrieved by the system divided by the total number of relevant documents contained in the system multiplied by 100. The precision ratio is the number of relevant documents retrieved by the system divided by the total number of documents retrieved by the system multiplied by 100. The two measures taken together indicate the filtering capacity of the system (Lancaster and Fayen, 1973, pp. 125–128).

Cleverdon (1970, p. 544) gave a similar explanation:

> On the one hand there are those devices which will increase the total number of documents retrieved, while alternatively there are those devices which restrict the number of documents retrieved. In the former case, recall will be improved, and in the latter case, it is precision. We know that improvement in the one of these measures can only be at the expense of the other so all that can be hoped for is to obtain the optimum solution. (Cleverdon, 1970, p. 544)

Earlier in the same article Cleverdon noted the historical "thorny problems of relevance decision, an aspect of testing that was to generate so much argument for many years" (1970, p. 543).

The Specialist in Relevance: Saracevic

The question of relevance, however, still intrigued some investigators, especially Tefko Saracevic, who continued to study it. He is responsible for purging a concept that had plagued researchers for a number of years. In 1969 and 1970 Saracevic (1969, 1970a,b) completed his basic work.

Approximately 10 years earlier, Maron and Kuhns (1960) had applied the calculus of probability to computer indexing in an attempt to establish a theory of relevance. In 1970, Saracevic applied Bradford's law of scattering with the same, or at least a similar, goal in mind. This area of investigation has been thoroughly researched and new insights may still emerge from the studies that have been conducted.

In 1976, Saracevic published a perspective of earlier times; he gave a clear account of what he and others had been doing and what their insights had been. This 1976 paper amounted to a philosophy of relevance not unlike Santayana's exploration in his "The Sense of Beauty" or Dalhaus' "Esthetics of Music." It was a significant and timely contribution, appearing after he had completed his basic research and had taken time for reflection. Tefko Saracevic surely qualified himself as a specialist on the subject of relevance.

Lancaster (1979, pp. 270–271) seems to have great respect for Saracevic's and other work on relevance accomplished in the Western Reserve studies but he does contend that

> much interesting and valuable work has been done on the relevance problem that has little direct application to the pertinence problem. Indeed, most of the investigations could not contribute directly to our understanding of the pertinence problem because they were conducted in controlled, experimental settings. Studies of pertinence can be done only in the context of a particular information system serving real users who have real information needs. The situation cannot be simulated in any laboratory setting. (Lancaster, 1979, pp. 271–272)

At a meeting of information specialists held in London on October 16, 1963, Rees set forth the Western Reserve position on the concepts of relevancy and pertinency:

> The difference between relevancy and pertinency is that relevancy is a property which corresponds to a question, while pertinency is a property which corresponds to a need. Relevancy is associated with the relationship between a document and a question, whereas pertinency is associated with the information need of which the question is a formal representation. The degree to which relevancy and pertinency coincide can be considered as a measure of the questioner's ability to represent his need in terms of a formal statement, the skill of the question analyst and the effectiveness of the indexing language. (Rees, 1963, p. 358)

The Specialist in Evaluation: Lancaster

Although from 1966 through 1985 statements regarding the testing and evaluation of information systems were forthcoming from various authors and investigators, it is Lancaster who has emerged as a leader in evaluation. His background is in vocabulary control (Lancaster, 1972a) and in principles of information retrieval, both manual (Lancaster, 1968b, 1979) and online (Lancaster and Fayen, 1973). In other words, Lancaster has an in-depth background for the specialty of testing and evaluation of information systems in current use. His experience is both national and international and in commercial, governmental, and university environments. While others should receive their due credit, Lancaster has been selected here as a model in the testing and evaluating of both conventional and nonconventional information systems.

In the field of information science one may note that there are specialists and there are generalists. Perhaps the generalists are the sounding boards for the specialists. The specialists are those who become known for their specialities—a truism. As in any science, the generalist is more aware of the spectrum. Fuller

(1970, pp. 20–29) might call the generalists the pirates, those who knew everything. But it is the specialists to whom one listens and looks for stability and objectivity. Each specialty may one day become a separate science. Testing and evaluation would surely qualify.

ERIC: Another Nonconventional Information System

At the same time that Taube was working out his computer-based information system and Luhn and Garfield were similarly engaged, Western Reserve University personnel were experimenting on their own computer, a GE-225, at their Center for Documentation and Communications Research that had opened in 1955. It was the first such installation to be affiliated with a library school in the United States. The center operated until 1961 under the leadership of James W. Perry, who first introduced both Luhn and Garfield to the information science field. After 1961, Dean Jesse H. Shera took over the management of the center when Perry left for the University of Arizona. Perry had co-authored a book on the punched-card systems (Casey and Perry, 1951). Among the activities at Western Reserve University Library School from 1955 through 1961 were several grants, research reports, and proceedings of conferences (Rees, 1963, p. 353).

The Western Reserve University Library School faculty were working with a computer-based information system that utilized roles and links, a semantic code subject system, when Allen Kent, a chemist by education, and colleagues received a grant from the U.S. Office of Education (USOE) to pursue a pilot project for what already had been named the Educational Research Information Center (ERIC) (Trester, 1981, p. 347), later to become the Educational Resources Information Center. The grant was received in 1961 and the report was completed and submitted in 1962 (Kent *et al.*, 1962).

According to what Trester found out in an interview on July 26, 1976, with Thomas D. Clemens, from the Media Branch at USOE, Kent had quickly drafted the preliminary proposal during an airplane flight to Puerto Rico (Trester, 1981, p. 8). Such informal acts were common practice in the early days of proposals and grants. The USOE felt confident that "the Western Reserve Center was competent to handle such an effort. Under Jesse Shera and Allen Kent the center had been active for 5 or 6 years (the principals over a longer time period) in the development of new tools and techniques for increasing the effectiveness of technical information dissemination" (Trester, 1981, p. 8). The study, entitled "The Library of Tomorrow—Today, and Information Service of Educational Research Materials," was carefully designed and executed. Many of its suggestions were utilized by the USOE planners who built upon its careful work. They did not, however, adopt what they considered to be the rather complicated subject system involving the telegraphic abstracts and semantic codes but rather opted for coordinate indexing, a decision that was "fully reviewed with the project people at Western Reserve" (Trester, 1981, p. 18).

The Western Reserve study had followed upon the heels of the rather unobtrusive study by Tauber and Lilley (1960), then on the Columbia University School of Library Services faculty, where the former specialized in classification and the latter in subject cataloging. Tauber was a Melvil Dewey professor and a graduate of the University of Chicago Library School, and Lilley was a Columbia Library School graduate. Their charge, under a USOE grant issued in 1959, had been to recommend subject classification for the emerging media research reports and collections that were accumulating. What they did was extensive research among educational professionals and the report reflected the findings, namely, that the whole field of education needed a subject-based coordinated information service. But their recommendations were modest: "It is the recommendation of the consultants that the 'Media Research Information Service' be considered as the first of two steps leading toward a coordinated information service that in time will embrace all educational research, and research in other disciplines that have implications for educational theory and practice" (Tauber and Lilley, 1960, p. 13).

This modest recommendation was almost immediately upgraded by those in authority at the USOE to include both the first and the second steps. Several things favored this approach: the stimulating report from Western Reserve that had already anticipated some of the organizational and other problems; the investigators' professionally astute utilization of the systems approach in conducting the research; the somewhat later availability of Lee Burchinal at the USOE, who was extremely interested in the concept of ERIC and who "had more than a little entrepreneurial–political talent . . . he had a sense of system and was viewed as a good manager" (quoted by Trester, 1981, p. 26, from the recommendations of Richard Dershimer, who knew Burchinal well); the increased funding that came from President Johnson's having signed the Elementary and Secondary Education Act (PL-89-10, 1965); and, not the least, the outside encouragement from prestigious and knowledgeable sources, including those in universities. Adkinson (1978, p. 82) recalled that "the ERIC program was an immediate success."

Many people were involved in preparing the ultimate system that we came to know as the fully-functioning ERIC information system. This system comprised: 16 to 20 decentralized clearinghouses that acquired and analyzed the documents; the ERIC facility that prepared *Resources in Education,* the document index; an administrative core at the central USOE; centers for dissemination, often in universities; the ERIC Document Reproduction Service (EDRS), which prepared the microfiche and was operated by Leasco; and another business firm, Crowell, Collier, and Macmillan Information Corporation (CCM), which prepared *Current Index to Journals in Education (CIJE)*. A more detailed account of the functions and changes that took place may be found in many information sources (e.g., Burchinal, 1971; Trester, 1981; Brandhorst, 1977).

ERIC has the honor of being the first computer-based system in a soft science. It stands as a model for other countries and other subjects, and has been used extensively in library schools for teaching the Boolean, postcoordinate search online. In general, it performs its education function at many levels.

However, there were and still are critics. There have been numerous tests and evaluations. Three of the most helpful have been: (1) the extensive study of use conducted by Bernard M. Fry of Indiana University (Fry, 1972; (2) the study of ERIC online procedures for searching by Charles Bourne (1974); and (3) the study on the efficiency of PROBE as a program for retrieval of ERIC bibliographic references (Kiewitt, 1979). There have been other studies, but the one that has had the most devastating effects is the Rand Report (Greenwood and

Weiler, 1972), not so much because of its content as the way it was handled by the inept management at the National Institute of Education (NIE) (Sproull *et al.*, pp. 211–212), under which ERIC had been struggling since August 1972.

Over the years there had been several reorganizational periods, first at USOE with a Management Review Group, next with the directors of the clearinghouses examining their own operations, and then the NIE-commissioned Rand Study (Greenwood and Weiler, 1972) that elicited so much controversy. The stated purpose of the latter study was to recommend alternate organizational plans for the clearinghouses.

In January 1973, Burchinal briefed the newly appointed NIE officials on ERIC and by February 1973, one month later, Burchinal left ERIC for what is often considered to be a loftier environs, the National Science Foundation. He was replaced at ERIC by Sam Rosenfeld from NASA, who had been appointed by Burchinal and was involved as a committee member of the ERIC Management Review Group (Trester, 1981, pp. 348–349). New and competent leaders emerged and ERIC regained its momentum of continuing improvement. By 1977, Brandhorst reported the almost unbelievable benefits that were accruing to users of the ERIC database. By 1978 the proposed budget was, for the first time, to reach more than $5 million. The budget included provision for an extensive overhaul of the "Thesaurus of ERIC Descriptors," which was accomplished and published completely revised in 1980.

This new thesaurus had a rather elaborate background. In 1960, Tauber and Lilley of Columbia University suggested a faceted subject system; in 1962, Allen Kent and others at Western Reserve University suggested the telegraphic abstract/semantic code subject system; in 1965, Lee Burchinal inaugurated the Panel on Educational Terminology (PET) with James L. Eller in charge. The various editions of thesauri followed; the first appeared in December 1967. It was subsequently explained (Eller and Panek, 1968) and evaluated (Hines and Harris, 1968a,b). This leads us to the completely revised edition, which included in its 1977 budget the ERIC Vocabulary Improvement Project. Here we have another first for information science: "The ERIC Vocabulary Improvement Project represents, to our knowledge, the first attempt of a widely used information system to systematically evaluate its vocabulary, to cross-check it against the database, and to let usage empirically determine the meaning and fate of each of its index terms" (Booth, 1979, p. 24).[1] This new thesaurus, completed in 1980, is another ERIC milestone. It is distributed by Oryx Press.

Two items must be mentioned before concluding this brief coverage of ERIC. First is the accomplishment of Trester's history (Trester, 1981) "ERIC— The First Fifteen Years." It is packed with facts, appears to be an objective account, and, although it covers only the first 15 years, is extremely helpful in portraying the broad scope of activities, and of problems overcome, during those early years. Second, we should emphasize how some professionals became dependent on their own clearinghouses.

ERIC/CLIS, the ERIC Clearinghouse for Library and Information Science, was established at the University of Minnesota in June 1967, with Wesley

---

[1]The authors have learned that perhaps an even more extensive revision of Medical Subject Headings (MeSH) has been carried out at the National Library of Medicine.

Simonton as Director. It moved slowly as most new organizations do. In 1970, as a result of open competition, it moved to Washington, D.C., under the auspices of the American Society for Information Science. Then things began to happen. Herbert R. Koller was the Director and Joshua L. Smith was Associate Director. Koller brought a sophistication to the clearinghouse that we later took for granted. Then in 1973 when Smith became Director, further cooperation developed with the American Society for Information Science (ASIS) and with other national and international organizations. The ERIC administration was pushing for dissemination. It was an effective push, especially since the ERIC Data Base Users Conferences were scheduled back-to-back with ASIS annual meetings. The ERIC Processing and Reference Facility was nearby with Ted (W.T.) Brandhorst as Director. There was a sense of unity and excitement as Ted, Josh Smith, and others from ERIC and from ASIS convened to discuss recent developments, especially in online retrieval. This was surely a renascent period for information scientists and for the many librarians who had by now crossed over, making friends with computers and databases.

In 1973, again through open competition, the ERIC Clearinghouse for Library and Information Science merged with Educational Media and Technology and moved to Stanford University under the Directorship of Lewis Mayhew. The name was changed to ERIC Clearinghouse for Information Resources. It remained there until January 1977, when it moved to Syracuse University, under Don Ely, where it remains today.

Research in Nonconventional Information Systems

Except for the discussion of the development of ERIC, which covers the two and one-half decades from 1960 to 1985, two decades have been represented in this chapter. The first, from 1948 through 1957, was one of germination of ideas and organization for change. We have focused on three creative designers of information systems out of several hundred if not thousands of researchers in the area of nonconventional information systems who contributed to the major changes from the traditional methods that existed throughout the United States and the world. By the end of 1957, Taube had set forth his goals and made waves; Luhn had joined the ranks of information retrieval from his engineering post at IBM; and Garfield had prepared for a unique future by publishing his seminal paper on citation indexes (Garfield, 1955).

The second decade, 1958 through 1967, was one of activity, close scrutiny by critics, and increased availability of funds for research and development in the field of information projects. The boundaries of these periods overlap but several trends can be drawn for each decade.

Between 1957 and 1969, the U.S. National Science Foundation, Office of Scientific Information Service, published two serials. The first to be reviewed here is *Nonconventional Technical Information Systems in Current Use* (*NTISCU*). This serial publication established that nonconventional information systems were operating. Bohnert (1977, pp. 71–90) summarized this serial that appeared irregularly between 1958 and 1966. The first edition was published in January 1958 with 43 pages and no index. It described 30 nonconventional systems in 25 organizations. The final edition, Number 4, appeared in December

1966 with 558 pages and 8 indexes. It listed 178 systems in 141 organizations. The final edition added the word *Scientific* to the title (*NSTISCU*).

The definition of nonconventional information systems kept changing. Originally it was "the information systems employing or embodying new principles for organization of subject matter or new principles using automatic equipment for storage and search" and, of course, they must be operating systems. At one point, supposedly because of their extensive use, the Uniterm Systems in use were no longer considered to be nonconventional. Most of the systems reported contained 25,000 or fewer documents and were used largely for organizing internal technical reports, but there were several much larger systems. In a 1961 issue of *NTISCU* Hans Peter Luhn is listed as having produced the first commercial permutated index, KWIC (Keyword-in-Context), for *Chemical Titles*, as well as SDI (Selective Dissemination of Information) systems.

Most of the nonconventional information systems reported were in commercial establishments. Of 289 organizations covered in this series, 60% were commercial, 25% were governmental, and only 15% were in nonprofit organizations (Bohnert, 1977, p. 80). By 1966 this series was terminated, having completed its mission. It has been said that there were not many new systems after 1965. This may or may not be the case.

Although much historical material was included in the series, some is missing because inclusion was voluntary. For example, although Garfield's *Science Citation Index* appeared in 1964, it is not mentioned in this series, which ran through 1966.

The second of these U.S. National Science Foundation publications is *Current Research and Development in Scientific Documentation (CRDSD), 1957–1969*, which was summarized by Wooster (1971). In historical perspective, it clearly established that there was extensive research and development in the information field. The areas of investigation and the investigators are identified but there is no mention of the amount of funding. After 1969, the *Annual Review of Information Science and Technology (ARIST), 1966–* and the then entitled *Documentation Abstracts, 1966–*, now called *Information Science Abstracts (ISA)*, were considered by the producers of *CRDSD* to have taken over its mission. Soon after the series terminated, sometime between 1969 and 1972, funds for research and development began to wane (Adkinson, 1978, p. 89).

In the *CRDSD*, research and development projects were reported in categories. Because there was no category labeled "Information Storage and Retrieval," Wooster reorganized the categories to show how much research was carried out in this area. Under this category from August 1956, when 13 projects were reported, until 1969, when 282 projects were reported, there was a near-doubling each year of the previous year's figures. In all, there were 489 projects in information storage and retrieval reported in a 10-year period.

It is interesting to note that in the last issue of *CRDSD*, 12 categories were reported. This number represented a growth from 4 categories and 19 projects listed in Volume 1 to 12 categories and 785 projects (all categories) listed in Volume 15, 1969, the last issue. These categories were:

1. Information Centers; Information Programs: Theoretical Studies
2. Information Use and Communication Patterns

3. Language Analysis
4. Machine Translation
5. Indexing and Classification Theory and Practice; Thesaurus Development
6. Automatic Content Analysis
7. Retrieval Systems
8. Publication and Announcement Operations
9. Library Operations
10. Performance, Analysis, and Evaluation
11. Pattern Recognition; Speech Recognition
12. Adaptive and Interactive Systems

This list, of course, was for documentation and was recorded a short time after documentation became information science. But it does confirm one of Harmon's criteria for a full-fledged discipline, namely, that it contain a full complement of subtopics. Harmon predicted that information science would appear by 1990. He admitted that his prediction "is only a crude approximate and . . . should not imply that further reconstellations of the present information science paradigm will not occur or that the name of the discipline will not change" (Harmon, 1971, p. 239).

The last issue of the *CRDSD* is bound in black, a symbol of the grief felt at the Office of Science Information Service with the demise of the publication. Could it be that with the birth of the *Annual Review of Information Science and Technology* and the *Information Science Abstracts* a new era was born and therefore the old one must die?

Several attempts have been made to replace these two publications on a permanent basis. It is fairly well agreed that the "1971 Encyclopedia of Information Systems" (Schmittroth, 1971) and its supplement "New Information Systems and Services: A Periodic Supplement" (Kruzas and Schmittroth, 1981) do extend, if belatedly, the serial *Nonconventional Scientific and Technical Information Systems in Current Use*. But, there is a problem with a system for continuing the type of information reported in *CRDSD*. In the United States the responsibility seems to rest with the Science Information Exchange (Freeman, 1968; Hales, 1980). At one time, there were at least 69 national centers for the control of research in progress, but at present, as explained by Werdel and Steele (1979), there are some problems arising on the international scene. A chapter in the *Annual Review of Information Science and Technology* (Hersey, 1978) covers information for both national and international researchers. This last *ARIST* treatment of research in progress, "Information Systems for Research in Progress" (*ARIST* **13**, 263–295) would appear to need updating.

Adkinson pointed out that government funds for R&D for the improvement of information services involved two groups: (1) 37 agencies with responsibility for large libraries and information centers feeding them, whose support of R&D was mission-oriented and whose results were often useful to other organizations; and (2) 6 agencies that "had missions to advance communications and information sciences for the benefit of the government and the nation" (Adkinson, 1978, p. 88).

More than 60% of the funding for projects listed in the *CRDSD* came from these six agencies: The National Science Foundation, the Air Force Office of Scientific Research, the Rome Air Development Center, the Office of Naval Research, the Army Research Office, and the Advanced Research Projects Agency. There was also general mission support to upgrade libraries in education and health-related areas. These funds came mainly from the U.S. Office of Education, the National Institutes of Health, and the National Library of Medicine. Other agencies that either had funded or were to fund information systems studies and library research were the Council on Library Resources, the Library of Congress, the National Bureau of Standards, the Patent Office, and the National Aeronautics and Space Agency (Adkinson, 1978, p. 88).

During this time there developed around Washington, D.C., an atmosphere not of competition but of cooperation, probably due to the leadership of Burton W. Adkinson and his close associates at the National Science Foundation. His leadership manifested itself in several ways, notably in the able group of federal administrators who, feeling the need to provide the best possible information services to the scientists and engineers who were receiving increased R&D funds, formed a group called IGRIS—Interagency Group for Research on Information Systems—an informal group that met regularly to exchange information on information problems. This group encouraged the National Science Foundation, Office of Science Information Service, to initiate the serial publication *Current Research and Development in Scientific Documentation* (Adkinson, 1978, pp. 94–95). The composition of the group assured a high level of information exchange and *CRDSD* was to become ''a major reference tool between 1956 and 1968 for information science investigators'' (Adkinson, 1978, pp. 94–95).

The accomplishments during these two decades were enormous. Considerable money was spent on R&D and the results were visible. By 1968 ''most libraries and information centers were routinely using such reprographic techniques as microfilm, microcard and microfiche . . . [and] some of the more advanced centers were using computer systems in answering user requests and a limited few were establishing networks based on computers and telecommunications'' (Adkinson, 1978, p. 75).

Summary

Innovation, communication, expansion, and research marked the 1948–1968 period. We reported in Chapter 1 that President Franklin D. Roosevelt, toward the end of World War II, had asked Vannevar Bush what should be done in the United States to bring research reports under control and what system could be developed to assure that new scientific research would be properly funded and appropriately directed. We know that one effect of the concept of Bush's Memex system proposal was to inspire creative individuals to action. Another Bush-inspired move was the establishment, in 1950, of the National Science Foundation. Four other visionaries of the period, Norbert Wiener, S. C. Bradford, Arthur C. Clarke, and Claude E. Shannon, brought vision and focus to this challenging and changing environment.

We featured Mortimer Taube as one of the creators of nonconventional information systems. His system, with the capability of postcoordination of terms, was to change the face of information retrieval techniques. Taube's contribution was followed by that of Hans Peter Luhn, whose interest was mainly in computer application to the problems of storage and retrieval of information, an area that continues to interest a tenacious group of researchers. Eugene Garfield, the third of our selected creators of the period, made his own contribution by adopting the citation index of the legal profession to the areas of science. Taube and Garfield became entrepreneurs, a trend that has persisted in the information field.

The National Science Foundation, which had sponsored and funded many of the early information science research endeavors, soon found itself in the company of other funding agencies: the Air Force Office of Scientific Research, which assumed responsibility for the Taube–Wooster Conference on Information Storage and Retrieval; the United States Office of Education, which backed the development of ERIC; and the Council on Library Resources, which would be instrumental in funding research to enable the Library of Congress to provide the Machine-Readable Catalog (MARC II). Expansion was occurring on a large scale.

ERIC encompasses the integrated systems approach as well as most of the features of Taube's nonconventional information system: terms (or descriptors as ERIC calls them) are assigned in depth (five for printout and others for computer-based retrieval). The same descriptors are assigned to all types of items. The descriptors can be postcoordinated, that is, the combinations can be determined at the time of the search. A microfiche copy of most of the report literature is available, and a thesaurus is provided to solve the problems that had been encountered with an uncontrolled vocabulary.

Conferences played a key role in the communication and exchange of ideas. Their practicality and inspirational nature assumed international significance, as shown by the 1948 Royal Society Scientific Information Conference held in London as well as the Taube–Wooster Conference and the International Conference on Scientific Information, both held in Washington, D.C., in 1958.

Two other environmental factors that emerged were evaluation of information systems, both traditional and nonconventional, an activity that had its beginnings in the mid-1950s and that is a continuing function of the methods and strategies of information science, and, of course, extensive research. The influence of information science has been estimated here by the extent of the apparent adoption of the new methods and especially the replacement of old methods by the new.

CHAPTER 3

Information Science Applied to Libraries

Introduction

The information science applied to libraries has been called "library automation," which is a misleading appellation (Reed and Vrooman, 1979, p. 193) but one that is likely to persist into the next century. We must be careful what we call things, and what we don't call them, for the errors we make live long after us. One librarian admitted that the principal automation in libraries is the thermostat on the wall. We suggest the Herculean task of flushing out the ingrained terminology, preferably by those who first conceived of its use in the library context.

Our objective in this chapter is to reveal some successful applications of information science to libraries. Our method of measuring the extent to which information science has been applied has been simply to observe and record to what degree its methods and strategies have replaced traditional library methods and strategies, and to observe by whom, where, and under what environmental influences this has occurred. Of course, this method may seem to be largely subjective, but much of the extensive activity of the past 30 years has been recorded, so that our observations can be confirmed.

Our challenge has been to select some aspects of information services that have contributed to updating our nation's libraries beyond what could have been accomplished using the traditional methods and strategies. We have focused on three libraries, three other information environments, three information specialists, and three technologies. These latter were not, in this case, presented as environments, but as diffuse, contributing factors.

Three Libraries

Each of the three national libraries, the Library of Congress (LC), the National Library of Medicine (NLM), and the National Agricultural Library

(NAL), has assumed a leadership role in the application of information science not only to the benefit of libraries in the United States but elsewhere as well. We place particular emphasis on the Library of Congress and on its MARC and RECON projects. The computer-based unit record with which both MARC and RECON are concerned is considered to be the module in the updating of libraries from which all other modules are derived (Avram and Markuson, 1967, p. 98; De Gennaro, 1968, p. 88, also 1971a; Kilgour, 1968b, p. 169).

Over the years there have been several projects inspired by information science, such as those at the University of Chicago (University of Chicago Library, 1968). The INTREX (Information Transfer Experiment) Project at the Massachusetts Institute of Technology (Overhage and Harmon, 1965), the cataloging project at the New York Public Library (Malinconico and Rizzolo, 1973), the BALLOTS (Bibliographic Automation of Large Library Operations Using a Time-Sharing System) Project at Stanford University (1975), and others both in this country and abroad. But the phenomena selected for presentation not only meet the criterion of having influenced many users but also have been successful operations. These criteria were met by each of our three national libraries and by each of our three other selected, operating establishments, which are treated here as environments.

Three Information Environments

The Council on Library Resources (CLR), the member libraries of the Association of Research Libraries (ARL), and the Ohio College Library Center (OCLC) represent successful information-based establishments. The Council on Library Resources has been instrumental in improving information science application not only through its funding capability but also through the insights of its first director, Verner Clapp. In 1955, after several years at the Library of Congress, and after having spent considerable time as a member of a famous planning committee in Washington, D.C., that included the information science advocates Ralph Shaw and Mortimer Taube, Verner Clapp left the LC to head the newly formed Council on Library Resources, which since the early 1960s has been a major source of funding of creative library projects.

It was largely Clapp's awareness of activities in Washington, D.C., that enabled him to develop the concept of the machine-readable unit record. This idea probably came to him not only from his discussions in "The Committee" but also from observing the development of NLM's new information system, MEDLARS (Medical Literature Analysis and Retrieval System).

By 1964, MEDLARS was operational, using the computer in the batch mode to provide on-demand search and retrieval of references to all types of materials. The marvel that the NLM identified during the process of developing MEDLARS was the concept of the unit record. The unit record for MEDLARS had been prepared manually for paper tape, then transferred to magnetic tape for computer manipulation. Although it was manual, it was a marvel in the minds of its developers.

By 1965, Clapp had another idea for the unit record. As director of the Council on Library Resources, he authorized funding and commissioned a study, to be conducted by L. F. Buckland (1965), to test the feasibility of making this unit record machine-readable and capable of manipulation for various purposes. The results of the study were positive. In the same year LC hired a systems analyst, Henriette D. Avram, and MARC was on its way to realization. These developments had tremendous implications.

By 1968, MARC II was available to subscribers. Among the subscribers was OCLC, the first bibliographic utility, whose director, Fred Kilgour, seized the opportunity to utilize MARC II in his service to member libraries. Over the years numerous other libraries were provided information-science related projects.

Also in the 1960s the Association of Research Libraries (ARL) became a powerful force in providing research scholars access to the world's literature. ARL members endorsed and participated in national and international conferences in support of changes that would improve MARC and that would encourage funding of RECON, the retrospective bibliographic control of research materials.

Vannevar Bush first pointed out that U.S. research libraries should acquire at least one copy of all research materials that were or would become available worldwide, and that collections be made available to research scholars. Bush's recommendation, when implemented, highlighted the need for international standardization, that is, standardization of the bibliographic format to allow computer utilization and control. MARC and RECON provided much of that control.

Three Information Specialists: Avram, De Gennaro, and Kilgour

Three specialists, Henriette D. Avram, Richard De Gennaro, and Fred Kilgour, were selected for this segment of the history, mainly because of their sustained capability for advancing and expanding the information science applications in libraries. All three had systems methodology backgrounds. Two had library degrees.

Henriette Avram was a key person in the development of MARC and RECON at the Library of Congress; Richard De Gennaro, through his publications over more than two decades, delivered current messages of recommendation to academic and other research libraries; and Frederick Kilgour developed OCLC, thus bringing modern methods to thousands of libraries. So OCLC is our third environmental establishment, and like the other two, it is considered to be an environmental factor by virtue of being outside of our three national libraries and yet still affecting what happens inside them.

Three Technologies

We also feature three technologies. Kilgour declared that despite the value of research and systems thinking, the key factor in updating libraries is the computer (Kilgour, 1968a, p. 163). His statement may be open to question. The three technologies, the computer, systems analysis, and research, however, are discussed later in this chapter.

Plan of the Chapter

The many variables considered in this chapter present an organization problem. The following facts were taken into account in determining the pattern of organization: (1) the activities of the three selected environments (CLR, ARL, and OCLC) permeate the full chronological span; (2) although the National Library of Medicine was the first of our national libraries to apply information science, it was soon followed by the Library of Congress, and somewhat later by the National Agricultural Library; (3) although the unit record was an idea from the NLM's new information system, MEDLARS, that was appropriated and computerized at the LC, it is the LC that is central to this chapter; (4) the LC is featured here because of its obvious and far-reaching application of information science to libraries through its creation of MARC (machine-readable cataloging) and RECON (retrospective conversion); and (5) MARC and RECON substantially increased the application of information science to research and other libraries as well as to OCLC. On the basis of these five aspects, we arrived at the following six-point organizational structure: Information Science Applied (1) at the Library of Congress, (2) at OCLC, (3) in Academic Libraries, (4) at the NLM, and (5) at the NAL, and (6) the Technologies Utilized.

So much had happened in this short period of time: from the NLM where the unit record was developed, to the LC where it came into direct contact with the computer, to OCLC and other places where the member libraries benefited from the application of information science to libraries. Expansion was the main result, but improved services were perhaps a more important outcome, as were enlightened users. It was at LC, though, that the miracle happened. After research into feasibility, after trial and feedback on MARC from users, many of them ARL members, MARC II became available worldwide as did the benefits of RECON. This history is discussed in the following sections.

Information Science Applied at the Library of Congress (LC)

In 1958: The Library of Congress Considered the Computer

The Library of Congress has had a long association with the computer. William J. Welsh, the Deputy Librarian, noted that they began to consider its capabilities as early as 1958 when computers were still rather primitive (Welsh, 1985, p. 2). Thereafter, the chronology of events is staggering. Subsequently, in the same year, the Committee on Mechanized Information Retrieval was formed (Rohrbach, 1985, p. 7). This committee was charged with examining such questions as "Is automation 'inevitable or even desirable'?" and "Should the library pursue a total system or a modular approach?"

In 1961: The CLR Issued a Grant to LC: The King Study and Report Ensued

In 1961 the Council on Library Resources ("an independent non-profit body established in 1956 at the instance of the Ford Foundation, incorporated in the District of Columbia, with the principal objective of aiding in the solution of library problems'') awarded the Library of Congress $100,000 so they could undertake ''a survey of the possibilities of automating the organization, storage, and retrieval of information in a large research library . . . not only from the point of view of the functioning of an individual institution but also from that of a research library whose activities are inter-related with those of other research libraries'' (a quotation in King *et al.*, 1963, p. 1). By December 1963 the ''King Report'' (or the Red Book as it was called at the Library of Congress) was issued, which set forth a blueprint for automation.

In 1963: The Power and Prestige of the Association of Research Libraries (ARL) Exhibited at the Conference on Libraries and Automation

Earlier, on May 26–30, 1963, a conference on ''Libraries and Automation'' (Markuson, 1964), sponsored by the Library of Congress, the National Science Foundation, and the Council on Library Resources, was held at Airlie Foundation, Warrenton, Virginia. More than 100 attended, and at least half of these were directors or other librarians from university and large research libraries. It was a veritable meeting of members of the Association of Research Libraries (ARL), but there were also some information scientists who had attended the 1958 Information Storage and Retrieval Conference five years earlier: Mortimer Taube, Harold Wooster, Joseph Becker, and Robert Hayes, for example. Others attending included information scientists as well as systems analysts, computer specialists, representatives from two library associations (the American Library Association and the Special Library Association), and representatives from each of the sponsoring agencies.

The subject matter that was presented included a statement of the problems that librarians wanted to solve by automation; a session on microform capabilities; some statements defending librarians and some questioning their dedication to change; problems of type fonts; a discussion of GRACE (Graphic Arts Composing Equipment) at the National Library of Medicine; and discussions of chain and other printers, of file structures, and of alternatives to the 3 × 5 catalog card.

The lasting impression on William J. Welsh of the Library of Congress came from a talk on modes of communication by three presentors from the telephone and telegraph companies. They discussed not how to communicate but how to organize people and components to form a system that would be in synchronization. Following is a quotation from their talk:

> It is of basic importance to consider the system—the library, computer, console, displays and communications—as an entity, not as a collection of parts. The choice of any one of the components of the system is a complex matter which interacts with others. It will take close cooperation from the very beginning among experts in the fields of library science, computers, graphics, and communications if a sound [unfortunate choice of words] system is to result. It is indeed a good omen that this symposium has recognized so early the many facets of the problem. (Welsh, 1966, p. 81, quoted from J. M. Emling, J. R. Harris, and H. H. McMains, ''Networks of Library Communications,'' (1966), pp. 203–219)

These presentors seemed to be advocating that librarians, computer specialists, university library directors, and government and private funding agencies merge their goals, try to understand each other, and strive to achieve goals as a unit. This may be what L. Quincy Mumford, then Librarian of Congress, had in mind when, in his opening remarks for this conference, he stated that

> we, the traditional librarians, may be facing the end of an era. Perhaps the future of library service will have to be entrusted to men who can manage large electronic computers and the mysterious array of machines associated with automation. I do not really fear this prospect, nor do I think that it is entirely realistic. There will be a need to state the intellectual requirements which machines will meet, and I am confident that librarians will develop the insights and abilities to specify these requirements in a way that can be understood by the technologist. I am also convinced that the library cooperation, which has accelerated over the past few decades, will be aided by automation . . . it is in this spirit of cooperation that I welcome you to this conference. (Mumford, 1964, p. 8)

In 1965: Buckland's Research Funded by the CLR
Justified "The Machine-Readable Form"

By 1965, Lawrence F. Buckland of Inforonics, Inc., of Maynard, Massachusetts, had prepared and presented a report entitled "The Recording of Library of Congress Bibliographic Data in Machine Form" (Buckland, 1965). The report was the result of a commission by the Council on Library Resources, who had requested that Buckland conduct a study to determine whether or not "there was a practical method of converting a bibliographic record, such as that represented on LC printed cards," that could also be manipulated by machine in a variety of ways (Welsh, 1966, p. 81; Buckland, 1965, pp. v–x). Buckland's results supported the concept. By 1966 the MARC (Machine-Readable Cataloging) concept was well on its way to realization and to becoming the most important library innovation of the decade and probably of the century.

From 1965 to 1986 and Beyond: Henriette D. Avram at
LC: Her Principal Contributions—MARC I, MARC II,
and RECON

Shortly after Buckland's study in 1965, Henriette Avram joined the Library of Congress as Coordinator of Information Systems. During her service there she was an inspiring coordinator. Barbara Evans Markuson was already established in the Information Systems Office of the Library of Congress and the two of them became a strong force aimed at modernizing the Library of Congress.

In 1966: Avram, Kilgour, and De Gennaro at the
Brasenose Conference Set the International Stage for
MARC II, RECON, and Systems Methods—ARL and
De Gennaro Supported RECON

In 1966 Avram and Markuson attended the Brasenose conference. They presented a paper entitled "Library Automation and Project MARC: An Experiment in the Distribution of Machine-Readable Cataloguing Data'' (Avram and Markuson, 1967). It is significant to realize that Henriette D. Avram, Frederick G. Kilgour, and Richard De Gennaro, who are featured here, attended the Brasenose Conference (named for the Brasenose College at Oxford, England, where the delegates were housed) on the Automation of Libraries. Two of these leaders, Avram and Kilgour, were presenters and the third, De Gennaro, assumed the role he was to play in the library automation scenario thereafter, that of the philosopher/decision maker. At this conference each of the three functioned as they would for the next two decades: Avram with systems and MARC (Machine-Readable Cataloging); Kilgour with systems and later with the designing of OCLC (Ohio College Library Center); and De Gennaro affecting fundamental decisions, at this time regarding RECON.

At the Brasenose Conference, De Gennaro was on the side of the winners. He had no hesitation in deciding that the MARC format must be applied not only to cataloging of new materials but retrospectively. He readily agreed that it was the retrospective files that distinguished libraries such as those at the British Museum and the university libraries, as well as other large, older libraries, but challenged the assumption that the project would be ''impossible financially'' (De Gennaro, 1967a, p. 22). We cannot know whether he was influenced in favoring the retrospective program, which turned out to be RECON (Retrospective Conversion), by such clear thinkers as B. E. Markuson of the Library of Congress, H. H. Fussler of the University of Chicago, and J. E. Skipper, Executive Secretary of the Association of Research Libraries.

ARL was at the time composed of 73 large research libraries whose composite cataloging bill, using the old methods, was estimated to have been $18 million a year. When the Higher Education Act of 1965 was enacted, the ARL determined, in consultation with Congress, to attract enough funds to assure comprehensiveness of the printed record, the best of it to be automated, and the manpower to perform the task to take advantage of the $50 million allocated for the first year and Congress's guarantee over the next three years of $19 million (Skipper, 1967, p. 126). The united front of the ARL was a powerful sanction for the MARC program.

At this conference the information scientists were completely overshadowed by the librarians from some of the largest and most prestigious libraries in the United Kingdom and the United States. This was a conference that set records and made history, mainly because it was the first time that representatives from these large libraries had met to plan and ultimately to act. Sir Frank Francis, Director and Principal Librarian of the British Museum Library, welcomed the conference attendees. Other librarians from the British Museum Library, the Cambridge University Library, the Bodleian Library, Oxford University, and other U.K. libraries attended presentations and exchanged ideas with personnel from the Library of Congress and the large university and medical libraries of the United States. The British editors of the conference proceedings put it this way: ''It was, of course, for the most part a matter of the American delegation expounding and the British listening and learning'' (Harrison and Laslett, 1967, p. vii). Imagine the reverse situation!

By 1968, under the leadership of Avram, MARC II was widely available, through subscription, to libraries both in the United States and abroad. In August 1969, the RECON Pilot Project was initiated (Avram, 1972, 1975), and in the late 1970s and early 1980s networking became the first order of automation business (see Chapter 5), especially the concept of a national network. All these projects and ideas had strong leadership and sanction from Avram. But a truly national network for the United States was not yet to be. Many factors were delaying national planning and realization, not the least of which were a tightening of funding and the appearance of the mini and microcomputers with the accompanying turnkey systems. These turnkey systems were to stimulate a return to individual local library systems.

Born in 1919, Henriette Avram was a pre-med student at Hunter College from 1936 to 1938 and a mathematics major at George Washington University from 1953 to 1955. From 1961 to 1965 she held the position of Senior Systems Analyst at the Datatrol Corporation. Her positions at the Library of Congress reflect her advancements: Assistant Coordinator of Information Systems and MARC Projects Director, 1965–1970; Chief of the MARC Division, 1970–1976; Director of the Network Division Office, 1976–1980; and Director of Processing Systems, Networks and Automation Planning, 1980–present (Lee, 1982, p. 19). From the time of her arrival at the Library of Congress in 1965 until her well-received presentation at the Texas Library Association in Dallas in April 1985, she has been and continues to be a prominent authority on library automation. By her own admission, Avram is a pragmatist; that is, when someone submits an idea that sounds good to her, she is likely to respond, "Let try it." She is also a subtle humorist. Less than a year after she had arrived at the Library of Congress, she remarked that at least she had learned what "the main entry" was (Avram and Markuson, 1967, p. 125). One is reminded of the student who asked a librarian if the library held a certain issue of a serial, whereby the librarian replied, "See the main entry." The student immediately went outside and gazed at the main entry of the building, expecting by some miracle to find the answer to her question. To outsiders, especially to students and to the systems analyst, librarians' nomenclature can seem slightly bizarre.

For the more than 20 years that Avram has been at the Library of Congress, she has made important contributions in the field of library modernization. Seven major accomplishments carry her trademark: (1) the MARC Pilot Project; (2) MARC II, the distribution projects; (3) the several MARC formats; (4) national and international approvals; (5) the effect of MARC on national and international standardization; (6) the RECON Project; and (7) her work toward a national network. These items are all tangible. The intangibles that contribute to Avram's success are even more impressive.

Avram is a prolific and competent writer. Her overview of the foregoing activities (Avram, 1975) convinces the reader that documentation is a necessity in any successful automation project. Avram's writing conveys compassion combined with both logical and cogent presentation.

In addition to Avram's 1975 comprehensive report, further lucid explanations of her principal activities are found in the following reports. These reveal the benefits of MARC that have been recognized both nationally and internationally through approvals, adoptions, and the beginnings of standardization, a necessity for efficient growth. These reports are: "The MARC Pilot Project" (Avram, 1968); "The MARC II Format: A Communications Format for Bibliographic Data" (Avram et al., 1968); "The Evolving MARC System: The

Concept of a Data Utility'' (Avram, 1970b); and ''RECON Pilot Project: Final Report'' (Avram, 1972).

Avram defined MARC ''as an assemblage of formats, publications, procedures, people, standards, codes, programs, systems, equipment, etc., that has evolved over the years, stimulating the development of library automation and information networks'' (Avram, 1975, p. 401). The MARC Pilot Project, which involved 16 participating libraries, was an experiment that permitted librarians to suggest changes for MARC II, the distribution project that followed. The MARC Pilot Project is now referred to as MARC I.

MARC II formats have been developed, at the Library of Congress, for books, serials, maps, films, manuscripts, and music and sound recordings. Each differs somewhat from the others in tags and content, but the structure or ''empty container,'' as it is called, is the same for all of them. There are fixed fields and variable fields, and the record itself is of variable length. There are three components of the format: the structure, or ''empty container''; the content designators, such as tags, indicators, and subfield codes; and the content, that is, the data such as the author's name, the title of the work, etc. (Avram, 1975, p. 383).

The MARC data are transmitted weekly on magnetic tape to the many subscribers. The tapes have been composed from the data utility (Avram, 1970b), which originates and rests at the central source—the Library of Congress. After these data have been distributed, especially to installations such as the bibliographic utilities, the largest of which is the Online Computer Library Center (OCLC), they are transformed into bibliographic records for use at their member libraries. There are currently four bibliographic utilities, three in the United States and one in Canada. They provide a variety of services to their member libraries. We shall emphasize the cataloging function.

The RECON Project involved the conversion of retrospective catalog records to machine-readable form. This project gave researchers access to huge collections that otherwise would not have been accessible in machine-readable formats. The RECON Project was begun in August 1969 and lasted until August 1971. A very important spin-off was the development of the format recognition process, which could also be used in processing MARC records. Several other organizations had tested automatic identification (Butler, 1974) but LC was ''the first actually to assign content designators and the fixed fields for full MARC II record by program'' (Avram 1975, p. 390). MARC II has been well received as a standard.

Approvals of MARC formats were forthcoming in the United States from the three national libraries, the federal libraries, the divisions of the American Library Association, the Educational Resources Information Center (ERIC), the Committee on Scientific and Technical Information (COSATI), the Association for Scientific Dissemination Center (ASIDIC), and others, in both the United States and foreign countries (Avram, 1975, p. 394). In fact, the early interest and approval expressed by the British National Bibliography (BNB) group was to influence the design of MARC II (Avram, 1975, p. 383).

Standardization grew out of the many applications of MARC II. Among the several advantages to libraries and ultimately to users are: (1) products and records from different libraries can mesh and be interchanged; (2) automation activities can be developed more easily in new locations; (3) ordering and cataloging can be more uniform; (4) there can be less duplication of effort; and (5) networking can be facilitated (Avram, 1975, p. 402). Despite these and other advantages, it is almost unbelievable that supporters such as the Council on Library Resources and the United States Office of Education have violated MARC standards by consistently funding programs that do not adhere to the standard (Markuson, 1976, pp. 56–57).

Several offspring of the original MARC Pilot Project have emerged, MARC II, of course, being the first. In alphabetical order, some of the others are COMARC, MICRO-MARC, MINI-MARC, PREMARC, REMARC, SUPER-MARC, TELE-MARC, and UNIMARC (Rohrbach, 1985; Reynolds, 1985; Avram, 1975). The MARC II success has fed directly into the bibliographic utilities to provide tremendously expanded services and to ensure the success of the utilities.

The Library of Congress must be credited with a fair share of the leadership in bringing library updates to so many libraries in the United States and around the world. The original impetus came in the late 1950s and early 1960s basically from the following sources: (1) the accomplishment of the information scientists in initiating the nonconventional information systems, which utilized the newly arrived computers; (2) the international and local interest manifested in the attendance at conferences held in Washington, D.C., and elsewhere, with LC personnel attending and often involved; (3) the increasing needs of research scholars for library materials; (4) the backlog of uncataloged and of unacquired library materials; (5) the availability of the computer; (6) the influence of key representatives of consulting firms and professional practitioners in both library science and systems design; and (7) funding sources. Better library service was the goal but technology was a magnificent enticer.

Kilgour and Others Comment on Attitudes of Librarians

From the beginning the LC personnel gave generously of their time and effort by hosting foreign and local librarians and researchers and accepting speaking engagements; however, librarians in general were slow to accept change. Eventually, several events contributed to an attitude change. MARC I and its scheme for involving libraries stimulated interest and MARC II accepted suggestions after they were weighed for their value. Entrepreneurs also became involved and began to serve even the smaller libraries.

The attitudes of librarians have changed significantly since the reviewers of the 1965 literature of library automation reported that "many articles were judged inappropriate . . . particularly those from a cynical school of conservative librarianship" (Black and Farley, 1966, pp. 273–274). Markuson noted in 1967 that at that time there were few librarians actually involved in library automation (Markuson, 1967, pp. 255–256). In 1968, Kilgour expressed his own concern and set forth some reasons why librarians found themselves in this position:

> One would like to hope that innovators would come forward in large numbers thirsting to have a hand in development of the new librarianship. But such hope would be false, for one cannot expect individuals to

participate in activities they have not chosen. . . . Librarians must not only
self-renew, but in many cases must retool intellectually to participate in
newer developments in their profession . . . the librarian also is going to
need to learn how to make the results of research and development a part of
his intellectual armament. (Kilgour, 1968a)

Information Science Applied at the Ohio College Library Center (OCLC)

From 1967 to 1980: Kilgour at OCLC—A Leader in Creating and Expanding the First Bibliographic Utility That Modernized Numerous Libraries

Fred Kilgour had originally planned to be a medical doctor. However,
after earning a bachelor's degree in chemistry from Harvard College and working
at Harvard's Widener Library, he became deputy director of the Office of Intelligence Collection and Dissemination in the Department of State. On leaving that
position, he earned a master's degree in library science from Columbia University, where he probably studied medical librarianship under Professor Thomas P.
Fleming. Then in 1948 he became medical librarian at Yale University Medical
Library (Weisbrod, 1974, also Lee, 1982). While in the medical library at Yale,
Kilgour participated in a project involving Professor Fleming at Columbia and
Ralph T. Esterquest of Harvard. The three formed the Columbia–Yale–Harvard
Medical Libraries Computerization Project, which was a forerunner of such
programs of library service as MEDLINE (MEDLARS online), also a precursor
of MARC (machine-readable cataloging). In 1965, Kilgour was appointed
Yale's first associate librarian for research and development. In this position he
conducted significant research into catalog use and, through the application of
computers to library problems, enhanced the development of the Yale University
Library (Weisbrod, 1974, pp. 402–405).

Kilgour's most rewarding years, however, must have been the 13 years
(1967–1980) he spent building the Ohio College Library Center (OCLC), of
which he became executive director in 1967. His insights into human nature and
behavior were exceeded only by his insights into modern business practices. He
respected the need for basic research along with development and was aware of
the need for a broader base of librarians who understood both libraries and
computers.

In 1967 the Ohio College Library Center was established as a not-for-
profit corporation. Its history goes back 100 years to 1867 in Ohio when a dozen
charter members formed the Ohio College Association (OCA) with the aim of
cooperation among academic libraries. By 1967, this group had changed its
name to the Association of Ohio Colleges (AOC) and it consisted of over 60 full
and associate members (Kilgour, 1968d).

A Special Committee had been formed in 1951 to suggest cooperative
activities that could be undertaken. The committee was revitalized in 1961 and
its major recommendation was the establishment of a bibliographical center to
facilitate interlibrary lending and cooperative purchasing of microprint by the

center. Two commercial firms presented proposals that were to cost a million dollars each. Consultants were busy evaluating the proposals when a new approach was suggested, namely, a centralized computerized catalog. The committee approved the recommendation of the consultants and in an October 1966 meeting empowered its president to form a corporation, employ a director, choose a location for the center, and arrange for the receipt of funds. A year later, in October 1967, the Ohio College Library Center was a reality (Kilgour, 1968d).

The executive director employed was, of course, Frederick G. Kilgour, who was an advocate of a systems approach to management. He had spoken a year earlier at the Brasenose Conference on the subject of system design (Kilgour, 1967), and now his abstract design could be adapted to the real world. This still tentative design included a set of definitions, an understanding of the lack of and need for suitable consoles, and a statement of broad objectives that included (1) future benefits to education by providing information to research scholars and (2) benefits to libraries through cutting costs by eliminating the funding formerly expended on duplicate library functions. In Kilgour's system, a book, for example, would now be cataloged only once. Kilgour was interested in cost-effectiveness with the user as a component in the system. From the beginning he envisioned OCLC as a regional center that could also perform as a node in a national center at some future time (Kilgour, 1968d).

Kilgour originally called his operation a computer utility but eventually it became known as a bibliographic utility. While cataloging, or creating the unit record as it was sometimes called, was a principal subsystem and the only subsystem considered in this history, the other subsystems were less widely used, with the exception of what may be considered a spin-off from the bibliographic record, namely, the interlibrary loan utility (Kilgour, 1979b). This was closely allied with CONSER (CONservation of SERials), which was actually a part of OCLC devoted to making it possible to search for serials. The tragedy for many was that despite the overwhelming success of OCLC in terms of widespread use of the cataloging subsystem, the originally envisioned subject access postcoordinate retrieval subsystem did not materialize. Near the end of the Kilgour tenure it was abandoned as a possibility, but at the very end he envisioned a subject system that would be quite different, precoordinated, and adjusted to the needs of all users. This will be discussed later.

The first major project of OCLC was to be shared cataloging with daily input of the MARC format from the Library of Congress (Kilgour, 1968d, p. 85). From the beginning this was intended to assure that the standard of cataloging would be uniform and compatible with that of existing and potential nodes in a projected national network. Local librarians, especially catalogers, were to have the freedom to change the content of the cards that they were ordering without changing the master at the center. Five subsystems were projected: (1) shared cataloging; (2) bibliographical information retrieval, including subject retrieval; (3) circulation control; (4) serials control; and (5) a technical processing subsystem that would also include management information (Kilgour, 1968d, p. 86).

OCLC had begun as an off-line batch-processing system in 1967, then went on-line in 1971 and remained a venture of the Ohio academic libraries. In 1972, however, the membership was extended to Ohio nonacademic libraries, and in 1973 it was extended to out-of-state libraries. Within four years there were 800 member libraries, many of them members of the Association of Research Libraries, but also many were smaller libraries. By 1977, OCLC (Ohio College Library Center) had changed its name to merely OCLC Inc., and in 1981 to OCLC Online, Inc. (Reynolds, 1985).

During his tenure Frederick Kilgour had brought the OCLC cataloging operation to full fruition. By the time he was ready to retire (1980), complaints were being heard. Competition was replacing cooperation, and other bibliographic utilities were emerging. The problem of governance had been corrected, but the subject access problem remained.

OCLC's Competition

By the late 1980s, the four bibliographic utilities were: OCLC, the online computer library center; RLIN (Research Libraries Information Network); WLN (Washington Library Network); and UTLAS (University of Toronto Library Automated Systems). OCLC no longer had the edge on the market, although it was the largest in terms of the size of its database and the number of its member libraries. It had also trained its users and many students in newer methods of performing certain library functions, but was still being challenged by the other bibliographic utilities. OCLC has always been a not-for-profit corporation and its member libraries are represented on its governing board (Katz, 1982b).

RLIN was organized in 1978 at Stanford University when the Research Libraries Group (RLG) merged with BALLOTS. RLIN differs from the other bibliographic utilities in several ways. Its clientele are the representatives of RLG, whose members own RLIN equally. The members form a corporation that is responsible for its programs and activities (Kershner, 1979; Kallenbach and Jacobson, 1980). By definition, "RLIN is the computerized bibliographic network that supports RLG's cooperative programs in collection development, preservation, and shared access . . . it is a technological tool, the means to an end and not an end in itself" (Kallenbach and Jacobson, 1980, p. 265). In other words, RLG is the organization, the authority, and RLIN is the bibliographic utility as we have come to know them. For our purposes, the enhanced search capabilities, especially the subject access, are significant and will be discussed later in this chapter.

WLN is the smallest of the four in the number of libraries that it now serves. It has some advantages over the others, mainly its "superior data-base records, which may be searched in a greater number of ways: that is, much more of the record is actually searchable" (Katz, 1982b, p. 216).

UTLAS is a Canadian operation, and since January 1985 it has been a subsidiary of the International Thomson organization with an American office in White Plains, New York. It offers services considered to be "second only to OCLC." In the future WLN and UTLAS are expected to be strong competitors (Katz, 1982b, p. 216), but currently the battle has been mainly between OCLC and RLIN.

Soon after the inception of RLIN a fierce competition began. RLIN was attracting some of the research libraries that formerly had been committed to

OCLC. This disturbed OCLC's equilibrium, and it retaliated by inviting the directors of all the members of ARL to a briefing at OCLC headquarters in Columbus, Ohio. Of course, OCLC needed the business of these same libraries. Having been challenged by others, OCLC began to examine its own monopolistic organization.

De Gennaro had predicted that when all was settled there would emerge a competitive pattern similar to that among the vendors of search services from large databases (De Gennaro, 1979b, p. 1217). Over the years De Gennaro's predictions have displayed a high degree of accuracy, and this one was no exception. Immediate reaction to the challenge to OCLC's monopoly resulted in compromises (Preston, 1982) and comparisons of the bibliographic utilities (Stratford, 1984; Reynolds, 1985). The outcome so far is that one can now partake of the services of both OCLC and RLIN at the same time.

OCLC Governance

It will be recalled that in 1970 Kilgour explained that OCLC was a not-for-profit corporation. The membership community consisted of Ohio colleges and universities, with each member institution appointing a representative to the center. From this group, the representatives elected nine trustees whose function was the same as that of a similar group in most corporations—supposedly to set policy (Kilgour, 1970).

By 1973, Hopkins noted that the OCLC had opened its membership to nonacademic libraries in Ohio, and that as of May 1973 there were a total of 54 members and OCLC was employing the concept of the computer utility by supplying both computer power and bibliographic information for member libraries, who were free to use the information according to their own needs (Hopkins, 1973). Throughout the rest of the 1970s and 1980s, OCLC expanded into other states and even other countries. Libraries were beginning to participate through membership in a regional network node. Headlines such as "Ivy Libraries to Use OCLC" [Ohio College Library Center (OCLC), 1973] and "OCLC Comes to the Southwest" (Dodson, 1974) were typical. There appeared to be a rush to join.

The enormous growth from 54 members to more than 1800, most of them affiliated with a regional network, highlighted the inadequacy of the governance structure growth. In 1977, N. D. Stevens published his seminal paper entitled "Modernizing the Governance Structure." By 1978 the Arthur D. Little study entitled "New Governance Structure for OCLC: Principles and Recommendations" (Little, 1978) was published, and almost immediately the following headline appeared in *American Libraries:* "OCLC BECOMES DEMOCRA-TIZED, NATIONWIDE CORPORATION," capitalized, underlined, and in red ink. This headline announced not only that the voting members of the OCLC board had authorized the recommendations of the Little study, but that a new 15-member board of trustees (6 more than the previous board) would manage (*sic*), that the new name would be OCLC, Inc., and that a Users Council of 15 members would be elected from the membership to represent the contractors of OCLC services. Six were to be elected by the Users Council, five others would be representatives of professions such as law, business, etc., three must be from the library profession, and one the OCLC executive director (OCLC, Inc., 1978).

By 1979, Kilgour had updated his information on the structure of OCLC governance (Kilgour, 1979a). He had been with OCLC since the early days and had only recently experienced some of the problems and quandries that had beset other pioneers such as Henriette Avram when pioneering machine-readable cataloging at the Library of Congress and Mortimer Taube when pioneering postcoordinate retrieval with the use of Boolean operatives at Documentation, Inc. Kilgour retired in 1980 to attack new problems.

In 1982 the new director of OCLC, Rowland C. W. Brown, reported on the status of OCLC. At the time there were more than 6000 library participants in the United States, Canada, Mexico, and Great Britain, plus the 20 regional affiliates and two service centers (Holmes and Armstrong, 1982). Brown and his 16-member OCLC board of trustees seemed to be working through their problems with grace and faith. They were located in a new building in Dublin, Ohio, and had announced the end of a former moratorium in expansion of regional centers.

OCLC: Lack of Subject Access

In the early days of systems design at OCLC, subject access and retrieval was listed as one of Kilgour's projected subsystems for OCLC (Kilgour, 1970). Kilgour, being user oriented, was considering the results of some research on subject access: at the University of Chicago Graduate Library School, in a study designed to determine the requirements for a catalog based on what the users remember about a book they had previously seen, the findings noted that retrieval from memory of the subject was possible in 70% of the cases, of the title in 23% of the cases, and of the author in only 16% of the cases (reported in Kilgour, 1969, pp. 319–320). Highfill (1969) found that the more access points per item, the more probable is success in retrieval. There is little wonder that subject access occupied Kilgour over the years.

OCLC, to a large extent, has built upon the Library of Congress system of subject cataloging and MARC II standards. On average, the assignment of subject headings for monographs, for example, is 1.41 subject headings per item (O'Neill and Aluri, 1979, p. 18). The subject headings that are assigned are precoordinated. For subject cataloging this figure is the bare minimum. They discovered that 85% of the records had 1–2 headings compared to 5–10 for ERIC and at least as many for items using MeSH.

Many research studies and informal proposals reflect dissatisfaction. A few examples are studies by Immroth (1971), Atherton (1978), and Gray (1979). The reactions of the Library of Congress have been either noncommital or negative. In 1978, Lilley wrote a letter to LC suggesting that utilization of the ERIC system for assigning subject headings for postcoordinate retrieval could be the basis for change. The reply was apparently ironical but is a fair example of their general attitude: "You have provided a viewpoint which had been unexpressed to us until now, and we appreciate having this alternative brought to our attention." (Library of Congress, chief, 1978). In 1979, Gorman proposed that the burden of responsibility be taken from LC. This was unacceptable to William

J. Welsh, Deputy Librarian of Congress, who replied, "we would caution anyone who thinks that basic tools such as a subject system could be subjected to a thorough overhaul by a 'democratic process'. Subject heading systems require revision and review by a full-time staff and do not lend themselves to maintenance by committee" (Welsh, 1979). In 1983, Pauline Atherton Cochrane reported that in a recent Council on Library Resources study of Online Public Access Catalogs (CLR/OPACs) it was found that "the great majority of library users are performing topical subject searches."

Both OCLC (Kilgour, 1979e) and the Library of Congress (Avram, 1985) have stated that they cannot afford to change the subject system. Kilgour stated that "further investigation of subject retrieval employing traditional postcoordination appeared to be so costly that we aborted the project . . . we immediately initiated a new research project to explore other avenues for subject retrieval. Avram's reply was similar regarding cost (Avram, 1985).

It is obvious that the Library of Congress is not likely to change its mind regarding the level of subject indexing if William J. Welsh's reply to Michael Gorman is taken, as it must be, as an authoritative statement (Welsh, 1979). The suspected reasons for the failure to change the LC subject system are that while the LC personnel chose to do the MARC and RECON projects, they would not be enthusiastic about a similar and probably more disrupting project at a time when funding was scarce and qualified subject specialists were even scarcer.

The subject dilemma will not go away despite the research and a finding by Katz (1982a, p. 82) that 50% of all requests in a library are for subject. Eventually, there will be a solution, and perhaps Kilgour himself may fathom it. That was the hint in his acceptance speech at the ASIS meeting when he received their 15th Award of Merit (Kilgour, 1980).

Kilgour's Writings and Awards

During Kilgour's tenure at OCLC for several years he was also editor of the American Library Association's *Journal of Library Automation (JOLA)*, beginning in March 1968 with Volume 1, Number 1. This was an ideal position for communicating the activities of OCLC as well as for encouraging other writing in the field of library automation. He also contributed to other professional meetings and publications, and often participated at the Clinic on Library Applications of Data Processing, held annually since 1963 at the University of Illinois.

Of the three specialists featured in this chapter, two of them, Kilgour (1969) and Avram (1971a), have each written a chapter on "Library Automation" for the *Annual Review of Information Science and Technology*. In 1984 a two-volume collection of Kilgour's writings was published by OCLC. Volume 1 consists of his pre-OCLC writings: Volume 2 contains the writings from his OCLC days (Kilgour, 1984a). In a review of the two volumes, a British critic praised the collection, asserting that the papers are as relevant today as when they were composed and that Kilgour had changed the face of the future of librarianship (Enright, 1985).

"If library automation has a single dominant figure in the United States, he is most probably Frederick Kilgour" (Hay, 1981). This comment is by George A. Hay, Acting President of Reed College, which in May 1981 celebrated its 50th anniversary of the Eric V. Hauser Memorial Library. Why did Hay say this? Probably because Kilgour had created "a system for cooperative cataloging and shared resources," because he brought to OCLC his imagination and vision, and because, "to use Kilgour's knowing phrase, the system has achieved an economy of scale that returns immense dividends to inter-institutional cooperation." Kilgour later asked for a reprint to include in the compilation of his own papers (Kilgour, 1984a, Vol. 2, pp. 463–466).

In 1974, Kilgour received the American Library Association's Margaret Mann Citation in Cataloging and Classification for his "success in organizing and putting into operation the first practical centralized computer bibliographic center and making the Library of Congress MARC data base a practical and useful product" (American Library Association, 1974). Kilgour also had an honorary life membership conferred upon him by the American Library Association in 1982 (Malinconico, 1982). But his most fulfilling award was probably in 1979 when the American Society for Information Science bestowed upon him their Award of Merit for

> transforming a state association of libraries into a national interlibrary bibliographic utility, OCLC, Inc., that has proved the feasibility of nationwide sharing of catalog-record creation and has helped libraries to maintain and to enhance the quality and speed of service while achieving cost control—and even cost reduction—in the face of severely reduced funding. This achievement may be the single greatest contribution to national networking in the United States. His work will have a lasting impact on the field of information science (ASIS Bulletin, 1980).

The bridge from library science to full-fledged recognition in information science was a difficult road. When he retired from OCLC in 1980 to pursue other creative activities, it was said that he had brought OCLC "from an intrastate network with two employees and assets of $60,000 to an international network with over 400 staff and $53 million in assets." He was a member of the search committee for his replacement (OCLC, Inc., 1980).

Information Science Applied in Academic Libraries

From 1966 to 1986: De Gennaro Provided Guidelines for Academic Libraries

Richard De Gennaro was born in 1926 in New Haven, Connecticut. He attended Wesleyan University from 1947 to 1951, working toward a bachelor's degree in government, and from 1955 to 1956 earned a master's in history. From 1951 to 1955 he was on a European Language and Cultural Program, mainly in

France and Spain. In 1956 he was awarded an AMP (Advanced Management Program) certificate from the Harvard Business School (Lee, 1982, p. 116).

De Gennaro's professional library work began after he earned a master's degree in library science from Columbia University in 1956. From 1956 to 1958 he was reference librarian at the New York Public Library. From 1958 through 1969 he was employed at Harvard University libraries, rising from the rank of Assistant Director to Associate University Librarian for Systems Development and on to Senior Associate University Librarian in 1969. He then moved to the Philadelphia area, where he has been employed as Director of Libraries at the University of Pennsylvania since 1970. He continues to maintain that the prestige of large research libraries will soon depend on their competence in connecting the user with sources in all formats and not on how many volumes a library holds. (Some will remember the days when Yale had a book retirement program and Harvard was reluctant to discard anything for fear of losing its lead in numbers.)

Since his arrival at the University of Pennsylvania De Gennaro has received several leadership, cultural, and intellectual honors. He held the Presidency of the American Library Association's Information Science and Automation Division in 1970–1971 and the Presidency of the Association of Research Libraries in 1974–1975, completed at least one foreign study, and directed many "lost souls" through the world of academic library automation. No other librarian/systems developer/writer has assumed as much responsibility for determining the appropriate activity for research libraries in the United States regarding all aspects of automation. For approximately 20 years, 1966–1986, De Gennaro has been unobtrusively in command in print.

The issues that he has attacked have been mainly seven: (1) the necessity to convert to machine-readable format the collections of research libraries; (2) the choices in the timing and extent of a library's automation program; (3) the relationship of the research library to the bibliographic utilities and to the database search services; (4) use of the minicomputer in serials control; (5) the move from monopoly to competition in the bibliographic utilities; (6) the proper response of libraries to threats from those who would dictate behavior of academic and other research libraries and (7) access versus collection building as a goal.

In 1966, while at the Brasenose Conference, and again in 1967, while he was still at Harvard University, De Gennaro (1967a,b) asserted the need to convert to machine-readable format the vast collections of American and foreign research libraries. In a 1968 article, De Gennaro answered the question of not only when and how to initiate an automation program, but which library function to modernize first. This 1968 paper has become a classic. Its value was immediately recognized by the editor (and others) at the American Society for Information Science, who received permission to reprint it in the first edition of "Key Papers in Information Science" (Elias, 1971). This paper, entitled "The Development and Administration of Automated Systems in Academic Libraries," set forth three choices of when to initiate automation and advised that cataloging or the creation of the unit record be the first change because all other functions depended on it. His discussion is of considerable value even today, nearly two decades after its first publication (despite De Gennaro's own statement to the contrary). At the time it was unusual for a librarian, even one with systems experience as De Gennaro had, to be readily included among authors of information science papers, although from its beginning in 1966 the *Annual Review of Information Science and Technology* (*ARIST*) has included a chapter on library automation in nearly every volume.

In 1973 the online retrieval of bibliographic references from large databases was a new service. There were about 100 available databases (by 1985 there were more than 2805; Williams, 1985c, Vol. 1, p. vii). Contrary to what was at first anticipated, however, libraries did not have to purchase the tapes on a regular basis but could serve, when properly equipped, as the interface or broker, thus making available to the user the many references held by vendors such as Lockheed and System Development Corporation—and later, of course, BRS. De Gennaro (1973) pointed out that this situation was much the same as when MARC II first became available by subscription.

By 1975, in an article entitled "Library Automation: The Second Decade," De Gennaro reiterated that not all librarians would, as originally thought, need to subscribe to the MARC II tapes. Rather the bibliographic utilities and regional networks would be expected to acquire the MARC tapes and provide the cataloging services to libraries, including catalog cards. At the time he made it clear "that the era of localized automation had effectively come to an end" (De Gennaro, 1975a, p. 4). By 1977, however, De Gennaro recommended that a minicomputer be used for a local library serials control system and that an online catalog be developed in view of the future online catalogs that libraries would be expected to initiate (De Gennaro, 1977).

In 1979, De Gennaro delivered the Richard Rogers Bowker Memorial Lecture. He discussed some history beginning with Rider's prediction that the research library would outgrow its space (Rider, 1944), proceeding to the ideas of Shaw (1951) and the Rand Corporation (Hays 1968) for miniaturizing the printed word, and on to Fussler's report to the Sloan Foundation entitled "Research Libraries and Technology" (Fussler, 1973). He continued with a discussion of OCLC, Inc., and the needs of the Research Libraries Group, Inc., and criticized the deteriorating relationship between publishers and libraries. From there he considered the three waves of technology—the copier, the computer, and telecommunications—that have significantly changed the environment of the library and made it a smaller and smaller participant in the total information services (De Gennaro, 1979a). Although in this lecture he praised everyone but the entrepreneurs, he did not clarify the positive direction for action that librarians had come to expect.

Changes were still coming rapidly. In 1979, De Gennaro warned of a general move from monopoly to competition. He was speaking, of course, of the bibliographic utilities. There were now three in the United States and De Gennaro was apparently cooling to OCLC. He had decided that "a single monolithic national network embracing all libraries and providing all types of services is neither a realistic expectation nor a desirable goal for a country with its traditions of diversity and free enterprise" (De Gennaro, 1979b, p. 1217). This is the first time in print that one can detect an ulterior motive on De Gennaro's part, but the evidence is not strong.

By 1984 he was openly calling OCLC to task. In his article "Will Success Spoil OCLC?" De Gennaro (1984a) was adamant. Earlier he had chastised Lockheed and System Development Corporation for, in effect, making scapegoats of librarians (De Gennaro, 1975b). Similarly he had attacked Giuliano and Lancaster (De Gennaro, 1982) not so much for their outrageous projections—Giuliano asking why libraries cannot or do not charge for their services (Giuliano *et al.*, 1978; Giuliano, 1979) and Lancaster suggesting a paperless society (Lancaster, 1978a,b)—but for implying that librarians were unaware of their choices. De Gennaro understood that their complaints had some value, but he disagreed with the negative light cast on librarians for their backward habits. He did not believe such attacks would help bring about change. His "message" to the database search firms was: "Libraries do not have the money to support them in the style to which they became accustomed in the sixties" (De Gennaro, 1975b, p. 457).

In 1984 he also presented for print a revised version of his 1983 Samuel Lazarow Memorial Lecture delivered at the School of Library and Information Science at the University of Pittsburgh (these lectures are sponsored by Eugene Garfield's Institute of Scientific Information). De Gennaro again went to the defense of libraries. The electronic age was here, he admitted, and as a consequence libraries must acquire as much technology as they will need in the future. But for the next 20 years traditional services will exist side-by-side with the electronic services. He emphasized that access was the major goal, especially for research scholars. To De Gennaro the next necessary step is the online public catalog (De Gennaro, 1984b); as usual he had predicted the closing of catalogs and the reduced demand for catalog cards nearly a decade earlier (De Gennaro, 1976). Users were to participate directly through online public access catalogs.

Information Science Applied at the National Library of Medicine (NLM)

The National Library of Medicine has become an international leader in automated service. Service has always been the library's main goal and as Dr. William B. Bean noted in the preface to a recent history of the NLM, "the word library is no longer adequate for the National Library of Medicine and its offspring . . . [it] has become the central nervous system of American medical thought and research" (Bean, 1982, p. iii). We might add that it is a major international resource as well.

The application of information science at the National Library of Medicine (NLM) probably originated in 1958 with then Director Dr. Frank B. Rogers and Seymour I. Taine, Chief of the Bibliographic Services Division. Dr. Rogers and his colleagues were thoughtful planners, especially since the 1950s when they had worked with "The Committee," which was composed of such giants as Verner Clapp of the Library of Congress, later to become the Director of the Council on Library Resources, Ralph Shaw of the National Agricultural Library, and Mortimer Taube, all three librarians (Taine, 1963, p. 10). New ideas were rampant and funds were forthcoming. By 1964 MEDLARS (Medical Literature Analysis and Retrieval System) was operational and although it had cost $3 million, the amount was considered to be "high but reasonable in view of the fact that it was the only publicly available fully operational electronics storage and retrieval system of its magnitude in existence'' (Miles, 1982, pp. 374–375). Even in 1959–1960, when the mechanized system that preceded MEDLARS was being initiated (Taine, 1961) to improve the output and production of the *Index Medicus*, workers at the National Library of Medicine were envisioning a computer-based system that could handle not only the publication programs but information retrieval for on-demand services.

Contrary to what was to happen under a future director, Dr. Martin M. Cummings, whose work is discussed later, at this time there was very little so-called ''research'' that preceded the conception and realization of the new information system, MEDLARS (Bracken, 1971, p. 215); ''NLM acted in an autonomous fashion in designing the MEDLARS system'' (Bracken, 1971, p. 216). But regarding the lack of research, as early as 1959 the library had contracted with a biomedical computer expert to ''conduct a study to investigate the feasibility of using electronic digital computers for publication of the *Index Medicus* and also as a basis for construction of an efficient reference and bibliographic service'' (Taine, 1963, p. 111). As it happened, of course, MEDLARS was conceived by NLM insiders who had or would acquire specialties in various fields: medicine, librarianship, computer technology, and systems analysis. No one would call their work basic research but their efforts did result in significant change and new knowledge.

By 1961, the specifications for the first stage of MEDLARS were completed and invitations to submit proposals were sent to 75 organizations, of which 25 replied (Taine, 1963, p. 117). In August 1961 MEDLARS was officially launched when General Electric's Defense Systems Department, located in Bethesda, Maryland, was selected to provide an outline for the new system (Schiller, 1963). By January 12, 1962, GE's system plan was received. It included a subcontract to the Photon Company, who would provide GRACE (Graphic Arts Composing Equipment), which has been so highly praised (although it was not delivered on the date promised).

Reminiscent of Greek astronomy, the number three looms large, at least in the details of the MEDLARS development. The scheduled plan consisted of three phases: (1) preliminary design; (2) detailed design; and (3) implementation (Taine, 1963, p. 118). There were three subsystems in the human interface with the computer operations: (1) input; (2) manipulation; and (3) output (Schiller, 1963, pp. 951–952). Subsystem 1 was to manually prepare a unit record for each article, monograph, book, or serial title selected for indexing (Schiller, 1963, p. 951). Provision was made for 12 types of data to be provided by the indexers, including the recording of the increased number of subject headings (Schiller, 1963, p. 952). The completed data sheet was sent to the typist for conversion into machine-readable form that the computer could utilize. These data were typed on machines that simultaneously produced typewritten copy and punched tape. The cumulated unit record on the original reel of paper tape was read into the computer. The following was an often heard quotation: ''The unit record is the life blood of the MEDLARS system'' (Schiller, 1963, p. 951; Taine, 1963, p. 118).

In subsystem 2 the computer converted the paper tape information to magnetic tape, reprocessed certain information to facilitate retrieval, and stored the various programs fed into it on magnetic tape.

Subsystem 3 was for the output of whatever product was needed— *Index Medicus, Cumulated Index Medicus, Bibliography of Medical Reviews,* or *Current Catalog*—as well as data for on-demand bibliographies and later for online retrieval. The procedure for cataloging books was further strengthened through an extension of the programs of MEDLARS (Austin, 1968, pp. 61–68).

The NLM was a prime example of a library equipping itself to upgrade its services. The criteria were: (1) it must be a computer-based system; (2) there must be a unit record from which all other output is derived; (3) the subject system must be considerably expanded beyond the two or fewer subject headings assigned to each item at the Library of Congress or in the original version of the NLM manual system. MEDLARS met all three.

There were nine (divisible by three) primary objectives of MEDLARS (Taine, 1963; Austin, 1968), from which the preceding three criteria were derived. MEDLARS also had three secondary criteria to be met after the basic objectives were realized (Taine, 1963, pp. 116–117). In addition, as mentioned earlier, there was an extension of MEDLARS that brought cataloging into line and made the system both an indexing and a cataloging system. Somewhat later the AIM/TWX was developed (Abridged *Index Medicus*/Teletypewriter Exchange Network), which ultimately became the AIM transmitted through TYMSHARE, a less expensive telecommunications method that was used to connect some 50 cities in the United States and Europe. Austin (1968) has called the NLM automated system "dynamic" and pointed out its many changes from the original intentions as well as its successes and some failures.

Besides MEDLARS, which became operational in January 1964, we now have MEDLARS II (Katter and Pearson, 1975). For this, in 1966 Director Cummings contracted with the Auerbach Corporation to draw up specifications and with the Computer Sciences Corporation to design the system at a cost of $2,037,505. A new computer was not included in the price. MEDLARS II was to have been developed in three phases and completed by 1971, but there was trouble with the contractor's performance. Cummings finally canceled the contract, perhaps partly because the System Development Corporation of Santa Monica, California, while working with AIM/TWX, had discovered some implications for an online system. Cummings awarded a new contract to SDC for the completion of MEDLARS II. It was completed in 1974 and accepted on January 3, 1975, by Davis McCarn on behalf of the NLM. In 1979 Director Cummings appointed Joseph Leiter to form a task force that would be capable of developing, you guessed it, MEDLARS III (Miles, 1982, pp. 389–390).

Most relevant for our purpose is the NLM treatment of the problem of subject headings. One may observe that unlike the Library of Congress, which still assigns an average of fewer than two subject headings per item, MEDLARS has been concerned with practically every aspect of subject headings. Even in the planning stages in 1959, Winifred Sewell revised the MeSH (Medical Subject Headings) list in anticipation of the computer-based system. Subsequently there were other changes (Sewell, 1964), presumably some of them to allow Boolean logic to operate effectively. At one time an in-depth subject analysis was used to provide the user with from 4 to 10 or even 12 headings. Some of the subjects were available only to the computer-based search, that is, they were not included in the indexes. When F. Wilfred Lancaster evaluated the on-demand retrieval system in 1966, he suggested further improvement in the subject categories, some involving the subject system (Lancaster, 1968b, 1969 and 1972b). Cummings ordered that Lancaster's recommendations be followed and that a quality control system be initiated that would exert control over search in terms of the degree of recall and precision attained (Lancaster and Jenkins, 1970). In MEDLARS II there was a seven-level MeSH file (Miles, 1982, p. 389). In 1984, Milstead pointed out that "the AID (Associative Interactive Dictionary) system" (Doszkocs, 1978) at the National Library of Medicine may presage the future" (Milstead, 1984, pp. 173–174).

Information Science Applied at the
National Agricultural Library (NAL)

In 1862 U.S. President Abraham Lincoln called for a Department of Agriculture "to acquire and diffuse . . . useful information on the subjects connected with agriculture" (Moran, 1976). It took more than 100 years to establish an agricultural library with national and international reputation. Of course there has been much progress in the dissemination of agricultural information over the past 130 years, but the original mission statement still holds.

The National Agricultural Library network now includes 69 land-grant universities, some of the larger public and government libraries, and, as the library of last resort in the network, the National Agricultural Library (NAL) (Moran, 1976). This national network is part of an international network that offers services worldwide with materials in more than 80 languages (Peters, 1981).

It was not until 1964 that the National Agricultural Library formed its "computer group." By 1970 a batch information retrieval system was in place, CAIN (Cataloging and Indexing), which carried references to both journal and pamphlet material from the "Bibliography of Agriculture" and book as well as technical report literature from the "National Agricultural Library Catalog" (Peters, 1981). This database also contains references to research in progress through CRIS (Current Research Information System), a system of abstracts (Katz, 1982a, p. 204n). A change was made in 1976 when CAIN (a batch system) became AGRICOLA (Agricultural Online Access) and again in 1979 when the MARC format was adopted and the file was split by date (Peters, 1981).

From the mid-1970s through the 1980s, the services at the National Agricultural Library appeared to decline. This was attributed to declining leadership ("NAL Overhaul. . .", 1983), but neither Katz (1982) nor Peters (1981) seem to have been aware of this. Their reports are, in the case of Katz, factual and neutral and, in the case of Peters, lavish with praise. Peters explains in detail the fine national and international services of AGRICOLA and of AGLINET, the international agricultural library network.

The AGRICOLA database includes all formats and is especially rich in state and local documents as well as those of Third World countries. AGRICOLA is listed in the new edition of "Computer-Readable Data Bases" (Williams, 1985c) and is available from the three principal vendors in the United

States: DIALOG Information Services, ORBIT (SDC), and BRS. Training workshops are held periodically for users and a free AGRICOLA User's Guide is available.

A central point in this history is that similar to the services of the other two national libraries, the National Agricultural Library is currently a leader in serving users both nationally and internationally, and automation is playing an integral role.

Technologies Utilized

Computers

It is a great temptation to talk of generations of computers that have contributed to the automation of libraries. The first generation (1946–1960) was the vacuum tube model, which required special environments, had relatively little speed or storage capacity, and performed its tasks in a linear mode. The second generation (1960–1965) was the transistorized computer; the third (1965–) is the integrated circuit computer; and the fourth (1980–) is exemplified by the experimental very large scale integrated circuit (VLSI) computer. The mode of performing in all four generations is linear, and they are all considered to be John von Neumann machines (Feigenbaum and McCorduck, 1983, p. 17; Becker and Pulsifer, 1973, for dates; Grosch, 1976, p. 225, for generations of library systems).

There is now anticipation of a fifth-generation computer designed by the Japanese, and possibly a comparable sixth generation by the Americans that will be completely new, expert-machine design, with a nonlinear mode of performing, and that can accomplish artificial intelligence (AI).

The British and American authorities, especially the British, are skeptical of these future models and are refusing funding for research. Some of the key British scientists in this field have migrated to the United States, where they may be able to continue some of their work. Major breakthroughs are needed to parallel the reported plans of the Japanese (Feigenbaum and McCorduck, 1983).

AI is a phenomenon that has interested researchers for many years, even those working on problems in librarianship and information science (Smith, 1979, 1980). AI represents the reputed "thinking machine" and over the years it has inspired such skeptical treatises as "Computers and Common Sense" (Taube, 1961), which was probably intended to offset Turing's early works of "Intelligent Machinery" (1947) and "Computing Machinery and Intelligence" (1950), as well as the more recent work by Dreyfus (1979) entitled "What Computers Can't Do: The Limits of Artificial Intelligence."

In contrast to the optimistic scenarios of AI research is the down-to-earth concern by librarians and computer specialists that computers need to be understood and integrated with current library systems. Therefore we have such works as "The Computer and the Library" (Cox *et al.*, 1967), "Possible Applications of Data Processing Equipment in Libraries" (Wertz, 1964), "Implications for Librarianship of Computer Technology" (Hayes, 1964), "The Coming of Age of Information Technology" (Taube, 1964), "Application of Computer

Technology to Library Processes—A Syllabus'' (Becker and Pulsifer, 1973), and two editions of Artandi's ''An Introduction to Computers in Information Science'' (1968, 1972), to mention a few. The amazing mini- and microcomputers are among the latest computers on the scene (Kesner and Jones, 1984; Pratt, 1984). The computer is the principal technology that has changed the face of libraries. Other contributing phenomena, however, are the organizing and problem-solving capabilities inherent in systems analysis.

Systems Analysis Applied

Systems analysis, which is no more or less than a ''hypothetical construct, a form of abstraction we use to identify patterns in the empirical world around us'' (Gough and Srikantaiah, 1978, p. 14), is nevertheless a powerful organizing and problem-solving technique. The term ''systems analysis'' itself is a dichotomy: it joins the concept of synthesis, an additive process, and the concept of analysis, a divisional or reductive process. This probably explains the rubric ''systems analysis and design'' that is frequently used in the fields of information science and librarianship.

General systems theory, from which the concept of systems analysis derived, owes its development to the work of men such as Ludwig von Bertalanffy (1968) and R. Buckminster Fuller (1970). The theory includes exciting notions such as negative entropy, open and closed systems, and equifinality. These are discussed by von Bertalanffy but also appear in some of the 336 references cited by Gough and Srikantaiah in their book ''Systems Analysis in Libraries'' (1978).

While general systems theory is by appellation applicable in the discipline of library and information science, the application seems to have come through the fields of mathematics and engineering as they have encompassed game, decision, and information theory and model and paradigm construction. The definitions utilized in the fields of library and information science are clear: ''Systems analysis is a formal procedure for examining a complex process or organization, reducing it to its component parts, and relating these parts to each other and to the unit as a whole in accordance with an agreed-upon performance criterion. Systems design is a synthesizing procedure for combining resources into a new pattern'' (Borko, 1967, p. 37).

How or why librarians so readily adopted the system concepts is not revealed in the literature that we examined for this history. But we do know that the participants in the designing of new patterns of librarianship were aware of the application of systems analysis and design. This is particularly obvious in the Library of Congress (Markuson, 1966), the Ohio College Library Center (Kilgour, 1967, 1970), and the National Library of Medicine (Bracken, 1971).

The reader will recall that the King report from the Library of Congress (the ''Red Book''), while setting forth recommendations, did not have available the data that would have made a thorough systems analysis and design feasible. One can only speculate that, lacking the necessary data to support the recommendations, someone stepped forward to keep the ''ball rolling''; we suspect it was someone from the Council on Library Resources, since it was they who financed the study by Buckland. Meanwhile, the Library of Congress set up a system staff in the Office of the Director and later in their own Information Systems Office (ISO), which had as its mission "the development and implementation of the main automation program for the Library and the co-ordination of all LC automation efforts" (Avram et al., 1967, p. 180). Markuson had already produced "A Systems Development Study for the Library of Congress Automation Program" (1966), which was reproduced with introductory remarks in The Library Quarterly.

The Markuson paper that presented the framework for the systems study was in fact an official Request for Proposal (RFP) that was mailed to 70 prospective contractors. It set forth seven tasks or phases to be accomplished. The first three included gathering the data that had been lacking as well as providing a functional flowchart of the current operations. The fourth task was a request for a complete systems plan with all details. The LC staff had made some relevant decisions since the King report, among them to approach the automation problem in segments or, as they have come to be called, modules. Although the basis for the design came from the King report, there were to be changes.

Kilgour, upon making a presentation at the Brasenose Conference in England in 1967, admitted that "unhappily, the word system has acquired so many meanings that it has become a coat which fits nearly every wearer" (Kilgour, 1967, p. 46). He then proceeded to demonstrate the benefits of systems design by explaining the requirements and the benefits to management's position. During Kilgour's tenure as Director of OCLC, he further showed his approval of systems analysis and design by applying its principles in his operations.

Although other writers had alluded to the systems process at the National Library of Medicine, it was Bracken (1971, pp. 34–93) who made clear the details of systems analysis and design as it was applied during the planning and design of the MEDLARS system.

Research Findings Applied

Library automation has been accompanied by numerous research studies that are noteworthy because of their almost immediate applicability. These studies might be termed "pragmatic research." Such research was carried out whenever it was needed for the projects reported in this chapter. Avram et al. (1967), for example, measured the frequency of occurrence of various aspects of the catalog record. Kilgour researched the degree of efficiency of truncation in the retrieval process (Kilgour, 1968c, 1973; Kilgour et al., 1970, 1971); Bloomquist (1963) measured the unmet library needs of medical school students; and Cummings approved continued monitoring of the retrieval process (Miles, 1982, p. 377) following Lancaster's evaluation of MEDLARS (Lancaster, 1968a,b; 1969, 1972b).

The various systems analyses and, of course, the feasibility studies (King et al., 1963; Buckland, 1965) are forms of research as are the trial-and-error processes noted at the Library of Congress when the first two computer programs for MARC failed and at the NLM when the mechanization project of 1958–1960 failed to satisfy the requirements of both publication and on-demand retrieval.

Cummings, who came to the NLM as Director in 1964, was definitely more research oriented than some of the earlier development staffs. His previous position had been as Head of NIH's Office on International Research (Miles, 1982, p. 394). At the NLM he made plans to set up a research and development wing and engaged Ruth Davis, who arrived on April 24, 1967, as the Library's associate director for research and development (Miles, 1982, p. 420). Later Cummings was to redesign the research program and place it at Lister Hill National Center for Biomedical Communications (Miles, 1982, p. 421), where a network for use in a wide geographic area was planned to utilize satellite transmission. This facility was dedicated on May 22, 1980 (Miles, 1982, p. 431).

Operations research, insofar as it was considered to be different from systems analysis, was rarely mentioned in the research literature utilized in this chapter. This is confirmed by Kraft and McDonald who pointed out that "sophisticated O. R. techniques have not played a direct part in the design or evaluation of automated library systems" (1976, p. 133).

The architecture of the various MARC formats, the design of the OCLC consoles to meet specifications, and the selection of TYMNET for combination with AIM (Abridged Index Medicus) for MEDLINE services are all examples of innovative thinking and application.

Summary

The main purpose of this chapter has been to delineate and reveal the process by which information science in the past 30 years has affected libraries in the United States. Three libraries, the Library of Congress, the National Library of Medicine, and the National Agricultural Library, constitute our national library. Each has utilized information science for the benefit of its users. In addition, we discussed other groups in the information environment that have contributed significantly to improving and expanding library services.

The Council on Library Resources (CLR), under its first director, Verner Clapp, authorized and funded the research that led to the machine-readable unit record, which was later developed into MARC II (machine-readable cataloging) at the LC. MARC II has revolutionized the cataloging process not only in the United States but throughout the world. Second, the Association of Research Libraries (ARL) encouraged the development of RECON (the machine-readable unit record for a selection of retrospective items), whereby not only current but the best of the retrospective records could be available to research scholars. Third, the Ohio College Library Center (OCLC), the first bibliographic utility, developed a massive online cataloging program, largely attributable to the availability of the machine-readable unit record. This program completely changed the traditional procedures in many libraries.

Three persons were selected to represent this period: Henriette D. Avram, Frederick G. Kilgour, and Richard De Gennaro. Selections from their writings have documented their dedication to their respective interests in promoting library updating. All three have made significant contributions toward extended and improved service to users who range from the most sophisticated scholars in all fields to the student in the public schools or the citizen using the public library. De Gennaro fought for improved academic and other research libraries; Kilgour fostered all types of libraries through a critical period; and Henriette Avram developed and supported numerous projects, bringing them to fruition.

CHAPTER 4

Online Activity
1940–1985

Introduction

Although in this chapter we pay some attention to activities such as the first recorded use in 1940 of a remotely located computer, the air defense system of the 1950s, and some experimental online bibliographic information retrieval in the 1960s, our main focus is the online bibliographic retrieval systems of the 1970s and 1980s. Online bibliographic retrieval from large databases, traditionally a reference segment of library information services, was the principal online interactive search and retrieval activity of the early 1970s. Library catalogs online (OPACs—On-line Public Access Catalogs) for immediate access by end users are a phenomenon of the 1980s, although earlier examples do exist.

There were three "revolutions" involving information science during this period (Kent and Galvin, 1978): (1) the introduction of nonconventional information systems with postcoordinating capability (see Chapter 2); (2) the development and extensive use of the machine-readable unit record (see Chapter 3); and (3) online interactive bibliographic retrieval—the most sophisticated application of information science to date. The capability for this third revolution resulted from the application of information science methods that replaced traditional ones. This change involved creative use of the machine-readable record, its manipulation, and its transmission.

The reader may question why these drastic changes are attributed to the application of information science to traditional methods. One might even legitimately ask: Is there an information science? This latter question was addressed by Williams (1985a, 1988), who has written of the vigorous research on information science. Much of that research has been applied in online retrieval and transmission of bibliographic information.

Plan of the Chapter

A considerable portion of this chapter is devoted to the history of the development of the man–computer relationship. We include a listing of a selected group of early online retrieval systems with various functions, a discussion of the 1970s when information retrieval had come of age, and an introduction to three phenomena that occurred principally in the 1980s: awareness of the effect of the user's mental model on performance of the online search and retrieval; full-text search and retrieval; and the online public access catalog (OPAC).

The order of presentation is as follows: (1) introduction; (2) a discussion of the history of man–computer interaction; (3) examples of early online activity: (4) online information retrieval from large databases; (5) the 1980s, including advances in human–computer interaction, retrieval from full-text databases, and the library catalog as a database, and (6) a summary.

Tables

The tables included in this and following chapters were inspired by the effectiveness of the CRT display in conveying additional information. Although these tables lack the electronic energy, they are portable, concise, and carry information for the reader's edification and interpretation. Table 1, for example reveals a shift from general or multidisciplinary degrees to degrees that are information or communication specific; it also shows a shift from East Coast universities to those in the midwestern and western states.

Specialists

Online activities involve several types of specialists. In this chapter we feature nine specialists, even though each, because of space limitations, could be only briefly profiled (Table 1). Each specialist was selected on the basis of sustained contributions to at least one of the subfields of online retrieval: Ruth M. Davis, J. C. R. Licklider, and Christine L. Borgman on man–computer interaction; Roger K. Summit, Carlos A. Cuadra, and Martha E. Williams on control and marketing of services from large databases; Donald T. Hawkins on online bibliography, bibliometrics, and front-end devices; Carol Tenopir on full-text information retrieval; and Charles H. Hildreth on the online public access catalog (OPAC).

The activities of the first six specialists involve four of the principal developments in the 1960s and 1970s toward the improvement of online retrieval activities; (1) the history of man–computer interaction, that is, how men and women came to use the computer as a problem-solving partner; (2) how the new business of online retrieval was started; the entrepreneurial developments of vendors, the expansion of their services and markets, the national and international appeal of their services, and their supply sources and clientele; (3) the emergence of a new literature, including directories of databases available, bibliographies, and selection and analysis of the literature through the *Annual Review of Information Science and Technology* on subjects related to online retrieval; and (4) the results—sophisticated intermediary and end users, improved educa-

TABLE 1
Nine Specialists in the Field of Online Retrieval from Bibliographic and Full-Text Databases and Online Public Access Catalogs

Name	Latest degree and institution	Position and affiliation
Christine L. Borgman	1984, Ph.D., Information Science, Stanford University[a]	Assistant Professor,[b] Graduate School of Library and Information Science, UCLA
Carlos A. Cuadra	1953, Ph.D., Psychology, University of California at Berkeley[a]	President, Cuadra Associates, Santa Monica, California
Ruth M. Davis	1955, Ph.D., Mathematics, University of Maryland[a,c]	Director, Center for Computer Sciences and Technology, National Bureau of Standards
Donald T. Hawkins	1970, Ph.D., Engineering, University of California at Berkeley[a]	Information Retrieval and Foreign Language Service Manager, AT&T Bell Laboratories
Charles H. Hildreth	1977, M.S., Library Science, University of Denver[d]	Systems Analyst, OCLC
J. C. R. Licklider	1942, Ph.D., University of Rochester[a]	Bolt, Beranek, and Newman, Cambridge, Massachusetts
Roger K. Summit	1966, Ph.D., Management Science, Stanford University[e]	President, DIALOG Information Services, Inc.
Carol Tenopir	1984, Ph.D., Library and Information Science, University of Illinois[a]	Assistant Professor, University of Hawaii at Manoa
Martha E. Williams	1959, Ph.D., Philosophy, Bryn Mawr College[a]	Professor of Information Science, University of Illinois

[a]*Dissertation Abstracts.*
[b]*Journal of Education for Librarianship: Directory.*
[c]"American Men and Women of Science," 12th ed., Vol. 2.
[d]Hildreth (1982a).
[e]"Who's Who in Librarianship" (Lee, 1982).

tion, and services far superior to any that had been available prior to the advent of online retrieval.

The activities of the other three specialists were felt in the 1980s. In the 1980s, the environment was quite different from that of the 1960s and 1970s—so much had been accomplished, and resources, particularly financial ones, were said to be scarce. Despite these limitations, a look at these three specialists provides insights into their innovative selection and use of the technologies available to them. Occasionally funding from private sources became available, especially for research for the online public access catalogs by the Council on Library Resources and by OCLC.

Man–Computer Interaction: 1940–1985

Considerable computer research and development had to be completed before the information specialists could work in the field of online interaction between man and the computer. A diverse group of experts from disciplines such as psychology, mathematics, and engineering, to name a few, entered the computer field as did representatives from the for-profit organizations, universities, and other institutions. In the beginning, research funds were relatively plentiful.

Cuadra, in his 1971 article entitled "On-Line Systems: Promise and Pitfalls" (1971a), and Becker, in his 1975 article entitled "A Brief History of Online Bibliographic Information Systems," have written about the early days and the beginning of online research. For Becker it began in 1958 when, upon visiting UCLA, he arrived at the same time their IBM 709 computer was being uncrated. A few months later the UCLA library school dean asked Becker to deliver a short talk, whereupon Becker proceeded to explain the two-way interactive man-machines with all the confidence of a newborn information specialist (Becker, 1975). Cuadra had to plead a similar case of ignorance early in his career (Cuadra, 1971a).

By 1976, Becker was in a position of authority. He succinctly reviewed some early research and highlighted H. P. Luhn's work on automatic indexing and the attempt by Maron and Kuhns to establish a theory of relevance through applying the calculus of probability to indexing by computer (Maron and Kuhns, 1960). Becker also discussed general work by experts such as Anthony Oettinger of Harvard University and Gilbert King of International Business Machines (Becker, 1976), and pointed out that J. C. R. Licklider, then of the Massachusetts Institute of Technology, was one of the first to bring to light the proposed benefits of computer time-sharing that have led to experimentation in online activity and man–computer interaction (Licklider, 1960). Man in this context, incidentally, does not exclude woman, who has researched and reported well on the relationship of the two entities, one alive and thinking; the other, electronically driven, and, at present, still usually in the command of man. Cuadra became a respected expert and is a major figure in the history of online information retrieval (Table 1).

Information science has been dependent on the development of the computer and, given the scarcity in the beginning of computer experts, it is easy to see how information science came to be called an interdisciplinary field. There were no formally educated computer scientists nor, of course, any academically prepared information specialists (or scientists as some like to call themselves), although a few did have a science degree plus a library or information science degree. The visionaries came from a variety of disciplines. Two computer conferences are of interest in this regard. They were, in fact, lecture series, the first held in 1961 and the second nearly 10 years later, in 1969–1970. Both sets of proceedings were edited by Greenberger (1965, 1971).

The list of people who participated in the first of these conferences held in Cambridge, Massachusetts, included mathematicians, psychologists, communications engineers, biophysicists, physicists, industrial administrators, and representatives of other specialties. Three of the attendees, Vannevar Bush, Norbert Wiener, and Claude Shannon, are among the five pioneers featured in Chapter 1. Arthur C. Clarke was also nearby since he had been invited to lecture at the 100th anniversary of Alexander Graham Bell, which was celebrated at MIT during this conference. Three of those present, Bush, Licklider, and Kemeny, proposed new types of information services. Besides Bush's well-known proposal for "Memex" (1945a), there were Kemeny's "A Library for 2,000 A.D." (1965), and Licklider's soon to be published "Libraries of the Future" (1965).

A short aside may be in order here. The Council on Library Resources commissioned Licklider to head an investigation that would lead to a proposal for a library of the future. This occurred after the 1961 conference, which Bush and Licklider both attended, but Licklider stated that he had not read Bush's proposal until after the study for "Libraries of the Future" was completed. Later still Licklider decided to dedicate the book to Bush: "Now that I have read it, I should like to dedicate this book, however unworthy it may be, to Dr. Bush" (Licklider, 1965, p. xiii).

The following treatment of the development of the human–computer interaction is expanded chronologically by using the progression found in the *Annual Review of Information Science and Technology* (*ARIST*). We emphasize the specialists Ruth M. Davis, J. C. R. Licklider, and Christine L. Borgman. The latter appears in a later section with other selected specialists of the 1980s.

Specialists: Davis and Licklider

Ruth M. Davis was awarded a Ph.D. in mathematics from the University of Maryland in 1955. Thereafter she was employed by the U.S. Department of Defense whose SAGE (Semi-Automatic Ground Environment System for Air Defense) online information system was the first large operational system of its kind. The original plans were developed in 1952 (Licklider, 1965, p. 17) and it was in operation by 1957. The SAGE utilized the IBM Q 7 computer, which at the time was the largest computer in the world—an impressive fact (Cuadra, 1971a). The SAGE did not, however, utilize time-sharing, although it functioned in real-time (Meadow, 1970, pp. 9 and 93). In fact, as much as time-sharing had been proposed and discussed, it was not a reality yet.

Dr. Davis was the author of a chapter entitled "Man–Machine Communication" in 1966, Volume 1 of the *Annual Review of Information Science and Technology*. Carlos A. Cuadra, who had earned a Ph.D. in psychology from the University of California at Berkeley in 1953, was the first editor of *ARIST*.

In her chapter, Davis identified the terminology used in the field of man–machine interaction. She limited the term "machine" to the computer, which is acceptable for information science, equated "interaction" with dialog, that is, communication, and explained how people could interact with and utilize the computer but that there had to be carefully timed interaction. The equipment and services needed were a console connected by telecommunications or cable to a central computer and programming that had to be synchronized with the needs of the user who might or might not be the console operator.

The history of the development of display devices was discussed in another article by Davis. She identified the years 1957–1960 as the time when these devices began to permit real dialog between the user and the computer. She found that consoles could be truly interactive and not just typewriters. The Rand tablet and other devices could be utilized in conjunction with the CRT-based input devices (Davis, 1965).

In a review of the 1965 literature Davis discussed the concept of time-sharing, which she said started with Licklider's 1960 paper "Man–Computer Symbiosis" (there was actually an earlier paper by Christopher Strachey cited by J. McCarthy, 1965, p. 222). The concept of time-sharing was conceived as a method for saving each user some money while at the same time providing the user with access to a large computer. This arrangement was considered to be the computer utility in the same sense that we now view the data utility (MARC II) and the bibliographic utility (OCLC and others). Each utility was intended to provide individual benefit with the cooperative sharing of the cost, that is, the benefit was intended to exceed the cost. As Licklider has pointed out, this was not always the case. Two reasons were that the use of a large, powerful, and expensive computer operated at less than full capacity was not advantageous and that users did not readily understand the interactive computer languages. There were also differences in time-sharing concepts, for example, time-slicing, dedicated time, and multiprocessing (Davis, 1966, p. 224; Meadow, 1970, p. 98). Of course, eventually computer experts and even not-so-expert users realized that it was not necessary to utilize time-sharing to experience interactive dialog with a computer.

Another perhaps more urgent problem, identified in 1967 (Borko, 1967, p. 52), has persisted to this day; namely, there were few reports on the design of online systems. In 1966 Davis had listed several suggestions that she thought would help designers of second-generation online systems; among the suggestions was that interactive time-sharing languages would differ substantially from the ones then in existence. This was due mostly to operations made possible by the remote console. She predicted that choice of languages would, in the future, be very important to optimal functioning.

Yet another problem was that accompanying theory did not exist. Systems designers had proprietary feelings regarding any recommended change, which erected barriers to the resolution of problems and integration of different systems. However, Gould and Lewis (1983) of IBM did publish an important study of design. There was also the matter of competition among the computer suppliers. At one time a major discussion was whether to provide general or specialized computers to better serve the emerging needs.

Davis (1966, p. 245) considered the following applications of interactive online systems to be important: education and teaching, and document handling (although Davis thought these systems were extremely primitive, and most needed government subsidy because of their exorbitant cost). There were also management and statistical applications as well as some in grammar testing and in medicine. Of course, each of these applications brought new users.

Early on experts in the field saw the need to increase the base of online bibliographic reference retrieval users to more than just the programmers, who were the ones most likely to understand the systems. In 1965, Kessler and others at MIT developed TIP (Technical Information Project) with the possibility for such user expansion (see Kessler, 1965). It utilized time-sharing, and with this system the user did not have to be a computer expert to query the system. It could accommodate 400 potential users and 30 could use it simultaneously (Kessler, 1965).

In 1967, Dr. Davis left the Department of Defense (DOD) when she was hired by Dr. Martin M. Cummings, Director of the National Library of Medicine, as the library's Associate Director for Research and Development (Miles, 1982, p. 420). In 1971 she became Director of the Center for Computer Sciences and Technology, U.S. National Bureau of Standards (Davis, 1971, p. 1).

It is interesting to speculate why Dr. Davis moved from one U.S. government information retrieval operation to another (DOD to NLM to NBS), although at this time there was a noticeable shortage of qualified personnel in the online information retrieval field, especially those oriented toward research. One can guess that there were sociometric reasons involved, because the DOD, in its early days, was closely allied with the System Development Corporation of California, which was in turn involved with the National Library of Medicine through having supplied ORBIT to the NLM during its transition from MEDLARS to AIM/TWX (Abridged *Index Medicus*/Teletypewriter Exchange Network) and then to MEDLINE (MEDLARS online). Also, Dr. Cuadra of SDC was in charge of the NLM project during the transition. The National Bureau of Standards, on the other hand, had been actively involved in monitoring certain changes in technology and the research accompanying it as had been recommended by several experts from the computer and human engineering fields.

J. C. R. Licklider is the second of our selected specialists. He received his doctorate from the University of Rochester in 1942. After conducting research on human communication and information processing at Harvard University and the Massachusetts Institute of Technology, he became President of the Acoustical Society of America. By 1961 he was the supervisory engineering psychologist of Bolt, Beranek and Newman, Inc., of Cambridge, Massachusetts, from which he was recruited by the Council on Library Resources to head a study on the library of the future.

Licklider accepted this challenge and began work in November 1961. In October 1962 he took a leave of absence to fulfill a special assignment for the Department of Defense. Research on the library project continued, however, and in 1964 the final report was issued and in 1965 "Libraries of the Future" was published (Clapp, 1965, pp. v–ix). The book may be more cited than read. It consists of crucial points that are difficult to attribute to any specific research. Future systems designers, however, may have benefited from some of the information and suggestions.

In 1968, Licklider published "Man–Computer Communication" in Volume 3 of *ARIST*. He was encouraged that some of the serious online programs were "perfected and exploited in a substantive way" (Licklider, 1968, pp. 201–202). The two first-generation online systems that he considered to be the leaders were CTSS (Compatible Time Sharing System) at MIT and TSS (Time-Sharing System) using the Q 32 computer at the System Development Corporation. A second-generation time-sharing system was also reported that could use more complex software and hardware. But all the problems had not gone away.

In reviewing the 1967 literature Licklider found several problems and changes. For example, the 360/67 computer from IBM was behind schedule, and the GE 645 ran in a "slow and faltering way," indicating that perhaps the total system was "too complex for man's present capability." More sophisticated users were needed. Also lacking was a sense of system—the integration of all the components including console, computer, communication lines, programs, sets of data, as well as memory storage and file and data management techniques. Some changes, however, were encouraging: an increase in computer graphics; debugging of all programming was now done online; with the advent of ARPA (Advanced Research Projects Agency), networking was rivaling time-sharing; and the emergence of a variety of sizes of computers, although the IBM 360/67 dominated the time-sharing market.

Licklider also set forth a plan whereby five types of man–computer interaction were sorted according to the size of the computer and the size of the task. This organization clarified the variety of uses in problem solving, for example, the idea of connecting a small computer with a large one, which acted as a satellite in either a batch or an interactive, multiaccess mode. So much had been developed in the past year that Licklider suggested the topic be subdivided in the future.

It soon became obvious that not only were new generations and types of computers needed, but also new generations of programming, new console and display designs, and new types of users with appropriate education. Telecommunications services in the beginning were inadequate to carry the increased loads demanded by time-sharing (Kemeny, 1971, p. 12). The advantage of time-sharing was that it served many people at once, which reduced costs and encouraged communication among its users. (Fano and Corbato, 1966). A disadvantage was the difficulty of finding sufficient users for optimally efficient runs.

Between the Davis (1966) and Licklider (1968) reviews, other suggestions were offered: debugging of programs needed two-way interaction; batch processing with its long delays was annoying; and rapid interaction was needed, for symbolic calculation and for teaching machines, so that the worker might proceed at his or her own pace. The question arose why Kemeny's modern library could not be realized in 1965 instead of the year 2000. The preferred terminal was already the more expensive CRT terminal that could project both graphics and text and could utilize the light pen and the Rand tablet (McCarthy, 1965).

Mills, in a 1967 *ARIST* chapter, had noted that the literature revealed concern for improvement in several areas. Lack of progress seemed to prevail. There had been no second-generation systems in operation; the principal terminal device was still the typewriter; visual coupling was scarce, except in special-purpose systems such as SAGE; the common language in use was still FORTRAN; and the computer was still not used extensively by the many people who perhaps could benefit the most but who had no understanding of computers. Yet new developments were encouraging: the concept of the computer utility whereby institutions would not need to own their computer but could subscribe to services online; Federal Communications Commission investigations promised some mutually agreeable policy decisions; and there was considerable evidence that bibliographic services from large databases were in the offing. Borko had worked on online displays that the SDC crew praised, although Mills considered their enthusiasm to be overstated. Perhaps the most significant development was an unforeseen aspect of time-sharing: the advantage inherent in a common intellectual community of users (Mills, 1967, pp. 240–243).

It appeared that in the future, user feedback to designers would be crucial. In 1965, Licklider had recommended several tangible items such as a light pen of a certain size, shape, and weight (Licklider, 1965, pp. 94–95). By 1971, Cuadra had set forth his 13 suggestions that were based on his philosophy that design should or could lead users to higher and higher levels of competence. His suggestions dealt mainly with flexibility of choices to extend and improve the search (Cuadra, 1971a). By 1972 *ARIST* was urging designers of online systems to focus mainly on accommodation of users with a lack of sufficient knowledge (Bennett, 1972). In 1973 *ARIST* noted that although theory had not preceded design, progress had been made in several respects. Languages had come to mirror the task rather than the computer's internal structure and storage and access had both been immeasurably improved (T. H. Martin, 1973). Focus could now shift to the conceptual aspects of interaction. Summit set forth the following encouraging developments: the online search was affordable; user rapport with the database had been achieved; search outcome was improved by the online thesaurus and index display; and improved search capability resulting from the incremental search formulation whereby the user could begin simply, then increase the request to a higher level of sophistication. He also noted that both indexed and full-text collections must be provided (Summit, "Evolution and Future of Computer-Assisted Information Retrieval," reported by T. H. Martin, 1973, p. 214).

In 1984, Christine L. Borgman completed a dissertation at Stanford University (1984b) as well as a chapter for *ARIST* entitled "Psychological Research in Human–Computer Interaction" (Borgman, 1984a). A precursor to this was "Mental Models: Ways of Looking at a System" (Borgman, 1982). One major breakthrough was manifested in the title change from "Man–Computer" to "Human–Computer." We must acknowledge advancement even when it occurs in small increments (Ramsey and Grimes, 1983; Borgman, 1984a). The Borgman dissertation is discussed later in this chapter.

By 1986 the 23rd Annual Clinic on Library Applications of Data Processing hosted its clinic on the topic of "What Is User Friendly?" This was not so far from Licklider's "Symbiosis"—or that of Kemeny or Strachey. For nearly 30 years, 1957–1986, humans and computers had been connecting on a regular basis. By 1975 online information retrieval had emerged to serve several types of applications: defense, airlines, and banking, to name a few (Frisch and Frank, 1975). Bibliographic information retrieval online systems had appeared in government establishments, academic institutions, and industry (Brandhorst and Eckert, 1972).

From 1966 to 1986, *ARIST* reviewers have covered the research, inno-

TABLE 2
Man–Computer Interaction: Relevant Chapters in _ARIST_[a] and Other Key Works, 1960–1970

Year	Volume	Author(s) and title	Affiliation
1960	NA	J.C.R. Licklider "Man–Computer Symbiosis"	Bolt, Beranek, and Newman
1965	NA	J. McCarthy "Time-sharing Computer Systems"	MIT faculty
1966	1	R.M. Davis "Man–Machine Communication"	Department of Defense
1967	2	R.G. Mills "Man–Machine Communication and Problem Solving	MIT
1968	3	J.C.R. Licklider "Man–Computer Communication"	See above
1970	5	H.D. Huskey "Computer Technology"	University of California at Santa Cruz
1970	5	R.L. Simms, Jr., and E. Fuchs "Communications Technology"	Bell Telephone Laboratories
1970	NA	C.T. Meadow "Man–Machine Communication"	National Bureau of Standards

[a]_Annual Review of Information Science and Technology._

vations, and problems in the field of man–computer interaction. Tables 2, 3, and 4 list some of these important reviews.

Early Online Systems: 1940–1970

The decade from 1960 to 1970 was a period of experimentation into online retrieval for various purposes (Table 5). Until this time, research in information science was conducted largely in Washington, D.C., or in one of the East Coast universities, particularly those whose personnel were interested in the computer as an ally in problem solving. Telecommunications problems had to be worked through; the concept of time-sharing had to be realized; and there was still much experimentation needed into methods for improving the man–computer interaction.

TABLE 3
Man–Computer Interaction: Relevant Chapters in *ARIST* and Other Key Works, 1971–1979

Year	Volume	Author(s) and title	Affiliation
1971	NA	M. Greenberger, ed. "Computers, Communications, and the Public Interest"	Johns Hopkins University, Professor of Computer Science and Director of Information Processing
1972	7	J.L. Bennett "The User Interface in Interactive Systems"	IBM Research Lab
1972	NA	J.G. Kemeny "Man and the Computer"	President, Dartmouth College
1973	8	T.H. Martin "The User Interface in Interactive Systems"	Stanford University
1976	11	P.L. Long "Computer Technology—An Update"	Phillip Long Associates, Inc.
1977	12	S.R. Bunch and P.A. Alsberg "Computer Communication Networks"	Center for Advanced Computation
1979	14	L.A. Hollaar "Unconventional Computer Architecture for Information Retrieval"	University of Illinois at Urbana

West Coast research centers such as the Rand Corporation, the System Development Corporation, and Lockheed Missiles and Space Corporation, as well as some universities, entered the mainstream of online retrieval through their research projects and by providing leadership to the national establishments such as NASA and the NLM. Two of our featured specialists come to mind: Roger K. Summit of Lockheed's DIALOG, who was instrumental in applying Lockheed's techniques to the NASA-RECON online bibliographic retrieval system; and Carlos A. Cuadra of the SDC, who administered the ORBIT II in the NLM's AIM/TWX experiment (Table 5).

The Real Beginnings of Man–Computer Symbiosis

Despite the early attempts to make the computer a symbiotic partner (Strachey, 1960; Licklider, 1960; Kemeny, 1972), the first recorded example of

TABLE 4
**Human–Computer Interaction: Relevant Chapters in *ARIST* and Other
Key Works, 1980–1984**

Year	Volume	Author(s) and title	Affiliation
1980	15	A.E. Cawkell "Information Technology and Communications"	Institute for Scientific Information
1981	16	P.W. Williams and G. Goldsmith "Information Retrieval on Mini- and Micro-Computers"	University of Manchester Institute of Science and Technology
1983	18	H.R. Ramsey and J.D. Grimes "Human Factors in Interactive Computer Dialog"	IIT Programming Technology and Development
1984	19	C.L. Borgman "Psychological Research in Human–Computer Interaction"	UCLA
1984	19	A.D. Pratt "Microcomputers in Libraries"	University of Arizona

a man using a remote computer as a working partner occurred when Dr. George Stibitz of the Bell Telephone Laboratories, at a meeting of the American Mathematical Society in September 1940, conducted a demonstration at Dartmouth College in New Hampshire while connected to a computer at the Bell Labs in New Jersey (Stibitz and Larrivee, 1957, pp. 53–54). The date of this activity was confirmed by Dr. J. W. Mauchly during a panel discussion at a 1961 conference (Greenberger, 1965, p. 238). Ruth M. Davis reported that the Bell Telephone Lab's first time-sharing system appeared "around 1950" (Davis, 1966, p. 226, quoting Samuel, 1965). This information is ambiguous. We now know that the first online interaction was 1940; the first time-sharing may have been and no doubt was a different matter.

Mauchly was himself a giant in the computer world, having co-invented and built in the 1940s, with J. Presper Eckert, the famous ENIAC (Electronic Numerical Integrator and Calculator) at the Moore School of Engineering at the University of Pennsylvania in Philadelphia. The ENIAC, the first electronic computer, was dedicated in 1946, six years after the first man–computer online interaction had taken place. Mauchly also co-designed and built the UNIVAC, the first commercial electronic computer after the Eckert–Mauchly Computer Corporation was absorbed by Remington Rand in 1947–1950 (Greenberger, 1965, pp. xvii–xviii).

TABLE 5
A Selection of Early Online Systems

Year Online	System	Function	Affiliation	Reference
1940	No name known	Demonstration	Bell Telephone Labs	Mauchly (1965); Stibitz and Larrivee (1957)
1952–1957	SAGE (Semi-Automatic Ground Environment System)	Air defense	Dept. of Defense	Licklider (1965); Cuadra (1971a)
1962	SABRE	Airline reservations	American Airlines	Parker (1965)
1964	TIP (Technical Information Project)	Bibliographic online retrieval	MIT	Kessler (1965)
1965–1967	BOLD (Bibliographic Online Display)	Online communications with computer	SDC	Borko (1966)
1964–1969	NASA-RECON (-Remote Console)	Bibliographic information retrieval online	Lockheed, NASA	Wente (1971)
1970	AIM/TWX (Abridged Index Medicus/Twx)	Experimental online bibliographic retrieval	SDC, NLM	Katter and McCarn (1971)

Most of the early online retrieval experiments occurred in the late 1950s and early 1960s. Examples are SAGE, SABRE, and TIP, which are air defense, airline reservations, and bibliographic online retrieval systems, respectively. We cite three additional experiments between 1965 and 1970 (Table 5) that illustrate the beginnings of the powerful online bibliographic retrieval systems that were developed at the Lockheed and System Development Corporation centers in California. BOLD was an experiment in display techniques (Borko, 1966), and ORBIT was to lead to MEDLINE. Similarly, Lockheed's development of NASA-RECON was to lead to a national and international system of the same name (Table 5). The West Coast was now involved in research and development, and the commercially oriented vendor was about to emerge.

Online Information Retrieval from Large Databases

An enormous new business was soon created. Equipment for remote utilization of the computer was designed, developed, and installed. Publications related to online retrieval emerged—directories, textbooks, bibliographies, and journals—and research studies of the effect of online retrieval on users were undertaken (Wanger *et al.*, 1976). The vendors collected databases from the producers, who developed their databases by organizing the documents created by researchers and other writers. The vendors then distributed portions to users upon online request.

Following the appearance of the earliest online systems, several other improvements were needed before massive retrieval of bibliographic references was possible. First, large, machine-readable databases had to be created. These were produced in increasingly large numbers in the 1970s. In 1974, for example, there were fewer than 100 such databases available (Williams, 1974), and by 1984 there were 2805 databases in 2509 separate entries according to one compilation (Williams, 1985c, Vol. 1, p. 11). Second, databases had to become available to libraries and information centers, mainly through vendors, or search services, as they came to be called. In the beginning these search services were principally from Lockheed (DIALOG) and System Development Corporation (ORBIT), with Bibliographical Retrieval Services (SEARCH) added in 1977 offering 10 databases (Reynolds, 1985, p. 118). (It is the vendors' programs for search services that are labeled DIALOG, ORBIT, and SEARCH; the latter is not often used as a name for the service.) For a considerable period these three were the principal vendors. In 1978, there were only eight commercial vendors in the United States; the new vendors were Battelle Memorial Institute, Informatics, Mead Corporation, New York Times Data Bank, and the Ohio College Library Center (Cuadra, 1978). This roster has changed many times (Neufeld and Cornog, 1986). Third, library and information center personnel had to learn how to use the vendors' services. It was a new experience; both the intermediaries in the libraries and information centers and their end users were faced with new roles.

Online Information Retrieval Comes of Age: 1971–1979

In 1971 several major databases listed in Table 6 either were online or went online. Salton's SMART, a batch experiment since the 1960s, was finally designed to go online. The book summarizing SMART research was also published (Salton, 1971b). Brandhorst and Eckert succinctly enumerated 11 of Salton's conclusions to this point. They also listed the databases on which the research had been based and their sizes (Brandhorst and Eckert, 1972, pp. 410–411).

Three significant and unique books also appeared in 1971. The first was

TABLE 6
A Selection of Online Bibliographic Systems Operating in 1971

System	Start-up year	Affiliation
OCLC	1967	Ohio College Library Center
MEDLINE	1964	MEDLARS online
ERIC	1966	Educational Research (later Resources) Information Center
NTIS	1964	National Technical Information Service
SMART	1961–1964	Experimental Automatic Retrieval System, Harvard and Cornell universities

a proceedings of a workshop on the subject of the man–machine interface. The workshop was unique in that it was conducted for and limited to experts in the information field (Walker, 1971). An equally important work was the King and Bryant (1971) publication on the evaluation of information services, which was the first comprehensive textbook on this subject. The third work was Lancaster and Fayen's textbook "Information Retrieval On-line," published in 1973.

In addition, following a meeting of the International Federation of Documentation (FID) in September 1972 (Fry, 1973, p. i), Bernard M. Fry, editor-in-chief of the international journal, declared in an editorial that his journal, *Information Storage and Retrieval* (later to become *Information Processing and Management*), had come of age. He announced that beginning in 1973 the journal would extend its coverage into practical applications in libraries, information systems, and networks, and increase its frequency from a quarterly to a monthly publication. Brandhorst and Eckert concluded their 1972 article in *ARIST* with a comment that the community of users was now increasingly sophisticated in performing computer searches (Brandhorst and Eckert, 1972, p. 416).

Tables 7 and 8 list some of the chapters that reviewed large databases, document retrieval and services, use of machine-readable databases, experimental techniques of information retrieval, database management, online systems and techniques, and education and training for online systems. The tables are intended to present an overview of the period. Table 9 lists publications related to databases and online retrieval that have specifically involved the specialists featured in this chapter.

Specialists: Williams, Summit, Cuadra, and Hawkins

Four specialists who made significant contributions to the historical development of online retrieval services will be discussed: Martha E. Williams,

TABLE 7
Online Information Retrieval from Large Databases: Relevant Chapters in
ARIST, **1972–1979**

Year	Volume	Author(s) and title	Affiliation
1972	7	M. C. Gechman "Generation and Use of Machine-Readable Bibliographic Data Bases"	Information General, Inc.
1972	7	W. T. Brandhorst and P. F. Eckert "Document Retrieval and Dissemination Services"	ERIC and NASA
1974	9	M. E. Williams "Use of Machine-Readable Data Bases"	University of Illinois
1974	9	R. K. Summit and O. Firschein "Document Retrieval Systems and Techniques"	Lockheed Palo Alto Research Laboratories
1975	10	P. B. Schipma "Generation and Use of Machine-Readable Data-Bases"	IIT Research Institute
1976	11	D. U. Wilde "Generation and Use of Machine-Readable Data Bases"	New England Research Applications Center, University of Connecticut
1979	14	M. J. McGill and J. Huitfeldt "Experimental Techniques of Information Retrieval"	School of Information Studies, Syracuse University
1979	14	M. A. Huffenberger and R. L. Wigington "Database Management Systems"	Chemical Abstracts Service

Roger K. Summit, Carlos A. Cuadra, and Donald T. Hawkins. They have earned Ph.D. degrees in the fields of philosophy, management sciences, psychology, and engineering, respectively (Table 1). Graphically they inhabit three different states: Williams in Illinois; Cuadra and Summit in California; and Hawkins in New Jersey. Each has been involved for several years in the relatively new application of information science—the online search and retrieval of bibliographic references from large databases. Cuadra, Williams, and Hawkins have

TABLE 8
Online Information Retrieval: Relevant Chapters in *ARIST*, 1976–1979

Year	Volume	Author(s) and title	Affiliation
1976	11	B. Marron and D. Fife "Online Systems— Techniques and Services"	Institute for Computer Science and Technology, National Bureau of Standards
1978	13	D.B. McCarn "Online Systems— Techniques and Services"	National Library of Medicine
1979	14	J. Wanger "Education and Training for Online Systems"	Cuadra Associates, Inc.

participated in major publishing projects related to online retrieval (Table 9). Their professional activities have been varied but focused.

Summit is President of DIALOG Information Services, Inc.; Cuadra is President of Cuadra Associates; Hawkins is Information Retrieval and Foreign Language Services Manager at the AT&T Bell Laboratories; and Williams is Professor of Information Science at the Coordinated Science Laboratory, University of Illinois. Williams is also Chairman of the Board of Regents of the National Library of Medicine, Chairman of the Board of Directors of Engineering Information, Inc., and Fellow of the American Association for the Advancement of Science. For a number of years she was co-author of a column in the *ASIS Bulletin* on the subject of databases; she is editor of the *Annual Review of Information Science and Technology, Online Review,* and *Information Market Indicators.* She is editor-in-chief of "Computer-Readable Databases: A Directory and Data Source Book" (1st, 2nd, 3rd, and 4th editions).

Martha E. Williams is an elected honorary Fellow of the Institute of Information Scientists of London, England, and in the United States has received the 1984 American Society for Information Science Award of Merit (Williams, 1985a). Her principal interest, aside from her obvious leadership, teaching, and research advisory roles, is assuring that the operation of the online search and retrieval activities becomes "transparent" to end users. She has summarized the history of the basic ideas leading to transparent retrieval methodology (Williams, 1986). Database monitoring has been another of her self-imposed responsibilities. A sampling of her papers reveals her numerous contributions and dedication (Williams, 1975a,b; 1977b,c,d; 1984, 1985b).

Roger K. Summit has been called the father of online retrieval (Herner, 1984). He was born in Detroit, Michigan, and migrated to California, where he earned three degrees: an A.B. in psychology in 1952; an M.B.A. in 1957; and a Ph.D. in Management Science in 1965—all from Stanford University. From 1965 to 1972 he was a research scientist in Lockheed's Information Science Lab;

TABLE 9
Emergence of Online Publications

Year	Author	Publication	Position
1966–1975	Cuadra	*Annual Review of Information Science and Technology,* Volumes 1–10	Editor
1976–present	Williams	*Annual Review of Information Science and Technology,* Volume 11–present	Editor
1976	Williams	"Computer-Readable Bibliographic Data Bases: A Directory and Data Source Book," 1st ed.	Editor-in-Chief
1977–present	Williams	*Online Review,* Volume 1–present	Editor
1977	Hawkins	"Online Information Retrieval Bibliography, 1965–1976"[a]	Compiler
1979–present	Cuadra Associates	"Directory of Online Databases" (quarterly)	President of Cuadra Associates
1979	Williams	"Computer-Readable Bibliographic Data Bases: A Directory and Data Source Book," 2nd ed.	Editor-in-Chief
1982	Williams	"Computer-Readable Data Bases: A Directory and Data Source Book," 3rd ed.	Editor-in-Chief
1985	Williams	"Computer-Readable Data Bases: A Directory and Data Source Book," 4th ed.	Editor-in-Chief

[a]Updated annually in *Online Review.*

from 1972 to 1977, Manager of Lockheed's Information Retrieval Service; from 1978 to 1981, Director of Information Systems at Lockheed's Palo Alto Research Lab; and from 1981 to the present, President of DIALOG Information Services, Inc. (Lee, 1982). By 1985 DIALOG Information Services, Inc., with Summit as president, offered more than 100 million records on many subjects from more than 200 different databases to its many customers in several countries (Camp, 1985).

There have been many changes and much growth since 1964 at the beginning of Lockheed's online retrieval system. At that time there were just two other systems that Summit, among others, considered to be precursors of it: Kessler's TIP at MIT and the experimental SMART system by Salton at Harvard (Table 5). Lockheed's second-generation design utilized "dialogue." The new system emerged slowly from a file size of 100 to 1600 to 8000 in steps called

Converse I, II, and III; in 1966 the latter was expected to switch from a tele-typewriter terminal to a CRT (Drew *et al.,* 1966). DIALOG later became the name of the retrieval program and later still the name of the company that divested from Lockheed, DIALOG Information Services, Inc., a full-fledged subsidiary. By 1967, Lockheed was well established in the area of interactive retrieval from their then few databases. In 1968 NASA contracted with Lockheed to design NASA-RECON (Table 5). Subsequent ventures made Lockheed a worldwide name in information retrieval. In 1971 Lockheed's commercial busi-ness was launched, and soon thereafter it was serving Europe as well as the United States with its first online bibliographic retrieval system.

NASA-RECON had cost from $200,000 to $300,000 plus an additional $700,000, for a total of approximately $1 million. This did not seem exorbitant at the time since IBM had developed the New York Times Information System at a cost of $3 million and ORBIT of the System Development Corporation had contracted with the National Library of Medicine to provide AIM/TWX at a cost that probably reached the $1 million mark. Subsequently the National Agri-cultural Library contracted for Lockheed services at a minimum of $16,000 per month. The direct system method of development for these large systems was clearly a costly way to go (Summit, 1975a). The method for developing online retrieval services would soon change. By 1974 this was manifested by the many databases held by a few vendors, with libraries and information centers acting as intermediaries. These intermediaries accepted requests from end users (Summit and Firschein, 1974).

By 1975, when Summit was officially Manager of the Systems Program Office at Lockheed Missiles and Space Corporation in Palo Alto, California, just four years after Lockheed had begun to operate the commercial services, it was obvious that this new type of organization was accepted, effective, and expand-ing rapidly. Many end users could now benefit from the services of one or several vendors. A completely new business had emerged. Unlike the beginnings of the earliest retrieval systems in the United States that had been government owned and operated, this new business was organized around a group of vendors that provided search services as private business establishments (Cuadra, 1978). There were three principal segments: (1) database producers who were usually also suppliers (the history of database producers is discussed later); (2) the vendors themselves, such as Lockheed and System Development Corporation, who received the citations on tapes, created standardized formats, and loaded the tapes onto random access storage devices for service (vendors could control only the acquisition and the pricing, putting them in a somewhat precarious position) (Williams, 1984); and (3) the information centers and libraries that in turn served the end users (Summit, 1975b).

In the early 1970s one of the problems that vendors encountered was how to advise their customers regarding the availability of documents. In the case of U.S. government report literature, a microfiche version could usually be acquired. The Institute for Scientific Information (ISI) offered a then unique service in their Original Article Tear Sheet (OATS) service whereby journal articles were provided (Summit, 1975b, p. 42). Of course, copyrighted books could not be supplied in this manner.

By 1979 the problem of procuring documents was solved to a large extent at Lockheed with their newly initiated Dialorder system, which involved placing an order with one of more than 70 document suppliers worldwide. The suppliers then pick up the orders electronically and mail the documents (Camp, 1985). SDC had used a similar service somewhat earlier—their Electronic Maildrop Service.

By 1981 when Summit became President of the recently divested DIALOG Information Services, Inc., sophisticated networking operations enhanced service to users around the world. Telecommunications engines at the front end of DIALOG routed incoming traffic from a variety of sources such as DIALNET, TELENET, TYMNET, UNINET, and In-Watts lines. These front-end devices are in the form of microcomputers that process the commands and send them out to the appropriate place for execution—to computers and to disk drives, for example (Camp, 1985). DIALOG added 93 databases between 1982 and 1984 and extended services to foreign countries. In 1985 they claimed 70,000 customers in 80 countries (Camp, 1985).

Saul Herner seems to have been correct in naming Roger K. Summit the father of online retrieval (Herner, 1984). Perhaps Summit's most notable achievement was the efficiency with which he expanded the user population from the public libraries in California (Summit et al., 1976; Summit and Firschein, 1977) to countries as diverse as Japan and Brazil (Camp, 1985). He has continued to upgrade services in the United States, including utilization of the latest technology and retrieval from full-text databases.

Carlos A. Cuadra graduated in 1953 from the University of California at Berkeley with a Ph.D. in psychology. Thereafter he was employed by the System Development Corporation whose first interactive online retrieval system, operating in 1960, was called the Photosynthex. This was a ''nonrecursive, non-Boolean system with a terminal that was hard-wired to the computer'' (Bourne, 1980, p. 156). It was a full-text approach to the contents of the ''Golden Book Encyclopedia,'' the predecessor of the Online Retrieval of Bibliographic Information Timeshared System, called ORBIT, that was first applied for the U.S. Air Force at the Wright-Patterson Base in Ohio (Bourne, 1980).

In 1969–1970 a revised ORBIT program was applied to form the AIM/TWX, a 30-terminal system at the National Library of Medicine that ultimately became MEDLINE (MEDLARS online). This ORBIT II program was sold to the National Library of Medicine, who called it ELHILL (Cuadra, 1978, p. 7). Cuadra provided expert guidance in developing these systems. Incidentally, the National Library of Medicine later provided the ELHILL (ORBIT) program to the British Library for BLAISE, the British Library Automated Information Service. BLAISE is not only a retrieval system but also a cataloging system (Hawkins, 1981, p. 189).

In 1966 and while still employed by SDC, Cuadra became the first editor of the *Annual Review of Information Science and Technology*. During the previous five years he had helped develop the guidelines and procedures for the *Annual Review*. Ultimately he was selected as its first editor, with the project partially funded for its first two years by the National Science Foundation with additional funding from the SDC (Cuadra, 1966, pp. 1–14). For 10 years *ARIST* had the benefit of Cuadra's unfailing tact and editorial acumen. In 1976 with Volume 11, Martha E. Williams became the second editor of *ARIST*.

At the same time that Cuadra was editor of *ARIST* he was sharpening his management skills and emerging as a leader in establishing economies. Some of his initiatives were the previously mentioned 13 suggestions for improving the online interaction between user and computer (Cuadra, 1971a, p. 111), his consideration of user education as a cost–benefit proposition, and an idea to increase users so as to cut cost for use of the time-shared computer (Cuadra, 1975). He also conceived of a cost-cutting activity involving the online hours of certain files that limited the need for additional online equipment while offering the user access to an increased number of files.

At SDC, Cuadra held several positions: Manager of the Library and Document System Department, 1968–1970; Manager of Education and Library Systems Department, 1971–1973; and General Manager of SDC Search Services, 1974–1978 (Lee, 1982). In 1968 he received the ASIS Award of Merit, and in 1969 he was cited as the author of the Best Information Science Book of the year for his work on Volume 3 of *ARIST*.

In 1978, Cuadra left the SDC and became president of Cuadra Associates, an independent consulting firm. While at Cuadra Associates he diversified: he served on the Board of *Online Review;* in 1979 began the quarterly "Directory of Online Databases;" in 1980 published an article titled "The Role of the Private Sector in the Development and Improvement of Library and Information Services" (C. A. Cuadra, 1980); also in 1980 was awarded the Information Industry Association Hall of Fame Award (previously awarded to Mortimer Taube and Eugene Garfield); in 1981 developed STAR, a microcomputer system for data entry (N. G. Cuadra, 1981); and in 1982 released a report of a prototype program "that provides the capability to capture search results from the three major U.S. bibliographic database services, convert the records into the user's format, automatically index them and make them an integral part of their own local electronic library system." The report was presented at the 1982 Online Conference held in Atlanta in November 1982 (Cuadra Calls for Ground-Rules on Downloading, 1983). In 1985, Cuadra published an article entitled "Integrating the Personal Computer into a Multiuser Database Environment." Clearly Cuadra supported the use of the personal computer. By 1986 one of his interests was the electronic library (Cuadra, 1986), following in the steps of Lancaster's paperless society (Lancaster, 1978b) and his own interests in electronic publishing (C. A. Cuadra, 1981).

Donald T. Hawkins is an engineer by academic preparation, having been awarded the Ph.D. degree in engineering from the University of California at Berkeley in 1970. Since then he has been employed at AT&T Bell Laboratories, first as information scientist (Hawkins, 1976) and more recently as Manager of Information Retrieval and Foreign Languages Services.

Hawkins is especially well known for his comprehensive bibliography entitled "Online Information Retrieval Bibliography, 1964–1979" (Hawkins, 1980a). This title is a compilation, or perhaps better identified as a cumulation. The bibliography first appeared in Volume 1, Number 1 of *Online Review* in 1977. With the cumulation and continued annual updates, this work constitutes an ongoing, reliable source of important information. The bibliography is comprehensive and covers online bibliographic, numeric, and other nonbibliographic information retrieval systems. Excluded, however, are hospital information systems, library circulation and cataloging systems such as OCLC, and teletext (such as Viewdata) systems (Hawkins, 1980a, "Introduction").

The cumulation covering the years 1964–1979 contains 1784 entries. Later editions have brought the count to well over 3000 references. From 1964 through 1966 there were but 11 entries—these were the lean years. The years 1974–1978 were the peak years with 144, 187, 223, 291, and 329 papers, respectively (Hawkins, 1978, 1980a). This corresponds to the period when information retrieval had "come of age," during which Hawkins (1978) discovered 19 journals with more than 5 articles each. Since that time there has been a steady but unspectacular growth in the online literature.

Hawkins contributed to the bibliometrics of the literature of online retrieval. He observed, for example, that in the early years literature was quite dispersed, but more recently it has been concentrated largely in three journals: *Online, Online Review,* and *Database* (Hawkins, 1981, p. 172). He also provided definitions to the profession (Hawkins and Brown, 1980) and helped with search strategy development for online search (Hawkins and Wagers, 1982).

In addition, Hawkins made a study of the advantages of online retrieval to the end users; these included completeness, modest cost, speed, expanded resources (compared to the local library), print copies of the results, Boolean capabilities, and increased productivity of researchers (Hawkins, 1976). These results are similar to those found by Wanger *et al.* (1976).

More recently Hawkins and Levy have reported increased benefits for end users in their search and retrieval activities. This interest has focused on use of the microcomputer, the concept of downloading, and the creation of appropriate programs for putting into operation various front-end devices (Hawkins and Levy, 1985, 1986a,b). Hawkins is a transitional figure among our nine specialists, having contributed his first bibliography in 1977 and a review chapter in *ARIST* in 1981. This places him in the 1980s with Borgman, Tenopir, and Hildreth.

The 1980s

In the 1980s there was an apparent convergence of technologies (Cawkell, 1980, p. 44) in what appeared to be a new information technology revolution (Borgman, 1984a). There were many new users of the personal computer, in fact, the market may have been saturated (Tenopir, 1986c). These computers were located in homes, classrooms, offices, and libraries (Table 10). They were used for word processing, that is, for composing and editing text, for information retrieval, including downloading, and for data entry (N. G. Cuadra, 1981). These personal computers were, of course, microcomputers, or even minicomputers, that could function in groups of their own kind or be connected to larger computers. They could be supplemented through video text whenever both text and graphics were needed or video text could provide graphics intermittently with online retrieval as in retrieval from full text. For communication with remote regions there was telecommunications and satellite technology. The

TABLE 10
The 1980s and Diversification in Online Retrieval: Relevant Chapters in *ARIST*

Year	Volume	Author(s) and title	Affiliation
1981	16	D.T. Hawkins "Online Information Retrieval Systems"	Bell Telephone Laboratories
1981	16	P. W. Williams and G. Goldsmith "Information Retrieval on Mini- and Micro-Computers"	University of Manchester
1982	17	P. B. Kantor "Evaluation of Feedback in Information Storage and Retrieval Systems"	Tantalus, Inc.
1984	19	A. D. Pratt "Microcomputers in Libraries"	University of Arizona
1984	19	C. L. Borgman "Psychological Research in Human–Computer Interaction"	University of California at Los Angeles
1984	19	C. Tenopir "Full-Text Databases"	University of Hawaii at Manoa
1985	20	C. R. Hildreth "Online Public Access Catalogs"	OCLC: Online Computer Library Center

Compact Disc Read-Only Memory (CD-ROM) was beginning to team up with the publication function to provide database transmission and storage.

There were other but perhaps less-noticed convergences. Traditional librarians were becoming information scientists by virtue of their new education and experiences; information scientists were advising library school graduate students in their researches; and retrieval from large databases, a function that had developed as a commercial enterprise, was moving into libraries, where the principal large database was the library catalog converted to a machine-readable, user-searchable convenience. The move had been accelerated when the Library of Congress closed its catalog. Previously the Library of Congress had provided printed cataloging data for libraries; now they themselves used only machine-readable records.

In the 1980s there was a noticeable elevation of the concept and activity of research in information science. One journal changed its name; another did not. The international journal *Library Research* was initiated in 1979. By 1983 its name was changed to *Library and Information Science Research*. The United States publication *Research in Librarianship*, initiated in 1965, by 1986 had not changed its title.

In 1984 the American Society for Information Science honored post-humously three high-level professionals who had generally been considered to belong neither to the library nor to the information science community. Fritz Machlup was the first honoree. His 1962 book ''The Production and Distribution of Knowledge in the United States'' (Machlup, 1962) is surely on the reading list of many graduate students in the library and information science programs. The same can probably be said of one outstanding work of the second honoree, Derek de Solla Price, whose ''Little Science, Big Science'' (1965a) was among his best-known works. The third recipient of this 1984 award, Ithiel de Sola Pool, whose writings concentrate on the technologies, could have been honored for any one of the many interesting works in the communications field: ''A Study of Worldwide Packet-Switched Data Communication and Information Retrieval Systems'' (de Sola Pool, 1974); ''International Aspects of Computer Commu-nications'' (de Sola Pool, 1976); ''The Problems of WARC'' (de Sola Pool, 1979); ''Forecasting the Telephone'' (de Sola Pool, 1983a); and ''Technologies for Freedom'' (de Sola Pool, 1983b). Several aspects of the cutting edge of communications technology had been explored by de Sola Pool.

New professional groups emerged, but that did not mean elimination of the older ones. Two new groups, National Online Meeting and International Online Meeting, emerged after the publication in 1977 of the *Online Review*. Both of these groups hold meetings and publish proceedings.

In the 1980s there were other new phenomena: new types of databases (Travis and Fidel, 1982; Tenopir, 1983; Carter, 1985a,b; Wanger and Landau, 1980; O'Leary, 1986); new front-end devices (Turtle *et al.*, 1981; Crystal and Jakobson, 1982; Hawkins and Levy, 1985, 1986a,b); new expert systems (Keh-oe, 1985); and newly educated researchers, for example, the following three specialists.

Specialists: Borgman, Tenopir, and Hildreth

The last three of the nine specialists featured in this chapter are Christine L. Borgman, Carol Tenopir, and Charles H. Hildreth. We shall explore the history of the 1980s by examining the following aspects of each of the specialists: (1) their main research topics; (2) their review chapters in the *Annual Review of Information Science and Technology;* (3) their academic backgrounds; and (4) their professional experiences.

Several of the principal concerns of the 1980s are the importance of psychological factors at the interface of the user and the computer, the need to test the relative efficiency of the search and retrieval from full-text databases, and the complexity of the design of online systems, particularly the online public access catalog.

Research Topics

It is interesting to speculate on what may have led Borgman, Tenopir, and Hildreth to their research interests and topics. Borgman's dissertation title is "The User's Model of an Information Retrieval System: Effects on Performance" (1984b). Ten years earlier Wasserman (1974) had outlined psychological factors in the information system design. Similar aspects of the topic had appeared in the literature since about 1960 (Licklider, 1960). By 1966, Paisley had co-authored a widely circulated paper that built on his dissertation at Stanford University and a paper published in the same year (Paisley, 1965a,b). In the 1966 paper Parker and Paisley considered problems that were also of concern to Borgman: the advantage to the psychologist/researcher of being able to monitor the user's behavior and the need for developing criteria measures for the design and evaluation of information systems. They also formulated the task of psychological research: to test the behavioral assumptions of systems designers through conducting basic research into the nature of human information-processing behavior (Parker and Paisley, 1966, also see 1971).

In 1983–1984, Paisley served on Borgman's dissertation committee as her principal academic advisor. Borgman (1983) had earlier researched the concept of monitoring the user at the computer. This time it was a conceptual problem that she was to test: How could a student learn to comprehend a system, form a mental model of it, and use it to his or her own benefit? Borgman admitted that her most surprising and disturbing finding was that some of the 43 undergraduate students in her sample experienced extreme difficulty. Only 28 of the 43 were able to complete the requirements of the experiment. Despite this, she was pleased that of the two conditions imposed on the subjects, the procedural and the conceptual models, the conceptual model worked better for the user when complex problems were encountered. Borgman also tried to answer several puzzling questions: Why did humanities and social sciences students, who were much heavier users of the library, not outperform the science students, who used the library less? Why did computer science students not demonstrate an advantage considering that the computer was involved, nor the philosophy students when it came to the use of Boolean logic? Why did so many students find mastering the Boolean logic such an extremely difficult chore? She found no difference in competence between the sexes. Borgman's study was co-advised and financed by OCLC, from whom she gleaned the database. Her advisor at OCLC was the Director of the Office of Research, N. K. Kaske. Her advisors at Stanford were from the departments of communications, psychology, and industrial engineering.

Tenopir's dissertation is entitled "Retrieval Performance in a Full Text Journal Article Database" (1984b). She used the *Harvard Business Review,* and preparation for the retrieval mode was quite extensive (Tenopir, 1985). Who or what may have been her inspiration for the selection of this topic? It could have been O'Connor, who 10 years earlier had conducted research into the retrieval of answer sentences and sometimes multisentence passages, but not yet on paragraphs from full text. O'Connor (1973, 1975), however, foresaw that eventually full-text retrieval would be possible. Or Tenopir could have been inspired by the success of full-text retrieval particularly in the field of law and in the similar retrieval of information from newspaper articles (Tenopir, 1983, 1984c). Clearly the subject was "in the air," and new researchers were picking up old problems for solution. Tenopir admits that she was inspired by her chief advisor and mentor, Linda C. Smith. Smith (1979) had received her doctorate on artificial intelligence from Syracuse University, and had published a chapter in *ARIST* entitled "Artificial Intelligence Applications in Information Systems" (1980). Two other familiar names associated with Tenopir are F. Wilfred Lancaster and Martha E. Williams. All three of them were on her committee at the University of Illinois Graduate School of Library and Information Science.

Tenopir's research was a comparison of results of a full-text database search of the *Harvard Business Review* on the BRS search system with the results from a titles, abstracts, and controlled vocabulary search of the same database. The full-text search yielded a greater number of documents, a greater number of unique documents, and higher recall. Its precision rate was lower and it cost twice as much, due mainly to the longer computer run. The searches utilized Boolean logic, word proximity, and truncation, as is common in modern online retrieval systems of this type.

The *Harvard Business Review* is the first journal to be available in machine-readable full text; on BRS in 1982 and on DIALOG in 1983. Since that time several science journals as well as journals on other subjects have become available as databases. In practice, Tenopir noted, the major reason for searching full text is to locate articles, not to browse or locate specific facts. Anyone familiar with the flippant titles in the *Harvard Business Review* will understand why Tenopir found its titles "virtually useless" as a search and retrieval mode.

Hildreth, on the other hand, found his research niche on the job at OCLC when in the early 1980s the OPAC researches became extensive under the funding by the Council on Library Resources (CLR). Hildreth's role in summarizing studies and charting new directions, as well as his work on nomenclature, was guided, to a large extent, by his interest and assignment in the area of user–computer interface.

It had been more than 10 years since some of the online public access catalogs had made their initial appearance for public use by the end user, so the subject was not new. The Ohio State University Catalog, for example, went online in 1975 (Hildreth, 1982b, p. 3). This was also the year that members of the library profession began to listen seriously to the rumblings from the Library of Congress of their intention of closing their catalog. Some of these librarians responded by participating in a series of landmark conferences.

Just as the publication of conference proceedings (Greenberger, 1965, 1971) was instrumental to an understanding of the origin and development of man's interaction with the computer, so proceedings also spurred the understanding of the need for OPACs in the middle and late 1970s. Two publications, "The Nature and Future of the Catalog: Proceedings of the ALA's Information Science and Automation Division's 1975 and 1977 Institutes on the Catalog" (1979) and

"Closing the Catalog: Proceedings of the 1978 and 1979 Library and Information Technology Institutes" (1980), reveal how these ALA-affiliated conferences attracted experts to the field of cataloging. These experts were verbal, articulate, even argumentative, and controversial. For example, Seymour Lubetsky and Frederick G. Kilgour had the opportunity to face each other in what other participants found to be a serious but hilarious confrontation. The principal institutions involved were the Library of Congress, the Association of Research Libraries, OCLC, and critics of AACR2, whose second edition had delayed the scheduled closing of the LC catalog. The catalog was later closed on January 1, 1981.

By the late 1970s the Council on Library Resources entered the fray by authorizing several exploratory studies (e.g., Cochrane, 1978). Then the Council increased activity. They funded literally dozens of studies on the major problems (Ferguson *et al.*, 1982; Hildreth, 1985, for listings). Next they set priorities based on the findings and assessed the status of the online public access catalogs. This was Hildreth's opening.

Hildreth was selected by OCLC to bring order and unity to the many research reports. As Project Manager, he filled in the gaps of language and information and published the results in a volume entitled "Online Public Access Catalogs: The User Interface" (Hildreth, 1982b). Various studies had focused on the variables in the online information retrieval systems, but Hildreth's charge was to extract which system elements at the user interface had the capability of affecting the success of an end user's search. His study became state of the art for design development strategy at that time, roughly 1982. The end user, however, and not the professional searcher, was always kept in mind.

At the beginning of this task, Hildreth found that the documentation statements that the various systems presented had little in common with each other: there was no common format, no manual for operation, and no uniform documentation that would allow comparison of features of the various systems. Often the same function was given different names. Therefore, he was unable to proceed until he had at least developed a common language of communication. The final glossary presented in this volume (Hildreth, 1982b) went through 20 editions, an indication of the intense interest in devising a common language. Hildreth provided a notebook on each system, and in turn each system provided him with access to the researchers who were the data collectors and designers. He found that these conversations with the designers were the most educational part of the study. Up to this point, despite the mountain of literature, the user interface had been "largely uncharted territory" (Hildreth, 1982b, p. 34). Although it was now understood that the OPAC required different user strategies than a card catalog, it was still unknown what the average library user expected from the card catalog. Perhaps the computer has brought us to our senses.

In commenting on the Hildreth contribution, Cochrane and Markey (1983) listed eight accomplishments but warned that his volume did not provide comparisons for the evaluation of individual systems. They noted that his work was a survey of systems rather than of users, in effect a detailed inventory of the systems features that could have an effect on system use. Hildreth (1983, 1984) followed through with a continuing study of the user–computer interface.

ARIST Review Chapters

At the risk of appearing to imitate Licklider when he admitted to not having read Vannevar Bush until he had completed the research for "Libraries of the Future," we did not realize at the outset that each of our nine selected specialists had written a review chapter for *ARIST*.

The *ARIST* reviews written by Borgman, Tenopir, and Hildreth were published in 1984 and 1985 (Table 11). Borgman's review covers selected literature for 1982 and 1983, with some from 1984 when reprints were available (Borgman, 1984a). Aside from works on methodology, the literature reviewed is mainly on text editing, text composing, and information retrieval. There is some coverage of psychological theory as it affects practice, especially the effect of mental models, which Borgman (1984a, pp. 36–37) defines as referring to a "qualitative stimulation of the system that 'runs' in the user's mind." According to Borgman (1984b, p. 50), the user's mental model is "so integral to the system's use that it should be a starting point for design."

Tenopir's review is the first *ARIST* chapter on full-text databases (1984a). It is limited to reviews of those works that deal directly or indirectly with retrieval performance of full-text databases. Her chapter is divided into five sections: an overview of the types of full-text databases; user studies; retrieval

TABLE 11
Nine Specialists in Online Retrieval: Relevant Chapters
in *ARIST*, 1966–1985

Year	Volume	Author	Title
1966	1–10	Carlos A. Cuadra, ed.	
1966	1	Ruth M. Davis	"Man–Machine Communication"
1968	3	J. C. R. Licklider	"Man–Computer Communication"
1974	9	Roger K. Summit and O. Firschein	"Document Retrieval Systems and Techniques"
1974	9	Martha E. Williams	"Use of Machine-Readable Databases"
1981	16	Donald T. Hawkins	"Online Information Retrieval Systems"
1984	19	Christine L. Borgman	"Psychological Research in Human–Computer Interaction"
1984	19	Carol Tenopir	"Full-Text Databases"
1985	20	Charles H. Hildreth	"Online Public Access Catalogs"

performance; related evaluative studies; and what she considers short-term future directions. She provides much information on when and with what success the various subjects and types of databases entered the field, how users viewed the use, and what seemed to be lacking from the user's viewpoint, for example, the visuals of the hard copy, which incidentally can be viewed from some terminals via video by pushing a function key and intermittently viewing while reading. Tenopir believed the future of full-text search and retrieval was expanding.

Hildreth's review (1985) is the first in *ARIST* on the subject of the online public access catalog (OPAC). He selected works on origins and development, data content, use and user research studies, the role of the library catalog, and the user interface. He noted that the literature of OPAC peaked in 1983 with the publication of nine monographs. At least 90% of the journal literature was in the library journals; only a small amount appeared in *Online, Database,* or *Online Review.* The leading source was *Library and Information Technology* with 24 articles. This is in contrast to Hawkins finding that a large percentage of online retrieval literature appeared in the first three journals (Hawkins, 1981).

Many have contributed to research related to the OPAC. Especially impressive is the large number of studies resulting from or inspired by the CLR nationwide study. The following is a sample list of OPAC references that appeared in Hildreth's review chapter (1985); Kaske and Ferguson (1980), a final report to the Council on Library Resources that is, in effect, a state-of-the-art report of OPACs with priorities suggested for research; Borgman and Kaske (1981) on determining the number of computer terminals needed in relation to the number of online catalog users; Mandel and Herschman (1983) and Cochrane (1982a,b, 1984) on subject access; Kaske and Sanders (1983) on the need for more specific subject headings; and Borgman (1983), an extensive study of the transaction logs of end users at Ohio State University. Similarly, Hildreth cites the Gorman study (1984), which focused on the impact of the online catalog on the library staff, organization, and administration. These studies funded by the Council on Library Resources represent a significant contribution.

Academic Backgrounds

The academic backgrounds of these three specialists include library and information or communication science. Christine L. Borgman, who concentrates on user–computer relations, earned a Ph.D. in information science from Stanford University; Carol Tenopir, who studies full-text search and retrieval, received a Ph.D. in library and information science from the University of Illinois; and Charles H. Hildreth, who has worked on the problems of online public access catalogs, with emphasis on the design of the user interface, added a master's degree in library and information science from the University of Denver to his master's degree in philosophy (Hildreth, 1982b).

Professional Experience

Both Borgman and Tenopir are faculty members at accredited library schools—Borgman at UCLA and Tenopir at the University of Hawaii at Manoa.

Hildreth (1982a) has been a methods analyst at the Chicago Public Library and a project manager at OCLC, Inc., of research into online public access catalogs. One of Borgman's concerns is the failure of systems designers to take into account the findings of researchers (1984a). This was articulated in the first review chapter of *ARIST* in 1966 (1967, p. 52) when Borko noted that as a reviewer he was "unable to discover any literature discussing the design methodology . . . no report made mention of the design problems." This problem still exists and may have gotten worse since 1984 (Borgman, 1984a, pp. 50–51, reporting on the Gould and Lewis study (1983) of 447 designers and other studies).

A central concern for Tenopir is the dilemma in the database industry. Outrageous growth is reported in both the number of available databases (30–40% annual growth rate since the first issue of the Cuadra Associates Directory in 1979) and the number of vendors (from 59 worldwide in 1979, to over 440 by 1986). Mergers are taking place, especially between different kinds of companies (e.g., Sears and IBM). There is a general realization that the personal computer need-to-know market is saturated, and the library market is near saturation. Although new markets are opening up internationally, many countries have their own databases, which tend to be small and unable to compete with the larger services. These concerns were expressed by Judith Wanger of Cuadra Associates and by Bill Marovitz, President of BRS, whose speeches Tenopir reviewed (1986c). One comes to the realization that, like medicine, information service has become big business, and is no longer the profession it once was.

Hildreth (1985) has focused on the disturbing fact that information retrieval researchers and vendors, on the one hand, and online public access catalog researchers and practitioners, on the other, operate from entirely different vantage points, publish in different journals, and rarely work together. It is important to remember that at times these separate factions have worked as one.

Hildreth himself reports (1985) that it was the DIALOG-RECON model that was used for the now famous SCORPIO (Subject Content Oriented Retrieval for Processing Information Online), an information system at the Library of Congress (Power *et al.,* 1976; Pritchard, 1981). The SCORPIO system provides access to the entire MARC monograph file as well as to several other files of value to the United States legislative body. The reader may recall that Hubert Humphrey (1970) at an ASIS Annual Conference in 1969 at San Francisco, pointed out with dismay the lack of current information for members of Congress before the advent of SCORPIO. This is one example of a cooperative effort that is sometimes overlooked.

In several of the turnkey systems, as Hildreth also pointed out (1985), subject access was becoming available; keyword, Boolean operators, and word proximity techniques were beginning to appear in integrated systems. These techniques must have been brought in from outside the traditional library complex. They appear to represent a melding of information science and library science. The National Library of Medicine was the first to have an integrated system, which was designed by the Lister Hill National Center for Biomedical Communications of the NLM in the 1970s. Their system has integrated from the start and included a user–system interface for patron access to online catalogs.

One of the papers reviewed by Hildreth explains this exciting history (Dick, 1984).

It should be recalled that the System Development Corporation first set up the online bibliographic information retrieval system for the National Library of Medicine's MEDLINE. There is plenty of evidence that information scientists and librarians were willing to cooperate on joint projects. On the other hand, it is also true that in the 1980s the development of the online public access catalogs in many libraries had not been of great interest to the information scientist. A similar situation existed in the early 1970s with the development of machine-readable record at the Library of Congress and the bibliographical utility at OCLC. Information scientists were not especially interested. The key people involved in this venture were Henriette Avram at the Library of Congress, Fred Kilgour at OCLC, and Richard De Gennaro at the University of Pennsylvania. The information scientists excluded themselves from library automation activities, although systems experts were deeply involved. The application of information science prevailed.

It is a fact that many of the first-generation information scientists did not know very much about library science. Yet, except for mission-oriented operations for the federal government, they had no laboratory except the library, no clientele except library users, and few educational institutions except the library schools. The only professional accreditation agency was the American Library Association. So to an extent the information scientist was trapped within his or her own professional society, the American Society for Information Science (ASIS), and later the Online Meetings. At the same time, in the 1970s Fred Kilgour, with his considerable formal library education and experience and building on the work of Henriette Avram and others at the Library of Congress, seized the day to develop his bibliographic utility. ASIS considered him to be an information scientist par excellence, and awarded him the Award of Merit in 1980. The future may require a closer alliance between information scientists and librarians. There have been many crossovers from librarianship to information science, and likewise there are remarkable examples of the information scientist functioning in the library schools.

Summary

In this chapter we have traced the activities and ideas of nine specialists in the area of online retrieval of bibliographic information. We discussed the following trends: (1) improvements in man–computer interaction, particularly in the pursuit of making the computer "user friendly;" (2) development of front-end devices and gateways to information or databases; (3) geographic expansion of services; (4) increase in types of databases, that is, full-text and numerical; (5) increase in subjects covered by the databases; and (6) increase in intermediary and end users. Four other changes were noted: (1) new types of professional leaders; (2) new publications; (3) new modes of communication and education; and (4) a newly sophisticated population of users.

In the 1980s there are still problems to be solved, and some are being approached in novel ways by a new group of professionals, usually in the graduate schools of communications or library and information science, or in commercial establishments with research divisions. Sometimes the new generation reinvents the wheel, for example, in the discovery that Bradford's law works for databases as it once worked when applied to the printed literature; namely, a small number of databases tend to furnish a large percentage of the references. Librarians have learned with the information scientists (which they have often become) how to query a file. The main job for the 1990s appears to be a mutual one—to help make access "friendly." The principal question may be: Is this a function of the designers of systems or of the educators?

CHAPTER 5

Networks
1965–1985

Introduction

Almost all the information services that have been developed in the past 20 years qualify as either networking services or components of networking services. Historically, networks have not always been called networks, for example, bibliographic utilities and online search and retrieval services from vendors. At the same time, entities that are not networks such as individual information systems, which usually are or can become components of networks, have frequently been viewed as networks.

Definitions of networks are plentiful. In 1968, Becker and Olsen declared that "broadly defined, a network is an interconnection of things, systems, or organizations," and that "in an information network more than two participants are engaged in a common pattern of information exchange through communications for some functional purpose." They reported that at that time no operating information network incorporated the four main characteristics of an ideal network: (1) formal organization, sharing a common information purpose; (2) communications, utilizing circuits that can rapidly interconnect dispersed points; (3) bidirectional operation, so information can move in either direction and each network participant can send as well as receive; and (4) a directory and switching capability (Becker and Olsen, 1968, pp. 289–291).

Hendricks (1973) discussed not only what networks are but also what they are not. At the time he was involved with medical libraries, and his definition made it clear, as Becker and Olsen had implied in 1968, that library systems (by extension we also take this to mean information systems) are not networks.

> Library cooperatives, consortia, or systems are not networks, but they may very well contain network elements. A group of individual libraries of the

> same type working together is a library system . . . when two library
> systems start interacting, then a true network activity develops. The interface
> of systems is the distinguishing feature that separates a system from a
> network. (Hendricks, 1973, p. 2)

Throughout the history of information science, particularly since 1971, networks
have been developing. Their various components, seen as technology, legislation, and creative information systems, preceded the establishment of the first
networks.

According to Hendrick's definition, the government-financed and -con-
trolled MEDLINE, AGRICOLA, and ERIC, as well as other similar information
systems, are not networks but rather information systems. Yet, when these
information systems are organized and serving users online in certain patterns,
they are considered to be networks, whether they serve homogeneous groups or
interface with crossover users.

An almost complete shift from government operation to commercial
operation occurred during the late 1960s and early 1970s when the database
vendors began preparing for online interactive search and retrieval services upon
request. These vendors were entrepreneurs. They acquired databases, re-
packaged them, and offered online interactive bibliographic retrieval of information services.

By 1977, Williams reported the tremendous success of online retrieval
services from these for-profit corporations (Williams, 1977b). She no doubt was
aware of the research and development contributions that the U. S. Government-
owned and -operated information systems had made and of the fact that most of
the resulting databases were by then also available from at least one of the three
vendors: Lockheed's DIALOG, the System Development Corporation's ORBIT,
and since 1977 from the Bibliographical Retrieval Services (BRS). Williams also
probably knew of the considerable pressuring and compromising that was needed
before the government contributions to some of these databases were conceded to
belong to the public and therefore should be available through commercial services. It was this availability that may have inspired Williams' comment that
"for the first time in history, computerized retrieval is in wide use and is
economically successful" (1977b, p. 14). The reader will note, however, that
she did not say that networking itself was working.

A similar change occurred for libraries in 1971, when OCLC (the Ohio
College Library Center) began functioning as the first online bibliographic
utility.

Williams (1977d) is among the relatively few observers who have considered online retrieval services from commercial vendors to be network services. Among other like-minded observers are Katz (1982a, p. 109) and Haas
(1982, p. 152). In 1982, Haas was President of the Council on Library Resources
and Katz was a professor and textbook author at SUNY in Albany. On the other
hand, Williams seemed to consciously exclude as networks the "library-type
databases and systems such as Ohio College Library Center." The key phrase
here is "library-type." In a similar vein, Rowland C. W. Brown, President of
OCLC, Inc., in a discussion of networking, assumed that his audience knew that
the bibliographic utilities were networks but gave no indication that he also

considered the commercial vendors' online services to be networks (Brown, 1982).

It is an unfortunate truism that there are few people who are capable of identifying and understanding the overview or larger picture. In the library and information science field, this phenomenon was demonstrated when librarians gave up their indexing and abstracting prerogative to the "documentalists" and forever lost this control and, at the same time, some of the prestige of their profession (Shera, 1966, pp. 26–27). Librarians went one way and documentalists, now information specialists and information scientists, went another, and rarely do the two groups meet on either a philosophical or a practical level.

Even in networking, there are few who participate in both types of online bibliographic service: online bibliographic databases available from vendors, which are usually produced by the indexing and abstracting services, and the online databases from the designated bibliographic utilities or the public access catalogs (OPACs). Similarly, to many professionals the gulf between the behind-the-scenes functions such as cataloging or interlibrary loan and online retrieval of bibliographic information for the end user is considerable if not insurmountable, in both concept and reality. This gap existed even before information science entered the arena.

Commercial bibliographic information retrieval services (Chapter 4) as well as bibliographic utilities (included in Chapter 3) were previously discussed but not as networks per se. The two types of operations are, however, information networks of the purest kind, that is, they meet the accepted definitions. Prototypes are Lockheed's DIALOG online search and retrieval services and OCLC's online cataloging and interlibrary loan services. The history of these services will not be repeated here; the basic information remains the same regardless of how one refers to them.

By 1973, only five years after Becker and Olsen had reported (1968) that there were no networks that met the criteria, several qualified, functioning networks were in operation. Greenberger reported on a research scientist in Hawaii who, in calling into service the index to the world's medical literature (presumably from the National Library of Medicine) in Bethesda, Maryland, activated a radio network, a telephone network, an international satellite, and a research network (probably ARPANET, Advanced Research Project Agency Network, developed by the U. S. Department of Defense) in the process of reaching Bethesda. Less than 5 seconds were required to reach this destination, and in 15 seconds the printout was appearing at the terminal in Hawaii (Greenberger *et al.*, 1973). Obviously, a mail request would have taken days if not weeks. We were in an electronic age. McLuhan (1964) saw it as media dependent and immediate; Daniel Bell (1973) called it postindustrial; and Toffler (1980) viewed it as the third wave.

We now knew that there were satellite networks, television networks, radio networks, telephone networks, computer networks, and information networks. These networks were also used in combinations to meet the user's needs. Part of the capability for combination was attributable to the famous Carterphone decision of 1971, which stated that upon meeting certain criteria, various organizations were permitted to attach equipment to and work in tandem with the communication lines of AT&T and Western Union.

By 1974 the interrelationship of computer, communication, and information networks (Penniman *et al.,* 1974) fostered the belief that they could complement each other and work together for the movement of messages: communication networks for telephone, radio, and television and information networks for interactive communication with machine-readable records with feedback in printouts according to the user's prescription. Also involved with the reception and movement of the messages were computer networks such as AR-PANET and value-added networks (VAN) such as TYMSHARE and TELENET (Greenberger *et al.,* 1973). Such interrelationships for the benefit of information networks had been anticipated by Licklider (1971) and a few others.

We could now think of networks as functioning combinations of systems for switching information from one place to another as mandated by the Weinberg Report (Weinberg *et al.,* 1963). We should discount the suggestions that networks might conceivably consist of scientific papers (de Solla Price, 1965b) or of people writing or using scientific papers, sometimes known as members of an invisible college or network (Crane, 1968). The networking concept had finally gained momentum. By 1978, Becker tried to clear the air and stated that a network was a concept to be explained and not an entity to be defined (Becker, 1979).

Library networks would eventually have their place in the sun, but not yet. Historically librarianship has been concerned with resource sharing, and bibliographical centers, consortia, and other cooperative arrangements have existed for many years, but until they became technologically, managerially, and organizationally modernized, they would not qualify as networks. By the late 1970s and early 1980s some of them did qualify, usually by virtue of their affiliation with a network such as OCLC. As Katz, at the School of Library and Information Science at SUNY in Albany, summed it up: "Nothing so revolutionized the working concept of networks as the computer." Katz did not dismiss the old library methods of exchange; he simply admitted that the new networking methods superseded the old methods but did not replace them (Katz, 1982b, pp. 207–208)—rather confusing terminology.

Although research and development funds were becoming increasingly available, and legislation had approved networking projects, the procedures for obtaining funds were not well known and librarians were reluctant to charge for services as well as pay for network membership and services. More than a decade later, while libraries were "automating," some librarians were still unwilling to charge for services or even to accept the new technology. In 1979, Giuliano had reproached librarians for failing to charge for their services, and as late as 1980 in a report of the Task Force on Implications of the White House Conference on Library and Information Services, it was claimed that besides funding, aware leadership, education in networking, and other factors, what was still needed was "to break down some of the attitudinal barriers against networking and technology" (Association of American Library Schools, 1980, p. 251). Obviously, the Task Force found that many librarians were behind the times technologically.

In the case of early interlibrary loan and other cooperative resource-sharing plans, the results often had been clumsy if not disastrous. The have-nots tended to gain at the expense of the haves. Large and successful libraries found themselves serving the smaller libraries at their own expense (Lorenz, 1977). Although there were some functioning programs designed to correct this discrepancy, the real breakthroughs in terms of both service and satisfaction were with the commercial and break-even networking operations, where technology, systems analysis and design, and entrepreneurial risk taking seemed to be solving the resource-providing function.

Early attempts were made by leaders in the library and information fields to increase the base of knowledgeable librarians. This entailed encouraging and explaining how modernization and technological improvements would allow better service. One example is Weinstock's 1967 paper to special librarians. Even so, special librarians, except those at the federal level, were slow to develop and utilize networks.

Types of Networks

Six types of networks are considered here. The first three were described in Chapters 2, 3, and 4. They are: (1) U. S. Government-owned and -operated networks, based on single information systems, such as MEDLINE, AGRICOLA, and ERIC; (2) bibliographic utility networks such as OCLC, RLIN, WLN, and UTLAS; and (3) online services from commercial vendors such as Lockheed's DIALOG, System Development Corporation's ORBIT, and BRS (Bibliographic Retrieval Services). The other three types of networks have not been described. They are: (4) geographical networks, that is, local, state, regional, national, and international; (5) the computer network, ARPANET; and (6) two of the several value-added networks (VAN), TYMSHARE and TELENET.

Plan of the Chapter

The outline for this chapter is chronological. Networks or their components are discussed in the order of their historical development and operation, especially as reported in *ARIST* or by one of our selected specialists.

Chapter 5 is divided into three periods: the first period, the beginnings, 1965–1971; the second period, planning and development activities, 1972–1978; and the third period, the retraction, diversification, and decentralization, 1979–1985. Evans (1979) perceived a similar three-period pattern.

Specialists

Information on our 16 networking specialists is mainly available in Chapter 3 for Avram, Kilgour, and De Gennaro, in Chapter 4 for Borgman, Cuadra, Davis, Hawkins, Hildreth, Licklider, Summit, Tenopir, and Williams, and in Chapter 5 for Becker, Evans, Markuson, and Martin (Tables 12 and 13). If the biographical information for the last four seems less complete than for the other specialists, that is mainly due to its more limited availability.

Many other individuals have contributed to the success of networking: Alphonse Trezza, Charles Stevens, Kjell Samuelson, and Alex Tomberg come to mind. There are also the inventors of mini- and microcomputers, those who earlier created the large computers, and those who improved them so that one

TABLE 12
Four Networking Specialists[a]

Name	Latest degree	Latest known position
Joseph Becker	M. L. S., 1955, Catholic University	President, Becker & Hayes, Inc., 1969–present
Glyn T. Evans	NA[b]	Administrator, SUNY[c] Libraries
Barbara E. Markuson	M. L. S. (NA) University of Texas	Director of INCOLSA (Indiana Cooperative Library Services Authority)
Susan K. Martin	Ph.D., LIS, 1983, University of California at Berkeley	Director, Milton S. Eisenhower Library, Johns Hopkins University, 1979–present

[a]Most of this information is from Lee (1982).
[b]Not available.
[c]State University of New York.

generation could improve and become the next generation. Other important researchers envisioned computer networks, time-sharing, packet switching, and value-added networks. Still others disseminated the new information through presentations, publications, developing and teaching networking curricula, or by advertising and promoting their services through in-service courses.

Overview of the Three Periods

A brief overview of the periods covered here reveals that in the beginning of networking, 1965–1971, the planners envisioned a national, centralized network with information services coordinated by one government institution. In the second period, 1972–1978, the critics, mainly information professionals, questioned the planned centralization. By the time the third period, 1979–1985, had ended a complete restructuring had occurred along the lines of natural organization. Networks of all types bypassed central leadership and flourished not only in the United States but internationally through the initiatives of institutions such as the Library of Congress, the National Library of Medicine, and the National Agricultural Library, as well as DIALOG Information Services, ERIC, and OCLC. In addition, networks emerged in foreign countries that reflected their own needs and capabilities.

The Beginnings: 1965–1971

The Needs of Science

The history of information networks began with the realization by information professionals and others of the need to provide scientific and technical

TABLE 13
**Sixteen Specialists in Networking or Networking Components
with Relevant Publications**

Author	Publication	Year
Henriette D. Avram	"The National Scene"	1971
Joseph Becker	"Library Networks: The Beacon Lights"	1973
Christine L. Borgman	"Human Factors in the Use of Computer Networks"	1985
Carlos A. Cuadra	"Library Automation and Networks"	1971
Ruth M. Davis	"The National Biomedical Communication Network as a Developing Structure"	1971
Richard De Gennaro	"The Role of the Academic Library in Networking"	1980
Glyn L. Evans	"On-line Networking: A Bibliographic Essay"	1979
Donald T. Hawkins	"Six Years of Online Searching in an Industrial Library Network"	1980
Charles R. Hildreth	"Online Public Access Catalogs"	1985
Frederick G. Kilgour	"Public Policy and National and International Networks"	1983
J. C. R. Licklider	"A Hypothetical Plan for a Library Information Network"	1971
Barbara E. Markuson	"Library Networks: Progress and Problems"	1976
Susan K. Martin	"Governance Issues for Automated Library Networks: The Impact of, and Implications for, Large Research Libraries"	1983
Roger K. Summit	"The Impact of Technology on the Governance of Library Networks: Response"	1979
Carol Tenopir	"Online Education: Planning for the Future"	1987
Martha E. Williams	"Networks for On-line Data Base Access"	1977

information to the research community. This realization, combined with the ingenious new techniques for information indexing, storage, search, and retrieval, led to the development of sophisticated information networks over which information could be transmitted rapidly.

Although officially we begin this segment of our history in 1965, we do go back through the years to identify five motivating forces that seem to have led to networking activity. Although all of the five are related to both science and technology, including information science, the fifth, perhaps somewhat more than the others, concerns the historical role of information professionals in providing improved services, especially over long distances.

The first of these motivations occurred in 1948 when the Royal Society of London convened a conference of librarians and documentalists to discuss appropriate methods for providing scientists with references and materials for their researches (Royal Society, 1948). A second motivating force occurred when, following his attendance at the 1948 conference in London, and while attending a 1950 conference at the University of Chicago, Mortimer Taube proposed what was to become mission-oriented services for the sciences (Taube, 1951; Adams, 1981). The third was the convening in the same year, 1958, and in the same place, Washington, D. C., of two conferences: an international one (International Conference on Scientific Information, 1959) that expanded the concept of and interest in providing scientific information and the Taube–Wooster conference that introduced new methods of information storage and retrieval (Taube and Wooster, 1958). A fourth impetus was more than a motivating force, it was a mandate. In 1963, President Kennedy's Science Advisory Committee, under the leadership of Alvin Weinberg, mandated that the dissemination of scientific information become a joint responsibility of scientists and information specialists (Weinberg et al., 1963).

The committee simply demanded that a way be found to disseminate the information that had already been generated and that would obviously continue to be generated as a result of the expanded research and development funds, particularly funds that were being spent by the federal government. Among the several strong demands made on all researchers and developers were two that are perhaps most relevant to the expansion of information networks: ''New Switching Methods Must be Explored and Exploited'' (Weinberg et al., 1963, p. 36) and ''The Technical Documentalist Must be Recognized and Supported'' (Weinberg et al., 1963, p. 29). The first would seem to have been satisfied by the initiation and continued improvement in the functioning of computer-based networking, the examination of the services of telecommunications, and the initiation of information networks such as NASA-RECON and MEDLINE, which had begun as information systems. The second resulted in increased research into information fields as reported in Chapter 2 and documented in ''Current Research and Development in Scientific Documentation, 1957–1969'' (U. S. National Science Foundation, Office of Scientific Information, 1969). Doctoral students who were to become documentalists, information specialists, and librarians also conducted research that resulted in an increase in dissertations in accredited library schools and elsewhere. The dissertation output increased, for example, in the library schools by a factor of five in the 1970s over the 1960s (data provided in C. Davis, 1980).

Information Science Arrives

A fifth and final motivating force discussed here emphasizes information science. In 1963 in Chicago, the members attending the Annual Meeting of the American Documentation Institute (ADI, soon to become ASIS) read for the first time a set of computer-based preconference papers ''engineered'' by President-Elect Hans Peter Luhn of IBM. Luhn had previously (1960) presented his now famous, computer-based ''Chemical Titles.''

During his short lifetime Luhn never ceased to propose new uses for the computer in the information field. He surely enhanced the 1963 meeting at a time when its members were already planning to change the organization's name and purpose: from the American Documentation Institute, with an orientation largely in microforms, to the American Society for Information Science, with a wide-open mission to accommodate the dreams of current and prospective information scientists. Luhn's computer-based document was a symbol of major changes that were to come in the modus operandi of the new professional society for information professionals. From 1965 forward, information science played a leading role in information services and publications.

By 1965 plans were near completion for the first edition of the *Annual Review of Information Science and Technology (ARIST)*. In 1966 the first volume appeared under the editorship of Dr. Carlos A. Cuadra, then employed by the System Development Corporation. For 10 years Cuadra was a faithful and competent editor. The first volume of *ARIST* made no mention of networks, but by 1967, in the second volume, the subject of networks was presented (Hammer, 1967). Thereafter, network activity occupied a fair share of the *ARIST* space (Tables 14, 15, and 16).

National and International Networks for Science

In the beginning it was expected that the federal government would play a major role in planning a national network. Representatives of government and other groups, as well as individuals, submitted plans and proposals; for example, the COSATI (Committee on Scientific and Technical Information) plan to handle scientific information (Knox, 1966) and the Meise proposal (Meise, 1969). Networks and document-handling centers were envisioned for both the national and international levels (Borko, 1968b; Samuelson, 1971a). Most of the plans were based on the need to disseminate the results of scientific and technical research and development for the benefit of future research.

Mission-oriented databases in all the major sciences and technologies became available; most of them were accessible at first only from specialized information centers, but later through the search and retrieval services of at least one of the database services vendors.

Libraries

Science held sway as far as planning went until President Lyndon Johnson in 1967 issued an executive order to establish two library-related groups: a National Advisory Commission on Libraries and the President's Committee on Libraries. Fourteen nongovernment appointees were to be named to the former (twenty were actually named) and five government appointees to the latter. The purpose of the former was to determine the role of libraries as sources of knowledge in the nation's communication resources; the purpose of the latter was to guarantee (at least to encourage) efficiency in and interaction between the government and private sectors.

Following these moves to line up the sources of library strength in 1967, President Johnson suggested his anticipated "Knowledge Network." This plan called for library and information services for everyone, which, though not original with Johnson, was to cause some consternation among librarians for a long time. In 1968 this "Knowledge Network" was funded as Title IX of the

TABLE 14
**Key Chapters in *ARIST* and Selected Conference Proceedings:
The Beginnings of Networks, 1965–1971**

Year	Volume	Author(s)	Title	Affiliation
1967	2	D. P. Hammer	"National Information Networks"	Purdue University
1968	3	J. Becker and W. C. Olsen	"Information Networks"	EDUCOM
1969	4	C. P. J. Overhage	"Information Networks"	MIT
1969	NA[a]	L. Carnovsky (ed.)	"Library Networks—Promise and Performance: 33rd Conference of the Graduate Library School, July 29–31, 1968	University of Chicago
1971	NA	R. A. Matzek (ed.)	"Network Concepts: Four Points of View"	Catholic Library Association
1971	NA	J. Becker (ed.)	"Interlibrary Communications and Information Networks," Sept. 28–Oct. 2, 1970[b]	President, Becker & Hayes, Inc.
1971	6	K. Samuelson	"International Information Transfer and Network Communication"	Institute of Technology, Stockholm University
1972	7	E. E. Olson *et al.*	"Library and Information Networks"	University of Maryland and Smithsonian Institution

[a]Not applicable.
[b]Proceedings of a conference sponsored by the American Library Association and the U. S. Office of Education, Bureau of Libraries and Educational Technology.

Higher Education Act. Progress at the individual library level was slow. For example, two years after the National Advisory Commission had made its final report with recommendations, there reportedly was no sign of action during either the Johnson or Nixon administration (Cuadra, 1971b, p. 17).

Many new and legitimate channels contributed to satisfying President Johnson's adopted goal of information for everyone. Not only had there emerged new sources of information that would apparently reduce the pressures on libraries, but libraries also initiated new programs of their own, an indication of the availability of funds.

Education

Throughout the 1960s educational television appeared, which was transmitted in closed circuit to many elementary and secondary schools as well as to undergraduate and graduate programs across the nation. In addition, public television programs such as "Sesame Street" and "Mr. Roger's Neighborhood" for the elementary level and formal college courses for the higher levels were aired.

There was also a distinct movement to bring computer-assisted instruction (CAI) to the classroom. Much later, C-Span (Cable Satellite Public Affairs Network) brought to the general public, as a public service, such educational programs as live coverage of the U. S. House of Representatives. Libraries, although an important source of information and documents, were not the only and perhaps not even the best knowledge source for many purposes. Johnson's dream had many ramifications.

Oettinger's 1969 essay titled "Run, Computer, Run" includes a section on the use of technology, mainly systems analysis and the computer, in the education of children. He concludes that after years of study he is convinced that, while the school system using technology has the potential for success, it also has many possibilities for failure. In contrast with these conclusions, we may consider the success of information services since the advent of the computer and ask: Why is it not as successful there as it is here? The answer may lie in the less complex system of the information services, the older participants, or the entrepreneurial spirit that permeates the modern information services establishment. These tremendous changes have taken place in the communications arena in only a few years.

Funding for educational purposes had already been substantial, some would think phenomenal. There had been ERIC (Educational Research, later Resources, Information Center), the first online search and retrieval system in the soft sciences. Funds from the Elementary and Secondary Education Act and from Title II of the Higher Education Act were widely available to support research and development, and finally Title IX was added to make the "Knowledge Network" a reality (Becker and Olsen, 1968). At the same time the states were working with Title III of the Library Services and Construction Act. All levels of government, local, state, and regional, were armed with funds—progress was inevitable.

At the college and university level, since 1964, EDUCOM (Interuniversity Communication Council) had been funded at $750,000 for five years. Members consisted of voluntary representatives from colleges and universities who were interested in planning for a not-for-profit network. A massive planning session resulted in a 1967 published report of a Summer Study of Information Networks (Brown *et al.*, 1967).

Librarians

The fact that representatives of many disciplines outside of librarianship contributed to the planning of library networks disturbed some librarians who considered this input to be an intrusion. Their ideas and proposals, particularly the guarantee that "there should be no poverty of information availability" (Hammer, 1967, p. 391), were unacceptable to those who understood libraries and the hardships of managing limited collections, personnel, and finances (Markuson, 1976, pp. 48–50). This assault from outside could not be forgotten.

The concept of availability, that is, total access—all users to all libraries—was being proclaimed everywhere that there were plans or moves toward development of library networks. Norman D. Stevens (1980, p. 40) speculated that this was a populist idea but admitted that the demand was unusual. Swanson, on the other hand, argued that "the NCLIS–ALA goal [for that must be what it was] of 'equal opportunity of access to information' is unintelligible" (1980, p. 97). Even if this was true, the whole idea hit a sore spot in a librarian's pride and capabilities, and, perhaps, their love of isolation. Recall the librarians' past objection, upon several occasions, to the merger of their professional associations, whether with the Medical Library Association, the Special Library Association, the American Documentation Institute, or the American Society for Information Science. No merger occurred, but the separations grew wider.

One of the main concerns was how to communicate that there were established criteria for networks and that nothing less than meeting these criteria would yield satisfactory networks. By 1969, Overhage, reviewing the network literature for the past year, reemphasized that citation-linked papers, such as those called networks by the information science giants de Solla Price in 1965 (1965b) and Garfield in 1967, were not networks, nor were organizational structures such as ERIC clearinghouses nor cooperative arrangements such as interlibrary loans. However, communication systems such as press wire services and computer-communications systems such as NASA-RECON were network examples (Overhage, 1969, p. 340).

The four criteria reported by Becker and Olsen seemed to hold. Overhage made an addition with the following statement: "It is the combination of computers, data circuits and user terminals that constitute information networks in the modern sense" (Overhage, 1969, p. 342). Ten years later Evans restated basically the same criteria using new terms when he listed prerequisites for making a network attractive to libraries: (1) use of online computing and telecommunications; (2) reduction in costs; (3) resistance to the labor-intensive nature of library and information services; (4) alleviation of the burden of the information explosion (too many materials to buy with too little money and space); (5) availability of standards, particularly MARC, machine-readable records; (6) new modes of publication (the paperless society); and (7) users' increased need for access to more materials than one library could hold (Evans, 1979).

Unlike in earlier periods, in this first period of networking, many librarians were concerned and interested in learning the new methods. In the following we briefly discuss three conferences that were convened for the purpose of increasing the awareness of librarians (Table 14).

In July 1968, the Graduate Library School at the University of Chicago held a conference entitled "Library Networks—Promises and Performance" (Carnovsky, 1969a,b). There were ten presentors, none of them among our selected specialists. Nine of the papers are included in the proceedings. There were seven librarians in key positions, one representative of a publishing company, and two representatives from government. Four were from the East, four from the Midwest, and two from the West. One of the presentors had been a member of President Johnson's National Advisory Commission so was well-versed in the concept of the "legal right of access . . . all libraries open to all users" (Lacy, 1969, p. 22). As previously mentioned, such a policy caused consternation among librarians (Markuson, 1976; N. D. Stevens, 1980; Swanson, 1980).

The papers of the Chicago conference emphasized the status quo, that is, lack of adequate library services to any but people living in the large metropolitan areas, lack of services to Blacks, few school libraries for anyone, and the need to form new governmental cooperative arrangements. Three papers mentioned the word "network" in their titles, several dealt with linkage or interrelations, and one praised traditional libraries, but hoped for change. Potential local, state, and regional cooperative arrangements were addressed. Legal arrangement, financing problems, and other salient aspects of networking were also discussed.

Although no mention was made of telecommunications nor of computer-based networks, this conference was representative of the first stages in the improvement in geographical coverage by libraries through networking. It represented the kind of planning that ALA had fostered over the years (Molz, 1984).

The second conference, which was representative of the movement toward updating the knowledge of librarians, was held on April 1, 1970, in Boston, under the auspices of the College and University Section of the Catholic Library Association. The resulting document is entitled "Network Concepts: Four Points of View" (Matzek, 1971). At this conference information scientists met with librarians. Richard De Gennaro repeated Becker and Olsen's four criteria (De Gennaro, 1971), and Carlos A. Cuadra spoke on the background and history of networking. He outlined the benefits to libraries and discussed the difficulties he had encountered in convincing his company, the System Development Corporation, that libraries could benefit from networking. He insisted that libraries and librarians who aspire to become involved in networking must be willing to make drastic changes in their preparation. Cuadra considered the most urgent problem to be "lack of training and preparation of people so that they can contribute to progress of individual libraries which will be the nodes of networks" (1971b, p. 18).

Henriette D. Avram spoke of the need to promote standards and advised that an optimal mix of librarians and systems experts be employed and that they make every effort to understand the strengths of each other. She noted that MARC II, to which many librarians had contributed suggestions, had celebrated its first anniversary of operation during the previous month and that MARC formats were now in place for every form of media. She answered one criticism, heard even today, by saying that all the possibilities for collecting data on each of the formats need not be completed; only what is needed or desired should be used (Avram, 1971b).

The third movement toward informing top-level information professionals was a second conference held in 1970. This one brought together practicing librarians, information scientists, and technology experts, mainly those in telecommunications. This conference, entitled Interlibrary Communications and Information Networks, was held September 28–October 2, 1970, and was sponsored jointly by ALA and the USOE Bureau of Libraries and Educational Technology.

This 1970 conference marked a turning point in that it was the first to introduce sophisticated concepts on a large scale to the practicing information professionals. At this time enthusiasm for a national network was running high. It was also the year that President Nixon signed the National Commission for Library and Information Science (NCLIS) into existence.

Five of our selected network specialists participated: Joseph Becker directed the activities and subsequent proceedings (Becker, 1971); Carlos A. Cuadra held the position of a leader in Network Planning; Ruth M. Davis presented a paper on the biomedical network at the National Library of Medicine (Davis, 1971); Henriette D. Avram spoke on the issue of a national network (Avram and Pulsifer, 1971); and J. C. R. Licklider submitted the hypothetical plan that introduced the computer network ARPANET (Licklider, 1971).

ARPANET, as well as telecommunications networks, were relatively new concepts in the information field at this time. ARPANET is a nationwide computer network designed to provide a variety of research and other problem-solving aids, mainly to personnel at the universities (Roberts and Wessler, 1970). Lawrence D. Roberts is credited with the original idea of ARPANET; the details were worked out with colleagues at MIT's Lincoln Laboratory under contract with the U. S. Department of Defense.

Associated with Robert's idea was that suggested by Wesley Clark, namely, that the computer network include IMPS (Interface Message Processors), small computers modified to facilitate connection to the host computers on the one hand and to telephone lines or other transmission links on the other (Heart et al., 1970). These IMPs were probably the first front-end devices for computer and information networks. The subject of telecommunications was the focus of 20% of the 31 papers, beginning with the keynote address delivered by Kenneth A. Cox (1971), Senior Vice President of the Microwave Corporation of America.

Early 1970 had witnessed the emergence of a fully operational value-added communications network, TYMNET, developed by TYMSHARE Inc. (Combs, 1973). Within a few years TYMNET was in use at the MEDLINE (MEDLARS online) operation for the NLM. Thus, librarians and information scientists at the top levels were made aware of the telecommunications advances that would eliminate the problem of distance and of a computer network that would provide unique services that could be shared.

Summary of Period One: 1965-1971

We have designated 1971 as the end of the first period of networking, an arbitrary move that coincides with the year that certain professionals declared that information storage and retrieval, as it was then called, had "come of age."

NASA-RECON, MEDLINE, and ERIC were already providing online services; OCLC was cataloging online (Chapters 2 and 4; Table 6); the commercial vendors Lockheed and SDC offered online bibliographic search and retrieval services; ARPANET had begun its operations; TYMNET was fully functional. No library network had yet come completely into the fold, although NELINET had established a cooperative arrangement to provide technical services for university libraries in New England. Other regional cooperatives were to follow. Many of them would affiliate with OCLC, thereby at least partially qualifying as participants in networking in the modern mode. State and local networks were also beginning to form.

With these beginnings, plans and criticisms of a national network occupied the next seven years, with quite unexpected changes. NCLIS became omnipotent; its critics matured. Plans for a White House Conference for Library and Information Services (WHCLIS) intensified the pace of events in the second period, 1972-1978.

Planning and Development of Networks: 1972-1978

Not only planning and development but also tremendous expansion and critical decision making characterize this second period, 1972-1978 (Table 15). Three levels of participants existed during this period: (1) the sophisticated entrepreneurs, that is, the database vendors, the bibliographic utilities personnel, and the representatives of other commercial firms, including vendors of technologies; (2) intermediary users, that is, the information professionals in libraries and other information centers; and (3) the end users.

Benefits of Networking

What were the benefits of networking to the entrepreneurs and to their institutions? According to the bibliographic utilities, the benefits were better information services and economies based on the number of people or customers served (economy of scale). In these early days, the best that librarians could hope for was that the Library of Congress or other card service would mesh with local cataloging. Even though countless libraries across the land were each cataloging the same book, no one attempted to estimate how much it had cost to catalog all the copies of the same title that had been acquired. Given this situation it was relatively easy for Kilgour at OCLC to explain the principle of one cataloging effort to serve all libraries, thus attaining cost-effective economy of scale. The more libraries that used the one record, up to a point, the cheaper it became.

Over the years much research, some of it financed by the Council on

TABLE 15
Key Chapters in *ARIST* and Selected Conference Proceedings:
The Planning and Development of Networks, 1972–1978

Year	Volume	Author(s)	Title	Affiliation
1974	9	R. F. Miller and R. L. Tighe	"Library and Information Networks"	NELINET
1977	12	S. R. Bunch and P. A. Alsberg	"Computer Communication Networks"	Center for Advanced Computation
1977	12	A. Tomberg	"European Information Networks"	EUSIDIC
1977	NA[b]	Proceedings of the February 1977 Information Science and Automation Division of ALA, Conference on a National Bibliographic Network		
1978	13	V. E. Palmour and N. K. Roderer	"Library Resource Sharing through Networks"	King Research, Inc.
1979	NA	A. Kent and T. J. Galvin, eds.	"The Structure and Governance of Library Networks"[c]	University of Pittsburgh

[a]*Journal of Library Automation* **10** (2): 101–180, June 1977.
[b]Not applicable.
[c]Proceedings of the 1978 Conference in Pittsburgh, Pennsylvania, Cosponsored by National Commission on Libraries and Information Science and University of Pittsburgh.

Library Resources, has been devoted to the subject of financing information services. Cooper has been an important writer in this area. He cited studies that stress factors such as the importance of collecting appropriate data, the use of models and formulas, the trade-off concept of cost-effectiveness, and more recently the concept of economies of scale (Black, 1969; Baumol and Marcus, 1973; Cooper, 1979, 1983, 1984, 1986; Cummings, 1986). What the researchers had not yet resolved, the entrepreneurs had at least temporarily figured out.

The database vendors had their own economic message—no need for every institution to purchase the database tapes (again economy of scale), because one database served many customers. Vendors had emerged to supply services to libraries and information centers that in turn needed to supply their end users. These intermediary users were the information professionals in each institution, and were usually the first point of contact by vendors (Chapter 4). They also congregated to form user groups and to receive instruction from vendors.

Warheit of IBM expanded on the concept of benefits to include benefits to libraries and information centers that could expand their services to end users by initiating online bibliographic retrieval from databases. These databases formerly were manual indexing and abstracting services, most of them with a considerable lag between the time items were published and the time that the alerting service became available. Warheit (1972) added the advantages of not having to purchase databases, online currency of references, and the capability of modifying the search.

What were the benefits to intermediary users? to end users? Intermediary users benefited by being able to offer sophisticated services with capabilities that manual services did not have. For example, those mentioned in the foregoing by Warheit as well as the fact that more access points are usually available for search from computer-based services than from the manual counterpart, even when the source of indexing is the same. The benefits to end users are fully enumerated and explained by Hawkins (1976) and Wanger *et al.* (1976) (Chapter 4).

Librarians

In the beginning most information professionals, especially librarians, had not heard of the two new services: online cataloging from a bibliographic utility and online information services from database vendors. To those just starting to use them, the services seemed revolutionary. It would still be a few years before the majority of librarians, and others, would understand these services and their benefits. The main problem for those who had designed and developed the new services was how to communicate their availability and their benefits to end users, and even to intermediary users at the centers for services.

Butler noted that it was virtually impossible to find in print a comprehensive account explaining the details and benefits of connecting with a network. He stated that there had been only one successful network (he referred, of course, to cataloging), OCLC, that met the rather "stringent and rigorous" network definition (Butler, 1975).

By the late 1970s, however, librarians were becoming aware of the situation and learning about their options. Services were now available to libraries through designated local, state, or regional service centers. This connection, if chosen, could in effect qualify librarians as participants in networking. Computers, terminals, and telecommunications connections were necessary before this was possible, however.

Promotion by Network Leaders

The cataloging network of Kilgour's OCLC had grown at a tremendous rate (Chapter 3). Librarians, especially cataloging librarians, and their clerical and technical staffs were pleased with the results and soon considered the new systems to be an integral part of their libraries. This satisfaction was a result of OCLC's open communication and cooperation with personnel from the technical services departments across the nation.

At the same time, the database services networks of Summit and Cuadra at Lockheed (DIALOG) and System Development Corporation (ORBIT), respectively, had grown at a similar rate (Williams, 1977b). What did Kilgour, Summit, and Cuadra have in common? They all, of course, were working with computers and with machine-readable records. But the real secret was probably their approach to and treatment of their customers. The cataloging services, from a not-for-profit corporation and the database services, from for-profit corporations were equally served by management's awareness of how to gain client acceptance.

The entrepreneurial spirit appears to be the central factor in the expansion of information services. Entrepreneurial spirit is a characteristic of leadership that works in any type of organization. Robinson (1980) asserted that the success of a third type of network in the late 1970s, the library networking system, was due to aggressive entrepreneurial service. The manifestation of dynamic leadership, a necessary quality for the kind of marketing that inspires trust, is required to expand the user population. This phenomenon apparently solved the problem of how to educate and inform libraries of the new library network services. A new type of leadership for librarians had emerged successfully.

Cooperation in many instances turned into competition. One competitor of OCLC was RLIN, but there were others that offered unique services. When OCLC was threatened or criticized in a constructive way (e.g., on its structure of governance), it initiated change. It responded to criticism with changes in governance structure, initiation of the interlibrary loan network, and later international expansion ("OCLC becomes Democratized, Nationwide Corporation," 1978; Kilgour, 1979b; Lewis *et al.,* 1986).

It also seems to be characteristic of networks and information systems that have survived adversity that they have the capacity to examine themselves critically, define their problem, adjust, and emerge stronger than before. ERIC, the NLM, and OCLC have each worked through serious problems and come out improved. Other examples are ERIC's response to the Rand study of ERIC clearinghouses (Greenwood and Weiler, 1972) and the 1960s preelectronic effort of the NLM to improve indexing and other services (Taine, 1961). John Gardner's "Self-Renewal" (1964) and the shorter "How to Prevent Organizational Dry Rot" (1965) reinforce the consequences of stagnation.

Expansion of TYMNET, ARPANET, and International Networks

Further expansion of networking during this period included more users of TYMNET and ARPANET. Each of these networks was intended to serve specific needs as well as to decrease costs. The telecommunications networks such as TYMNET overcame the barrier of geographical distances, while ARPANET was useful not only by fulfilling users' needs for sophisticated programs that could be shared, but also by serving as a model in understanding basic computer technology and packet-switching (Bunch and Alsberg, 1977). Both types of ARPANET services functioned mainly at the university level.

International networks services also increased. EURONET (Voight, 1976) and the UNESCO-planned UNISIST, a network for STI (Science and Technology Information), were planned in the early 1970s (Tocatlian, 1973) and were operating shortly thereafter. International networks reveal an interesting phenomenon that is unfamiliar to networks in the United States and Canada, namely, that these are the only countries whose Postal Telephone and Telegraph services do not provide digital data services. EURONET and other international networks rely on Postal Telephone and Telegraph (PTT), as does England's TYMNET (Bunch and Alsberg, 1977).

In 1977, Alex Tomberg described the international networking scene by reporting that in Europe "the term 'information network' was used to mean a telecommunications facility involving at least one dedicated circuit and enabling more than one organization to access online one or several services in the field of scientific and technical information (STI)" (Tomberg, 1977, p. 219). Tomberg defined European as "operating in Europe or planning to operate there"; he added, with a little humor, that the "state of Europe is that it is not a state" (1977, p. 220). He confirmed that networks are government controlled through postal services and that even the Europeans do not understand how post offices came to be in their present peculiar position.

The National Network—Progress Delayed

All had not come up roses in the development of a national network. Readers will recall that at the 1970 networking conference, the director announced that President Nixon had signed the bill authorizing the National Commission for Libraries and Information Science (NCLIS). This new body is composed of the Librarian of Congress as a permanent appointment and 14 commissioners appointed by the President with the advice and consent of the Senate for five-year terms. Let us state at the beginning that President Nixon had not been enthusiastic about NCLIS since it had grown out of the presidencies of John F. Kennedy and Lyndon B. Johnson (Molz, 1984). Nevertheless, he had "gone along" with its authorization.

To the appointees and to many others, the formation of this body assured that there would be a central policy-making and coordinating national leadership. In 1970 there was no indication of how the information services leaders would come to bitterly oppose any hint of central control by this newly formed institution. NCLIS was slow to staff and establish itself and to develop and publish its principal document [National Commission on Library and Information Science (NCLIS), 1975] and plan for action. In the meantime all appeared to be friendly, but the grumbling had begun.

At a 1977 ISAD Conference on the subject of networking, the members of ARL were prevalent with only one representative from NCLIS—its then Executive Director, Alphonse F. Trezza (Trezza, 1977a). Besides NCLIS, also represented were the University of California at Berkeley, the Association of Research Libraries Group, the American Library Association, and the Library of Congress (*Journal of Library Automation*, June 1977). Like all good politicians, the presenters couched their questions in soft language: Why are standards needed since they are in a constant state of flux? Why should technical services continue to introduce esoteric information when only the few specialists in technical services are concerned with them? Then the hard questions followed: What should be the role of NCLIS? of the Council on Library Resources? What was the probability that a national library and information services network could be realized? If so, what should be the nature of its governance?

A second relevant conference cosponsored by the University of Pittsburg and NCLIS was entitled The Structure and Governance of Library Networks. It was held in November 1978 and was definitely an NCLIS conference. The principal controversy was a presentation by John W. Bystrom entitled "A Proposal for New Federal Legislation." It contained a plea for a federal policy-making authority (Bystrom, 1979). Papers were also presented by three NCLIS personnel: Chairman Charles Benton (Benton, 1979), Executive Director Alphonse F. Trezza (Trezza, 1979), and William D. Mathews (1979). Three other presentations were given by our selected specialists: Joseph Becker (1979) and Roger Summit (1979) gave reaction papers, and Henriette Avram (1979) presented "The Governance of Library Networks: A Call for Action."

One of the participants at this conference pointed out the value of large integrated circuit computers as opposed to the microcomputers. He also valued the customer's choice to enter and exit at will (Summit, 1979). Another participant expressed acceptance of the range and benefits of the new technologies to the performance of network governance (Hayes, 1979).

In a second phase of the discussion, questions were directed toward NCLIS as a national leader group. General criticisms seemed to oppose the prospect and reaffirmed that choice in an atmosphere that encourages creativity is important to innovation and success (Summit, 1979; Hayes, 1979). Summit simply concluded: "To paraphrase an ancient wisdom: Beware of bureaucrats bearing gifts" (1979, p. 151).

Mathews of NCLIS sprinkled some loving advice upon the shoulders of librarians: "Librarians and library networks should discard their accustomed xenophobia and join forces with the rest of the information community . . . it is time to march together on this broad front or to be left dusting books" (1979, p. 137). There had been considerable tension at both of these conferences, and more was to come before the White House Conference on Library and Information Services. The general atmosphere was labeled "frightening" by one onlooker (Moffett, 1979).

Mad Dash by NCLIS

Certain librarians and others to be responsible in the proposed national network, but especially those affiliated with NCLIS, seemed bent on making the right impression at the White House Conference and may have contributed to the tension at the previous conferences. At the same time, however, they were concerned, even disturbed, by the stated purpose and program of NCLIS. One persistent and nagging question was that of access for all. This access was to be the theme of the WHCLIS, and it had already elicited strong criticisms. Counteracting these concerns, however, were efforts and plans to make the conference a huge success (Becker, 1979; Trezza, 1977a, 1979; C. H. Stevens, 1977, 1979).

Meanwhile, relevant studies were investigating the feasibility of providing a central periodicals bank (NCLIS, 1977), who should be responsible for interlibrary loan services, and the probable structure and concerns of the national network (Palmour et al., 1972, 1974a,b). Most of the studies were funded by CLR, who later concluded that some of the recommendations "were not feasible" (Council on Library Resources, 1986, p. 15).

The unpopular NCLIS scheme was conducted over eight years (1970–1978). Its true nature was perceived by only a skeptical few. Miller and Tighe (1974) reported intense publishing activity that seemed to reflect a benign beginning largely focused on a planned White House Conference on Library and Information Services. This conference was planned for 1976; but did not occur until 1979.

The Library of Congress

In the meantime, the Network Advisory Group at the Library of Congress appeared to be cooperating toward the NCLIS networking goal. Continued planning and studies were focused on a central cooperative plan. Efforts toward a bibliographic component for the national network consumed considerable time (Avram and Maruyama, 1977).

Summary of Period Two: 1972–1978

The principal message from this second period (1972–1978) was expansion. In the following we give a brief report of each type of network covered in this history with selected references that are of particular importance.

First, we considered three examples from the U. S. Government-owned and -operated networks developed from sophisticated information systems: MEDLINE (Miles, 1982); ERIC (Trester, 1981); and AGRICOLA (Peters, 1981). Each report confirms the modernization and expansion of services.

Second, the bibliographic utilities were represented by OCLC. In "OCLC from Concept to Functioning Network," Long (1973) recounts the development of this first bibliographic utility that for a long time operated as a nonprofit monopoly, but which in our second period was faced with its first competition. The complete papers of Frederick G. Kilgour (1984a) cover much of the same period and extend to 1980, when Kilgour retired from OCLC.

Third, vendors of database services were represented by DIALOG (Camp, 1985). Both intermediary and end users increased as expansion extended to international locations, new databases were added, and promotional activity was widely visible. New technologies improved services. Other leading vendors experienced similar growth and expansion of databases (Reynolds, 1985; Williams, 1985b).

Fourth, geographical networks included local, state, and regional library networks, the concept of a national network, and international networks. All levels experienced expansion, although a national network did not develop as was earlier envisioned. Robinson (1980) gave an account of the growth of geographically located library networks, while individual administrators, Evans (1973) and Charles Stevens (1979), conveyed the representative activity in the state and regional centers (SUNY and SOLINET, respectively). Although the national network dream as planned by NCLIS did not materialize, services nonetheless were drastically improved through efforts such as OCLC's role in raising the status of library networks, the expansion of services of database vendors, installation in libraries of turnkey systems, and the prevalence of personal computers in the process of information retrieval.

Fifth, this second period was also the time when the computer network

ARPANET came of age. Evidence of its acceptance is documented by Kehl (1973), Borko (1975), Wyatt (1973), and Sher (1974). Williams (1979b) and *ARIST* reviewers were also aware of its progress.

Several universities came to depend on the services of ARPANET. William Kehl, then Director of the Campus Computer Network of UCLA, reported that the UCLA ARPANET program was under the sponsorship of the National Science Foundation (NSF). It provided services similar to those that are now spoken of as "expert systems." Borko (1975), a professor at the UCLA Graduate School of Library and Information Science, reported on the cost savings and program advantages of ARPANET use in universities. ARPANET services had the potential for increasing each university's access to new programs. It was used mainly by faculty and other researchers at UCLA, but the regular university computer services were still available. On the other hand, some universities, Harvard and the University of Illinois, for example, eliminated their large computers and relied totally on ARPANET services (Wyatt, 1973, quoted by Kessler, 1974, p. 6); Illinois depended on ARPANET "almost exclusively since 1972." The advantages were not only cost-effectiveness and increased services, but also communication among users (Sher, 1974).

Sixth, telecommunications networks that were necessary to the operation of library networks became better known and understood among librarians. Published proceedings and attendance at conferences had improved communication (Becker, 1971; Markuson and Woolls, 1980). Combs (1973) explained TYMNET, while Roberts (1976) discussed TELENET, explaining how he had worked on the development of this first public network and on international standards to improve its chances of expansion. Kessler (1974) revealed that while the much publicized EDUNET did not materialize, "something probably much better occurred," namely, "EDUCOM became the forum for network 'experimentors' and for the exchange of thoughtful views that helped shape the field" (p. 2).

Retraction, Decentralization, and Diversification: 1979–1985

Retraction from the concept of a national information service network during this period was immediate and complete. A concept that had potential in the late 1960s and the 1970s fell upon hard times during this later period. A formal national network was no longer viable.

Although this third period officially covers the years 1979–1985, the preceding three to six years had set its tone. These earlier years had witnessed the publication of the NCLIS program statement (NCLIS, 1975) and at about the same time a study by the American Library Association of the institutions that had become powerful and that were headquartered in Washington, D. C. Some of the institutions included in this acronymic conglomeration were ALA, ARL, GPO, NIE, USOE, LC, CLR, and NCLIS (Plotnik *et al.*, 1975).

The results of this study were numerous. Here we note only two impressions that are relevant to the beginning of retraction from the idea of a new national leadership. The study found that Avram, at the Library of Congress, deserved accolades for her sustained efforts not only in the pursuit of the conversion of records to machine-readable form but also for her work to promote a quality national networking service. NCLIS received mixed reviews depending on who was asked (Plotnik *et al.*, 1975).

Doubts arose at several meetings as expressed by members of various groups. Readers will recall that at the 1978 Pittsburgh conference on the structure and governance of networks, a few members of the audience reacted vigorously following an NCLIS-sponsored presentation by Bystrom (1979) on the subject of proposed federal legislation. Strangely, however, the audience did not react negatively to three NCLIS speakers: Chairman Charles Benton, Executive Director Alphonse F. Trezza, and the Staff Associate for Information Technology, William D. Mathews. It probably was the proposed legislation and not, at the time, NCLIS itself that elicited opposition.

Similar concerns were echoed at a later conference, Networks for Networkers (Markuson and Woolls, 1980), held in Indianapolis on May 30–June 1, 1979, just five months before NCLIS found itself in charge of the White House Conference on Library and Information Services (WHCLIS; Table 16). Swanson, the keynote speaker at the conference, opposed national leadership on the following grounds: (1) a self-regulated market was preferred over central control; (2) there was no desire among libraries to surrender autonomy; and (3) there would be no faith in the benevolence and incorruptibility of those in the central power positions (Swanson, 1980).

Probably the strongest statement came from Markuson, who declared that decentralized (local, state, and regional) as opposed to centralized leadership in the development and control of library networks was mandatory. She pointed out that "there was insufficient attention to both the decentralization of libraries and the fact that no national organization or agency has any responsibility whatsoever for local library services" (Markuson, 1980, p. 14). Appearing to agree were De Gennaro, who spoke for academic libraries, and Evans, who, in declaring this the best of the pre-White House conferences, took the negative (thereby dramatizing support not only for decentralization but for diversification) in a debate centering on the question "Should state-level networking evolve principally from the state library agency rather than the cooperatively governed member library network?" (Summary of a Debate between Roderick G. Schwartz and Glyn T. Evans, 1980, pp. 342–344). Evans, who at the time was executive in charge of the cooperative computer-based network at SUNY, played a realistic role in expressing opposition to any rigid control.

Decentralization prevailed in library networking. Markuson (1980) apparently spoke for all local, state, and regional library networks when she publically stated the preferred and necessary condition. National leadership by NCLIS was summarily rejected.

NCLIS officiated at the White House conference held in Washington five months after the networks conference. It produced 64 resolutions, several related to the proposed national network. These resolutions were communicated to the White House in a letter dated March 1980, signed by Charles Benton, then Chairman of NCLIS. President Carter received the letter. Thus from 1970 to 1985, five presidents had been involved (whether or not they knew it). NCLIS

TABLE 16
**Key Chapters in *ARIST* and Selected Conference Proceedings:
The Retraction, 1979–1985**

Year	Volume	Author(s)	Title	Affiliation
1980	NA[a]	B. E. Markuson and B. Woolls, eds.	"Networks for Networkers"[b]	Indiana Cooperative Library Services Authority
1980	NA	—	U. S. White House Conference on Library and Information Services[c]	U. S. Government Printing Office
1981	16	G. T. Evans	"Library Networks"	State University of New York
1982	NA	A. Kent and T. J. Galvin	"Information Technology: Critical Choices for Library Decision Makers"[d]	University of Pittsburgh
1985	20	J. A. S. Segal	"Networking and Decentralization"	Association of Research Libraries

[a]Not applicable.
[b]Based on a conference sponsored by several Indiana professional groups and funded by the U. S. Office of Education, Office of Library and Learning Resources, held May 30 through June 1, 1979, in Indianapolis, Indiana, with 136 attendees, 21 of which were delegates to the White House Conference on Libraries and Information Services.
[c]SUMMARY, 1980.
[d]Third Conference held at the University of Pittsburgh, November 1981.

was conceived during the presidency of John F. Kennedy; it was articulated by President Lyndon Johnson; President Richard Nixon signed NCLIS into existence; and by 1980 President Carter would receive this letter from the 1979 WHCLIS. The letter carried subtle signs of a NCLIS demise. President Ronald Reagan, however, did continue appointments on seemingly shaky grounds. After the networking segment failed, NCLIS was advised to revise the submitted resolutions to exclude those pertaining to networking leadership. This did, however, leave other activities to NCLIS.

After the WHCLIS, Trezza tried to counter the various arguments against central control for libraries and information services, including networking, when he pointed to the success of the National Library of Medicine's integrated system (Trezza, 1981). This NLM integrated system, a prototype, was previously mentioned in Chapter 4. It should be remembered, however, that there were significant differences between the NLM and NCLIS. Nevertheless, shortly thereafter Trezza (1982) left NCLIS and took a position at the Library of

Congress, where he intended to work with NCLIS on his then new proposal for a Federal Library and Information Services Network.

NCLIS Slippage

From 1979 onward NCLIS suffered from limited funding and, lacking a strong mission, seemed to create its own agenda under a changing leadership (NCLIS, 1983, 1983–1984, 1984). In 1985 it offered a proposal for services to the elderly (Moore and Young, 1985), for example.

NCLIS's hope of leading a national network had formally died. NCLIS itself published the following announcement in its 1983/84 Annual Report: "With the rapid development of nationwide networks, such as OCLC and RLIN, regional and state networks, and the linking together through the Linked Systems Project, the concept of a single national network with strong federal leadership is no longer appropriate, nor does the library/information community want it" (NCLIS, 1983–1984, p. 43).

While NCLIS had not succeeded in becoming the leader of a national network, the program succeeded to a large extent in proving that information professionals usually can decide what they can and will do, what obstacles need to be overcome, and what does or does not fit into their own scheme or inclinations. At their own pace, and using their own criteria, libraries applied information science to their networking component of services.

NCLIS Still Extant

It seemed ironic that, even with the concurrence of NCLIS that its major goal of a national network leadership was "not appropriate" and with the confidence of information professionals toward NCLIS completely depleted, NCLIS programs were still being planned in the face of limited funding (federal funds were still appropriated). There must have been a reason for reluctance to close down. Perhaps, with a foot in the door at the national level and a few personnel and a budget (however limited) in place, NCLIS was secure as an appendage to the U. S. Government structure. A second WHCLIS is scheduled for 1989.

Network Environment in the 1980s: Diversification

Some of the leaders of the acronymic establishments were still active in the 1980s. Three speakers at a November 1981 conference (Kent and Galvin, 1982), Haas, Brown, and Avram, added considerably to the optimism of the application of information science to traditional environments.

Warren J. Haas had recently become President of the Council on Library Resources (CLR); R. C. W. Brown was the new head of OCLC; and Henriette D. Avram from LC continued the dependable and industrious efforts that she had shown throughout the period of the application of information science to information services activity.

At this conference Haas spoke mainly on two issues: the librarians' failure to make decisions on the type of technology that is offered them and their failure to understand the workings of the library networks from top to bottom. He called for technological unity within the diversity that was evolving and displayed considerable knowledge of the advances and problems of the library network field (Haas, 1982).

Brown, on the other hand, while agreeing with Haas on the position of librarians in the decision-making process, immediately turned to more inspiring issues. He discussed how OCLC was in the midst of a far-reaching planning process that was setting priorities such as international linking, new telecommunication opportunities, home delivery services, and many collaborative and joint ventures with the commercial world and with the government. Librarians and local networks would also be involved. OCLC, from a position as the only undifferentiated network in terms of the types of libraries that it serves, was preparing to work with various levels of task forces to assure that each level of library or other user would receive the new OCLC services in the most convenient and acceptable way. In response to a criticism in the Rush/Stevens report that no evaluation of network services had taken place, Brown assured the audience that the customer would choose the suitable services, and that this would be evaluation enough. After a reiteration of IBM's criteria for leadership that included trust, reserves of energy and strength, and integrity, Brown added characteristically "effective, informed followship" (1982, p. 183).

In Avram's presentation, entitled "Network-Level Decision: Basic and Key Issues," she pointed out that great strides had been taken in the library community due to the bibliographic utilities, the Library of Congress, the National Library of Medicine, and the commercial database services, but there was still not coordination. Links from one service to another were needed. Her report summarized the progress networking had made during the past 20 years and identified one of the main objectives for the future—linking (Avram, 1982).

By the middle 1980s, while Segal (1985) was reporting expansion of services, she was also concerned with the total spectrum of library networking: decentralization, diversification, linking, and the various configurations of integrated networks, ring networks, and hierarchical networks. Her report of the literature introduced open systems, interface, gateways, distributed databases, distributed (computer) processing, the decentralized (computer) network, and centralized processing (Segal, 1985). Only the last term might have been familiar to the "old" librarian.

Summary of Period Three: 1979–1985

The most outstanding phenomenon of this third period, 1979–1985, was continued expansion beyond that of the second period. Although further improvements would come, at last library networks had developed into sophisticated operations. New services such as OCLC's interlibrary loan program brought increased use. Intermediary and end users increased as did types and numbers of databases and the geographical areas covered. International networks also developed and expanded, and DIALOG and OCLC, in particular, continued to seek and acquire new clients.

Individuals with microcomputers were now capable of downloading and gaining access to the specific databases that allowed the creation of highly individualized information systems. Each person could begin to control his or her own search and retrieval activities.

Retraction occurred mainly in the concept of the national leadership of NCLIS; decentralization characterized local, state, and regional operations; and diversification was becoming difficult to manage, if it needed management at all. The choices had become so numerous, the structure so diverse, and the institutions in charge so disparate, that as Wedgeworth (1980) pointed out, the United States may eventually find itself unable to decide what individuals or groups could coordinate national programs or represent the United States on the international level.

A Pause

Cleverdon summed it up when he noted in 1970 (Chapter 2) that the main thing Taube did with his often called outrageous Uniterm Information System (it was nonconventional) was to shake up certain libraries that would not have responded without the shake (Chapter 3).

By the mid-1970s, information science personnel who were infiltrating libraries were receiving comeuppances from librarians. They came to be viewed as incompetent or overly clever, as suggested by Tighe's title "Hoist by Their Own Petard" (1974, pp. 3–4). De Gennaro had also found this to be the case (Chapter 3). At the time information science was considered to be moving too fast and with too much arrogance; needless to say librarians were adamant. Tighe herself became an information specialist in networking. She worked for NELINET, co-wrote a chapter for *ARIST* (Vol. 9; pp. 173–219, 1974), and planned the ASIS Annual Conference for Boston in 1975. However, differences remained between librarians and other information professionals.

The influence of information science continued apace, however. This influence came not only from Taube but also from Shannon, Wiener, Bradford, Clarke, Bush (Chapters 1 and 6), and other visionaries and designers who made possible such innovative instruments of information science as the machine-readable record, on-line transmission, and networking. Now that information science had been widely applied and accepted, perhaps all had been accomplished, thus heralding the need for a new paradigm as forecast by Harmon (Chapter 1).

Summary of Network Specialists

All 16 of our selected networking or networking component specialists are remarkable for their sustained and significant work. A brief summary of each of the specialists follows.

Davis initially worked with the National Library of Medicine and with its Biomedical Communications Network. She moved to the National Bureau of Standards, where she led evaluation teams to determine the extent of the technology contributions to the information processes. Later, she became one of the first women to join the Council on Library Sources (CLR), the institution that in the 1980s funded much of the research that was related to the application of information science to libraries and networks. (CLR was originally a branch of the Ford Foundation, but later combined funding from 10 to 12 private and government sources, including the National Science Foundation and the National Commission for Libraries and Information Science). Davis has projected the future of libraries for the community. Young people and senior citizens will come to read the newspaper. Information services will be separated. She foresees a split between libraries and what she calls the Information and Knowledge Network (Davis, 1987, p. 1–6).

Licklider continues to be cited, especially by designers of information systems. Several of his insights are basic: for example, man–computer symbiosis, the value of information sharing over time-sharing in interactive multiaccess, and the use of various-sized computers for various-sized jobs. His major accomplishments will not readily become outdated.

Summit, who has been called the father of online retrieval, received his Ph.D. in management science from Stanford University and went on to develop information services that resulted in DIALOG Information Services. DIALOG eventually divested from Lockheed, the operation that had been central to its history of online services from databases. DIALOG has continued to grow and is now considered to be the largest operation from databases in the United States, and probably in the world. The expansion of users was one of Summit's guiding principles. In 1987 he proposed that online information retrieval education be expanded in high schools (Summit, 1987).

Williams, the longtime monitor of databases and database services, recently conducted research that predicts that online information services will become more understandable and transparent to the end user by 1990.

Cuadra explored the role of microcomputers, investigated electronic publishing, directed the activities of Cuadra Associates, promoted library networks, and initiated online information services from the System Development Corporation. He recently declared that in the 1990s the user will again be in charge. Through the use of the personal computer, the user's searching autonomy is increasing (Cuadra, 1987).

Hawkins' goal of making information retrieval transparent to the user is similar to that of Williams'. Hawkins studied front-end devices and gateways in an effort to ease and embellish the user's access. He developed a powerful network for Bell Laboratories.

Tenopir is a researcher of renown on the topic of search and retrieval from full-text databases, particularly *Harvard Business Review*. In the late 1980s she explained some of the new technology (1986b,e) and advocated drastic improvement in professional education in the graduate library and information science programs (Tenopir, 1987).

Martin is interested in network governance and completed a dissertation on the subject. The populations that she studied were related to RLIN and RLG: the network directors, the 26 members of the Council of Computerized Library Networks (CCLN), and the directors of the Association of Research Libraries (ARL). She applied Mathew's definition of governance (Mathews, 1979, pp. 132–133), which, she explained, is not the traditional concept of the policymaking and advisor role but one of management and administration. The focus is more on testing, evaluation, and retesting of the structure to obtain the optimal result. Among her findings related to governance of networks, the most salient was that while there was support for federal involvement in library networks, the same library directors admitted to feeling more comfortable with a vendor–customer relationship (Martin, 1983).

Borgman conducted considerable computer-related research; one of her recent studies examined the user's mental model of an information system. She earned a Ph.D. from Stanford University in the field of communications; W. J. Paisley was her principal advisor. Her research was funded in part by OCLC.

Becker and Avram, two of the most avid advocates of a national network, seem never to tire of work toward that end. Although the original plan did not materialize, their dream was partially realized through distributed networking. One of Avram's principal goals is the establishment of standards. She believes that linking is crucial to future advances.

Both Markuson and Evans tirelessly promoted their library networks that would provide the decentralized services that clientele needed—Markuson in Indiana and Evans for the New York State universities. Both rejected central control and rigid organizational patterns.

For more than 20 years, from the Brasenose Conference in London in 1966 to the Networks for Networkers Conference in 1979 and beyond, De Gennaro has continued to support the best interests of academic libraries as they adjust to the application of information science. His concentrated efforts and acute judgment have resulted in recognition by his peers as a trustworthy authority.

Kilgour's talents and accomplishments are by now well known. At OCLC he proved to be a master of entrepreneurship although it was a not-for-profit organization. His interests include management strategies, application of technologies, the traditional methods of information services as well as research into new ones, and the education of personnel regarding the application of information science principles.

Hildreth, who worked at OCLC, assumed the task of organizing the results of several research studies related to OPACs in order to determine the design problems affecting the computer–user interface. This research problem involved communication with designers, organizing the data collected, defining terms to allow easier communication, and analyzing the needs of end users.

Dippers and Concentrators

Each of our 16 featured specialists probably falls into one of the following types of professional: the concentrators, who focus on one or several special interests, or the dippers, who diversify their interests and energies. De Gennaro, Davis, Licklider, Avram, Summit, and Hawkins are all concentrators, each in his or her own aspect of information networks. Carried to extremes the concentrators could become monomaniacs, so intense is their pursuit. Any of these six could conceivably win a Nobel Prize, or at least a Peace Prize, for advancing the science of network philosophy.

On the other hand, some of our specialists attempt to achieve unity through diversification. Becker, Williams, Kilgour, and Cuadra are the dippers. They dip into one aspect of the discipline and discover a solution for a problem in another. They dip into history and see the future. They remind us of Buckminster Fuller's pirates, who know everything. The American Society of Information Science (ASIS) apparently favors the dippers. Both Becker and Williams received the ASIS Award of Merit in 1984; Kilgour received it in 1979; and Cuadra in 1968. Cuadra also received the ASIS Best Information Science Book Award in 1969.

It is too early to categorize our other specialists, Markuson, Martin, Evans, Borgman (she may already be a dipper), Tenopir, and Hildreth. Both dippers and concentrators are needed, and most of our specialists have elements of both. All of them have continued to make profound contributions to the development of information and library networks. The two decades from 1965 through 1985 have been stimulating for information professionals. Lacking the government funding that was available in the 1970s, these specialists have nevertheless been both resourceful and productive.

Summary

The big event is that the National Commission on Library and Information Science (NCLIS) failed to establish itself as a national network leader. This failure, however, seems to have had little effect on the implementation of its program of access for all. The program has succeeded under a completely different structure from that envisioned by NCLIS. Ironically, the information professionals who expressed opposition are among those who advanced the program. Despite NCLIS and according to the opposition's own principles and strategies, networks of all types expanded and improved their services. Private funding and entrepreneurial leadership, both inside and outside for-profit institutions, proved that it is just as important to know what will not succeed as what will succeed.

Why did the proposal for NCLIS leadership founder? The Council on Library Resources (1986, p. 14) admitted that "in retrospect the concept of a tightly structured national bibliographic system was naive." Kilgour noted that the structure of our government with its separation of executive, legislative, and judicial powers, militates against a central authority, especially one that would set information policy (Kilgour, 1983, also 1986). He surely meant to include local, state, and regional responsibility.

We have already presented NCLIS's own statement that library and information professionals did not need nor want NCLIS leadership (NCLIS, 1975). There may be other reasons for its failure. One possibility is the fact that although ALA has a long history of leadership in planning the future of national information services, with the emergence of NCLIS, ALA relinquished that responsibility (Molz, 1984). Consider also that ALA has not been a leader of all factions of library and information services.

Except for the Library of Congress, which appears to be strongly represented in ALA membership, the national libraries and information centers are not significantly identified with ALA. Even the Association of College and Research Libraries, which is a division of ALA, at times has considered breaking away. This was evident in 1978 when for the first time this group met by itself in Boston (Association of College and Research Libraries, 1979).

Of course the Special Library Association is separate, as are the library associations of medicine, law, music, etc. Each is seldom associated with ALA. Vendors of database services and their supporters seem to favor membership in the American Society for Information Science (ASIS) or National and International Online Meetings, as well as ACM, IFLA, and FID. On the other hand, the Library of Congress, at least in the case of exporting MARC II, had tremendous leadership impact on other national libraries and on our own federal libraries as well.

Scholars and practitioners may speculate far into the future on why things fell apart for NCLIS network leadership. One obvious reason is that we already have successful, strong, and sophisticated national libraries: the Library of Congress, the National Library of Medicine, and the National Agricultural Library. We have information networks of every conceivable sort, strong academic and other research libraries, effective information systems such as MEDLINE, ERIC, and SCORPIO, and access to citation indexes through SCISEARCH, SOCIAL SCISEARCH, and ARTS & HUMANITIES SEARCH, and to the Library of Congress holdings through DIALOG. There are also the new CONSER and OCLC's Interlibrary Loan System, increased and enlarged database holdings from vendors, growing school libraries and learning resources centers, and improved public libraries.

Centers at the local, state, and regional levels bring services to the smallest communities. Increasingly sophisticated systems serve researchers in business, law, science, and other fields, some of which use full-text data bases. Numerical databases are used mainly by business, science, and technology. Finally, as Cuadra foresaw, end users are beginning to control their own information search and retrieval destiny.

CHAPTER 6

Conclusions

Introduction

This book has presented a history of successful trends in information science in the period 1945–1985. It does not always emphasize the adversity that some may have experienced along the way, nor does it necessarily agree with other accounts that may draw different conclusions from the same data.

This is a history of the revolution in information availability. One significant development has been the "economy of scale," that is, the more who use a service, the cheaper it becomes. These cost-effective information services are not only readily available now, but are cheaper and better. This is also a history of people, specifically the 24 featured specialists, whose vision, creativity, education, and diligence have contributed to both the refinement in information services and the increase in sophisticated users over the last few decades.

Major Successful Trends

The major identified trends are concisely summarized for each of the five chapters: (1) information science emerged; (2) nonconventional information systems were created; (3) information science applied to libraries began seriously with MARC II at the Library of Congress and with OCLC's cataloging program; (4) online activity developed and was adopted by both OCLC and the vendors who provided services from data bases; and (5) networks expanded services largely by eliminating the barrier of distance. These trends have been cumulative beginning with new information systems and progressing to the machine-readable record, the bibliographic utility, and the removal of geographic barriers through networks.

There have been and still are two separate streams in information science: indexing (database) services and cataloging (library OPACs—the online public access catalogs—are one example). The first is included in information science partly because of the early abandonment of indexing by librarians, and the second is considered a part of library science that many information scientists still do not warmly embrace. Since the early 1980s, sources of funding, probably more than any other factor, have tended to merge information science and library science. For example, OCLC and CLR collaborated in funding Borgman and other researchers. At the service level there has been a recognized need for formal linking, coordinating, and converging.

Information science has had an impact on library science that is similar to the impact of the early visionaries on information science. The time lag for change has been relatively short—only 40 years. Information science originated as a discipline that provided mission-oriented services from specialized information centers, new avenues for research, new possibilities for organizing technical reports, and the capability to switch information from one place to another, and it has eventually subsumed and now controls all types of materials, subjects, and formats. Much of this progress can be attributed to the machine-readable record, the vendors of database services, the bibliographic utilities, and online services including networks. Meanwhile, public access catalogs and continuing research into the habits of users as well as into the nature of new technologies were advanced by specialists such as those discussed in this history.

The Selected Specialists

We have classified the 24 specialists featured in this history to be five visionaries, three creators, six concentrators, four dippers, and six still unclassified (Table 17). In 1945, at the beginning of this history, the visionaries Bush, Wiener, Bradford, Clarke, and Shannon breathed life into information science. Three creators emerged: Taube, Luhn, and Garfield; 16 other specialists functioned in various capacities. We classified Davis, Licklider, Avram, De Gennaro, Summit, and Hawkins as concentrators: they focused on specific issues, including increasing the population of users and improving services. Kilgour, Cuadra, Williams, and Becker were classified as dippers: they dipped into different areas and focused their wider experience on their work. The six remaining specialists were not classified. The principal contributions of each and the chapter in which we discussed their background and work are listed in Table 17.

The first five specialists were visionaries, thinkers, and catalysts. They envisioned and developed the National Science Foundation, the electronic versus mechanical feasibility of computer function, the use of a binary versus base of ten system in computers, Bradford's law, the futuristic vision of satellites around the earth, and the first mathematical theory of information in the realm of telecommunications. This latter breakthrough was a harbinger of the increased role that telecommunications would play in information and communication services.

The next three specialists were creators. Their creations included an

TABLE 17
The Twenty-Four Featured Specialists and Their Principal Contributions

Name and classification[a]	Chapter reference(s)[b]	Principal contribution(s)
Vannevar Bush (V)	1	Inspired establishment of the National Science Foundation (NSF)
Norbert Wiener (V)	1	Inspired modifications in the first electronic computers
S. C. Bradford (V)	1	Created Bradford's Law
Arthur C. Clarke (V)	1	Envisioned the earth satellites
Claude E. Shannon (V)	1	Wrote "The Mathematical Theory of Communication"
Mortimer Taube (C)	2	Created an information system for use with coordinate indexing so that "retrieval is by logical operations of the product, sum and complement on the codes in the store" (Taube and Wooster, 1958, p. 8)
Hans Peter Luhn (C)	2	Created the KWIC/KWOC indexes and Selective Dissemination of Information (SDI) systems
Eugene Garfield (C)	2	Created citation indexes, first for science and later for social sciences and the arts and humanities
Henriette D. Avram (Co)	3, 5	Work on MARC I, MARC II, RECON, and toward a national information network
Richard De Gennaro (Co)	3, 5	Monitored the academic and other research library activities in library automation and networking and advised a large population through his publication
Frederick G. Kilgour (D)	3, 5	Created the first and largest bibliographic utility (OCLC)
Ruth M. Davis (Co)	4, 5	Man–computer interaction
J. C. R. Licklider (Co)	4, 5	Man–computer symbiosis
Roger K. Summit (Co)	4, 5	Management and expansion of DIALOG
Carlos A. Cuadra (D)	4, 5	Proponent of library networks, information networks, the personal computer, and electronic publishing; editor of *ARIST*, Vols. 1–10

(*continued*)

TABLE 17 (*Continued*)

Name and classification[a]	Chapter reference(s)[b]	Principal contribution(s)
Martha E. Williams (D)	4, 5	Monitor of database services; researcher, professor, and editor of *ARIST*, Vols. 11–20
Donald T. Hawkins (Co)	4, 5	Bibliographies through ONLINE; information services for Bell Labs; work on front-end devices
Christine L. Borgman (U)	4, 5	Human–computer interaction
Carol Tenopir (U)	4, 5	Retrieval from the full-text database; new technologies
Charles R. Hildreth (U)	4, 5	Man–computer interface; OPACs
Joseph Becker (D)	5	Worked toward a national information network
Glyn T. Evans (U)	5	Developed a library network in New York State
Barbara E. Markuson (U)	5	Developed a library network in Indiana
Susan K. Martin (U)	5	Research into governance of library networks

[a]V = Visionary; C = Creator; Co = Concentrator; D = Dipper; U = Unclassified.
[b]Refers to chapters in this book.

information system that, in its purest form, lent itself to the immediate application of postcoordinate search and retrieval, a computer for automatic indexing that could compose KWIC/KWOC indexes and SDI systems, and a citation index applied to periodical articles.

The other sixteen specialists, already reviewed in the summary of Chapter 5, included six concentrators, four dippers, and six unclassified individuals. They were largely responsible for improving the positions of the library intermediary and end users for information services. These specialists researched, developed, monitored, and promoted many aspects of information services. Their areas of concentration were diverse; man–computer symbiosis, research and evaluation, machine-readable records, multiple MARC formats, bibliographic utilities, the philosophical and pragmatic monitoring of the evolution of the academic and other research libraries, the human–computer interface, the full-text database, the governance of networks, and considerable research, much of it in the graduate schools of communications and of library and information science. These sixteen disseminated their ideas through conferences, presentations, and publications and encouraged international expansion and cooperation,

TABLE 18
Selected Major Conferences and Specialist(s) Who Attended

Year	Location and conference	Specialist(s) who attended	Chapter reference[a]
1948	London, Royal Society Science Conference	Taube	2
1950	Chicago, University of Chicago	Taube	2
1958	Washington, D. C., Taube–Wooster Conference	Taube, Luhn	2
1958	Washington, D. C., International Conference on Scientific Information	Taube, Luhn, Garfield	2
1961	Cambridge, Massachusetts, MIT Lecture Series, 100th Anniversary of Alexander Graham Bell	Bush, Wiener, Shannon, Clarke	1
1963	Warrenton, Virginia, Conference on Libraries and Automation, sponsored by LC, NSF, and CLR	Taube, Becker	3
1963	Chicago, American Documentation Institute Conference	Luhn, Garfield	2
1966	London, Brasenose Conference on the Automation of Libraries	Avram, De Gennaro, Kilgour	3
1968	Chicago, University of Chicago Library Networks—Promise and Performance	None	5
1970	Boston, Network Concepts: Four Points of View	Avram, Cuadra, De Gennaro	5
1970	Warrenton, Virginia Networking	Becker, Avram, Davis, Licklider, Cuadra	5
1977	Place not indicated, ISAD (Information Science Division of the ALA) Conference	Avram	5
1978	Pittsburgh Conference on Structure and Governance of Library Networks	Avram, Becker, Summit	5

(continued)

TABLE 18 (*Continued*)

Year	Location and conference	Specialist(s) who attended	Chapter reference[a]
1979	Indianapolis, Networks for Networkers	Markuson, De Gennaro	5
1979	Washington, D. C., White House Conference on Library and Information Services (WHCLIS)	Becker, Cuadra	5
1981	Pittsburgh, Information Technology Conference	Avram	5

[a]Refers to chapters in this book.

standardization, and the application of systems methods. Some of their individual accomplishments and important conferences are cited in Tables 17 and 18.

Information Environments: Conferences

Most of our specialists attended and participated in conferences (Table 18). Conferences were one of the principal environmental factors that enhanced the decision-making process as information science was maturing. These professional meetings fostered cooperation and communication among scientists and promoted MARC II internationally and, eventually, the expansion of all types of online information networks. Malinconico has stated the missions that institutes serve:

> To address two major professional needs: first, to serve as a means of providing continuing education regarding the rapidly evolving ambience being shaped by the application of technology to librarianship, and second, considered equally important . . . to fulfill a need for public fora in which the consequences of the application of technology can be openly discussed while decisions and policy are still malleable. (Malinconico, 1977, p. 102)

The same may be said for conferences.

Sociological Patterns

In the early 1980s, Evans studied sociological change as he reviewed the literature of networks for the *Annual Review of Information Science and*

Technology (Evans, 1981). This awareness of trends has prompted us to examine subtle changes as well as to observe the more obvious ones. The concept of trends was discussed by Naisbitt (1982) in ''Megatrends: The New Directions Transforming Our Lives.'' In our history of information science we have noted trends toward an information society, high-tech/high-touch systems, decentralization (distributed systems), free market tendencies in providing services, and networking in several forms. It is difficult to imagine what life would now be like if we had remained on ''the road that we were taking'' (apologies to Robert Frost).

Technological Climate

There are three key trends related to technology that have persisted throughout this history of information science and that have permeated every conceivable aspect of the discipline and services: (1) the relationship of humans to the computer; Licklider (1960) started the inquiry in the United States when he submitted his famous symbiosis paper, and Davis, Borgman, Hildreth, and hundreds of others from designers to personal computer users have pondered the problem; (2) the development of the computer network, with ARPANET in the vanguard in establishing a nationwide network, initiating the IMPs, and sharing the unique expert contents that appeal mainly to the research community; and (3) the value-added networks (VANs), which have been the principal means of geographic expansion.

The mini- and microcomputers are not only the fashion in the 1980s but are the means of providing access from small operations to larger ones; they are also indispensible in establishing distributed activities and have many other uses due principally to their relatively low cost, easy availability, and flexibility in many situations (see Table 10 for relevant references). These small computers are still constructed on the von Neumann model. Other models are being developed and will probably be produced in the near future.

Unfinished Business

A subsequent volume of the history of information science should include the following topics: education for all information professionals; management (governance); the professional associations and societies; the literature; international developments; and forecasting.

It is a difficult task to present the successful trends in information science that have occurred over the past 40 years. We are reminded of a simple but profound recommendation made at a conference held in the early 1960s: Problems can be effectively attacked and solved through a careful reading of the literature. All we would add to this formula is a little insight and energy.

APPENDIX A

Acronyms
and Abbreviations

AACR2	Anglo-American Cataloging Rules, 2nd edition
ACM	Association for Computing Machinery
ACRL	Association of College & Research Libraries
AD	*American Documentation*
ADI	American Documentation Institute
AEC	Atomic Energy Commission
AFIPS	American Federation of Information Processing Societies
AFOSR	Air Force Office of Scientific Research
AGLINET	Agricultural Libraries Information Network
AGRICOLA	Agricultural Online Access
AGRIS	Agricultural Information Science (International Information System for the Agricultural Sciences and Technology)
AI	Artificial Intelligence
AIM	Abridged *Index Medicus*
ALA	American Library Association
AMA	American Medical Association
AOC	Association of Ohio Colleges
ARIST	*Annual Review of Information Science and Technology*
ARPANET	Advanced Research Projects Agency Network (DOD)
ASIDIC	Association of Scientific Information Dissemination Centers
ASIS	American Society for Information Science
BALLOTS	Bibliographic Automation of Large Library Operations Using a Timesharing System (since 1978 this has been RLIN)
BLAISE	British Library Automated Information Service
BRS	Bibliographic Retrieval Services
CCLN	Council of Computerized Library Networks
COMSAT	Communications Satellite Corporation
COSATI	Committee on Scientific and Technical Information
CRIS	Current Research Information Services (abstracts)
CRT	Cathode Ray Tube
C-Span	Cable Satellite Public Affairs Network
DIALOG	DIALOG Information Services (formerly DIALOG Service of Lockheed Information System)
DOD	Department of Defense
EDUCOM	Interuniversity Communications Council
EDUNET	Proposed Network of the Interuniversity Communications Council
ELHILL	ORBIT modified at the NLM and at BLAISE
ENIAC	Electronic Numerical Integrator and Calculator

ERIC	Educational Research (changed to Resources) Information Center
EURONET	European (packet-switching) Network
EUSIDIC	European Scientific Information Dissemination Centers
FID	International Federation for Documentation (since 1986 the Federation for Information and Documentation)
GE	General Electric Corporation
GRACE	Graphic Arts Composing Equipment (NLM)
HBR	*Harvard Business Review*
IBM	International Business Machines
IFIP	International Federation of Information Processing
IFLA	International Federation of Library Associations and Institutions
IGRIS	Interagency Group for Research on Information Systems
IIB	International Institute of Bibliography
ILL	Interlibrary Loan
IMP	Interface Message Processor
INTELSTAT	International Telecommunication Satellite Consortium
ISAD	Information Science and Automation Division (of ALA)
ISI	Institute for Scientific Information
JOLA	*Journal of Library Automation* (organ of ISAD)
KWIC	Keyword-in-Context (index)
KWOC	Keyword-out-of-Context (index)
LC	Library of Congress
LCCS	Library of Congress Classification System
LJ	*Library Journal*
MARC I	Machine-Readable Cataloging (experimental)
MARC II	Machine-Readable Cataloging (operational)
MARC Format	The format for transmission of machine-readable cataloging data; developed by LC personnel
MEDLARS	Medical Literature Analysis and Retrieval System
MEDLINE	MEDLARS online
MESH	Medical Subject Headings (NLM)
MIS	Management Information System
NAL	National Agricultural Library
NASA	National Aeronautics and Space Administration
NBS	National Bureau of Standards
NCLIS	National Commission on Libraries and Information Science
NELINET	New England Library Information Network (later NELINET)
NIE	National Institute for Education
NLM	National Library of Medicine
NSF	National Science Foundation
OATS	Original Article Tear Sheet (ISI)
OCLC	Ohio College Library Center (in 1977 changed to OCLC, Inc.; in 1981 to OCLC Online, Inc.)
OPAC	Online Public Access Catalog
ORBIT	Online Retrieval of Bibliographic Information Tymshared (SDC)
OSI	Open System Interface (a linking service)
PTT	Postal, Telephone, and Telegraph Utility
RAM	Random Access Memory
RECON	Retrospective Conversion of Catalog Records (to machine-readable format at LC); also NASA-RECON for the use of Lockheed's Remote Console terminal for space science and technology (utilized software that is now outmoded)

RLG	Research Libraries Group, Inc.
RLIN	Research Libraries Information Network (formerly BALLOTS, now owned by RLG)
SAGE	Semi-Automatic Ground Environment Systems for Air Defense (DOD)
SCORPIO	Subject Content Oriented Retrieval for Processing Information Online (at LC)
SDC	System Development Corporation
SDI	Selective Dissemination of Information
SLA	Special Library Association
STAR	*Scientific and Technical Aerospace Reports* (Taube)
STAR	Microcomputer System for data entry (Cuadra)
STI	Scientific and Technical Information
TELENET	A commercial telecommunications network
TIP	Technical Information Project (MIT)
TYMNET	Commercial telecommunications network of TYMSHARE
UBC	Universal Bibliographic Control
UNISIST	United Nations Information System in Science and Technology
USOE	United States Office of Education
UTLAS	University of Toronto Library Automation System
VAN	Value-Added Network
VLSC	Very Large Scale Integrated Circuit Computers
VSAT	Very Small Aperture Terminals (satellite)
WHCLIS	White House Conference on Library and Information Services
WLN	Washington Library Network
WRU	Western Reserve University

Chronology

1800	Library of Congress (LC) established.
1836	National Library of Medicine (NLM) established.
1839	National Agricultural Library (NAL) established.
1847	American Medical Association (AMA) established a committee on medical literature.
1859	George Boole wrote a treatise containing accounts of his development of symbolic language.
1876	American Library Association (ALA) established.
1890	Documentation begun in Europe.
1892	Paul Otlet and Henri Fontaine formed the International Institute of Bibliography.
1895	Institute of International de Bibliographie formed.
1908	The International Federation of Documentation (FID) established at the Hague, Netherlands.
1909	The Special Library Association (SLA) broke from the ALA.
1937	Documentation transported to the United States when Watson Davis decided to organize the American Documentation Institute (ADI).
1938	*Journal of Documentary Reproduction* became the official journal of ADI. It ceased publication in 1943.
1939–1943	MARK I computer assembled at Harvard under the direction of IBM's Howard Aiken.
1940	Dr. George Stibitz went online with a computer at Bell Labs, New Jersey, from a mathematical conference in New Hampshire.
1945	Vannevar Bush's paper "As We May Think" and his book "Science, the Endless Frontier" published, giving impetus for new nonconventional information systems, development of the National Science Foundation, and improvement in the collections and facilities of the nation's principal libraries.
1945	Arthur C. Clarke's paper "Extra-Terrestrial Relays" published, alerting the world to his concept of earth satellites.
1946	Bush's "Endless Horizons" published.
1947	First U. S. chapter of FID established with Vernon Tate as its official representative.
1948	S. C. Bradford's "Documentation" published.
1948	C. E. Shannon's "The Mathematical Theory of Communication" published.
1948	Norbert Wiener's "Cybernetics or Control and Communication in the Animal and the Machine" and "Human Use of Human Beings" published.
1948	Mortimer Taube attended the Royal Society Scientific Information Conference in London, 21 June–2 July, where several of his ideas were confirmed.

1950	The National Science Foundation (NSF) established.
1950	At the 15th Annual Conference of the Graduate Library School, University of Chicago, Taube presented a paper on his concept of mission-oriented information services for science.
1951	First commercially available electronic digital computer—Remington Rand's UNIVAC I.
1951–1953	Eugene Garfield employed on Army Medical Library Project at Johns Hopkins University.
1952	Taube left the Atomic Energy Commission (AEC) to form Documentation, Inc.
1952–1957	SAGE (Semi-Automatic Ground Environment System for Air Defense) conceived at the Department of Defense (DOD); it became operational in 1957 using the IBM Q 7, then the largest computer in the world. It was not a time-sharing operation; it functioned in real-time.
1953	First large-scale evaluation of nonconventional and conventional information systems conducted at LC.
1953–1959	Mortimer Taube *et al.* published five volumes of "Studies in Coordinate Indexing" for Documentation, Inc.
1953	Hans Peter Luhn published "A New Method of Recording and Searching Information."
1955	Eugene Garfield's paper "Citation Index for Science" published.
1955	James Perry and associates established the Center for Documentation Communications Research at Western Reserve University (WRU).
1956	Garfield formed his own business.
1957	IBM named Luhn to be Manager of Information Retrieval.
1958	Luhn was on the planning committee for the International Conference for Science Information held in Washington, D. C., sponsored by the National Academy of Science, the American Documentation Institute, and the National Science Foundation.
1958	Taube–Wooster Conference on Information Storage and Retrieval held in Washington, D. C., sponsored by the Air Force Office of Scientific Research (AFOSR).
1958	National Aeronautics and Space Administration (NASA) established.
1958	Office of Scientific Information Service (OSIS) established at the NSF with Burton W. Adkinson as its first director.
1958	LC considered the capabilities of computers.
1959	NLM contracted with a biomedical computer expert to plan for the future.
1959	Winifred Sewell at the NLM revised MeSH (Medical Subject Headings).
1960–1965	Second-generation (transistorized) computer developed.
1960	Maurice F. Tauber and Oliver L. Lilley completed subject classification research that led to the ERIC information system. USOE funded this study.
1960	*Chemical Titles,* a current awareness tool for chemistry resulting from Luhn's research, published its first volume on April 5, 1960.
1961	The Council on Library Resources (CLR) commissioned Licklider to research the library of the future.
1961	Publication of the King Report (Red Book), an exploration of the feasibility of modernizing LC.
1961	Specifications completed for the first stage of MEDLARS (Medical Literature Analysis and Retrieval System) at the NLM.

1962	General Electric (GE) received MEDLARS contract.
1962	GE awarded subcontract to the Photon Co. for GRACE (Graphic Arts Composing Equipment).
1962	Allen Kent and others completed feasibility study for ERIC; funding from U. S. Office of Education (USOE).
1963	May 26–30: Members of the Association of Research Libraries strongly represented at Conference on Libraries and Automation.
1963	Beginning of the annual meetings of the Clinic in Library Applications of Data Processing at the University of Illinois.
1963	Luhn was program director for the annual meeting of the American Documentation Institute (ADI) that was to become ASIS. He introduced the first computer-produced technical papers (ADI preconference papers).
1963	In January, the first issue of *STAR* (*Scientific and Technical Aerospace Reports*) appeared.
1963	The Weinberg Report, "Science, Government and Information," released by President Kennedy's Science Advisory Committee.
1963	*Science Citation Index* first published.
1964	The National Agricultural Library computer group formed.
1964	Winifred Sewell again revised MeSH (NLM).
1964	MEDLARS became operational at NLM.
1965	ARPANET conceived by Laurence G. Roberts.
1965	Third-generation computers (integrated circuit) appeared.
1965	ERIC went into trial production at WRU with "Catalog of Selected Documents on the Disadvantaged."
1965	Buckland's research into the feasibility of the machine-readable record for LC commissioned by CLR.
1965–1971	Period when the concept of a national information network was prevalent.
1965	Licklider's "Library of the Future" published.
1965	Kessler's TIP (Technical Information Project) established at MIT; 400 people are potential users. The first public awareness of the need for an expanded user population.
1965	First communication satellite (Early Bird), Intelstat I, launched by COMSAT (Communication Satellite Corporation).
1966–1968	MARC I and MARC II developed at LC.
1966	Avram, Kilgour, and De Gennaro presented MARC and RECON to international audience during Brasenose Conference in London.
1966	ERIC firmly established with 11 clearinghouses.
1966	ALA-ISAD (ALA's Information Science and Automation Division) established.
1966	*Annual Review of Information Science and Technology* (*ARIST*) appeared with Carlos A. Cuadra as editor.
1967	First ERIC Thesaurus published.
1967	Dr. Ruth Davis left the DOD for the NLM, where she became the Associate Director of R & D.
1967	Fred Kilgour went to OCLC, where he developed an off-line batch-processing system for cataloging.
1967	President Lyndon Johnson proposed the "Knowledge Network."
1967	The Interuniversity Communication Council (EDUCOM) published its "Summer Study of Information Networks."
1968–1980	Libraries attempted to enter networking at an acceptable level.

1968	*Journal of Library Automation (JOLA)*, organ of ALA-ISAD, appeared.
1968	Fred Kilgour became the first editor of *JOLA*.
1968	ARPANET services began to rival time-sharing.
1968	The term "documentation" was changed in the United States to "information science."
1968	NASA contracted with Lockheed to design NASA-RECON at a cost of one million dollars.
1968	MARC II data available to subscribers.
1968	EDUNET proposed.
1968	President Johnson's "Knowledge Network" funded as Title IX of the Higher Education Act.
1968	Becker and Olsen state four necessary standards for the ideal network.
1969	ARPANET operational.
1970	IMPS (Interface Message Processors) included in ARPANET configuration.
1970	Cuadra, De Gennaro, and Avram promoted "rigid" networking criteria at a Catholic Library Association meeting in Boston.
1970	TYMNET operational as the first VAN (value-added telecommunications network).
1970	President Richard Nixon signed NCLIS (the National Commission for Library and Information Science) into existence.
1970	Batch retrieval information system operational at NAL.
1970	Off-line batch processing operational OCLC.
1970s	Third-generation computers utilizing integrated circuits appeared in such powerful mainframes as the IBM/360 and 370; comparable computers made by Honeywell, Sperry Rand (UNIVAC), and the National Cash Register Company, for example.
1970	Joseph Becker headed a networking conference.
1971	RECON (Retrospective Conversion of Catalog Records) to machine-readable format at LC. This operation is not to be confused with NASA-RECON—the use of Lockheed's Remote Console terminal for space science and technology.
1971	OCLC went online.
1971–1980	Period of decline in the concept of a nationally led information network.
1971	First microcomputer, Intel 4004, became operational.
1971	Carterphone Decision permitted attaching equipment to telecommunications lines.
1971	MEDLINE (MEDLARS online) operational at NLM.
1971	ERIC online.
1971	Lockheed's commercial information retrieval business launched.
1971	Dr. Ruth Davis moved from NLM to NBS, where she became Director of the Center for Computer Science and Technology.
1971	Cuadra offered his 13 suggestions for improving man's interaction with the computer.
1972	Summit submitted five facts of encouragement for online retrieval.
1972	OCLC extended membership to Ohio nonacademic libraries.
1973	OCLC extended membership to out-of-state libraries.
1973	Lancaster and Fayen's "Information Retrieval On-line" published.
1973	Hendricks proclaimed what is not a network.
1973	Greenberg reported on sophisticated information networks, including

	telecommunications, computer, information, and satellite operations.
1974	MEDLARS II completed and accepted at NLM.
1975	Online retrieval of bibliographic information utilized in several fields.
1975	Eugene Garfield awarded the American Society for Information Science Award of Merit.
1975	NCLIS published its program statement in "Toward a National Program for Library and Information Services: Goals for Action."
1975	CAIN (Cataloging and Indexing) became AGRICOLA (Agricultural Online Access) at the NAL.
1976	Martha E. Williams became editor-in-chief of the 1st edition of "Computer-Readable Bibliographic Data Bases: A Directory and Data Source Book"; 2nd ed., 1979; 3rd ed., 1982; 4th ed., 1985. Titles vary slightly.
1976	Martha E. Williams became second editor of *ARIST*, beginning with Volume 11.
1977	J. G. Williams as well as Aronofsky and Korfhage set forth criteria for evaluating information networks. At the same time the entrepreneurs contended that sales are proof of value to the customer.
1977–1978	NCLIS function questioned.
1977	Eugene Garfield received the Skolnik Award for outstanding contribution to the field of chemical information.
1977	BRS (Bibliographic Retrieval Services) operational.
1977	*Online* appeared in January.
1977	*On-Line Review* appeared in March (hyphen removed in Volume 2).
1977	OCLC became merely OCLC, Inc. (no longer an acronym).
1977	Stevens' seminal paper on OCLC governance published.
1978	Arthur D. Little Study of OCLC governance published.
1978	OCLC initiated a new governance structure with a 16-member board.
1978	RLIN organized at Stanford University, where RLG had merged with BALLOTS.
1978	Carlos A. Cuadra left SDC to become president of Cuadra Associates.
1979	Cuadra Associates published 1st edition of a quarterly journal, *Directory of Online Databases*.
1979	NAL adopted MARC format.
1979	"Structure and Governance of Library Networks," edited by Kent and Galvin, received ASIS Award for Best Information Science Book.
1979	Fred Kilgour received ASIS Award of Merit.
1979	MEDLARS III developing.
1979	Dialorder system installed at Lockheed.
1979	Giuliano suggested that libraries may need to charge for services.
1979	NCLIS headed the WHCLIS in Washington, D. C.
1980	Library networks functioning mainly through OCLC affiliation.
1980	Cuadra awarded the Information Industry Association Hall of Fame Award.
1980	Fourth-generation, very large scale integrated circuit (VLSI) computers appeared.
1980	Computers were becoming "user friendly."
1980	Kilgour retired from OCLC; Rowland C. W. Brown assumed the position of president.

1980	Hawkins' "Online Information Retrieval Bibliography, 1964–1979" published.
1980	LC closed its catalog on January 1.
1980	*Harvard Business Review* (*HBR*) became the first journal to offer a machine-readable full text for search and bibliographic retrieval.
1980	*HBR* available for search from BRS.
1980	*HBR* available for search from DIALOG Information Services.
1984	Tenopir predicted increased use of full-text databases.
1984	Williams promised that information systems will be increasingly "transparent" to end users by 1990.
1984	DIALOG Information Services, under the leadership of Summit, offered 100 million records on numerous subjects from more than 200 different databases, and claimed 70,000 customers in 80 countries.
1987	OCLC completed 13 million interlibrary loan requests between 1980 at the inception of its new system and 1987.
1989	Second White House Conference on Library and Information Services scheduled.

References

Adams, S. (1981). "Medical Bibliography in an Age of Discontinuity." Medical Library Association, Chicago, Illinois.

Adkinson, B. W. (1978). "Two Centuries of Federal Information." Dowden, Hutchinson & Ross, Stroudsburg, Pennsylvania.

American Library Association (1974). Margaret Mann Citation, Frederick G. Kilgour. *Libr. Resour. Tech. Serv.* **18**(4), 402.

American Men and Women of Science (1972). "The Physical and Biological Sciences," 12th ed., Volume 2 (D–G), p. 1350. Bowker Co., New York.

American Society for Information Science (1979). Best information science book award. *In* "The Structure and Governance of Information Networks" (A. Kent and T. J. Galvin, eds.), p. 25. Dekker, New York.

American Society for Information Science (1980). ASIS awards presentations for 1979. *Bull. Am. Soc. Inf. Sci.* **6**(3), 32.

Aronofsky, J. S., and Korfhage, R. R. (1977). Telecommunication in library networks: A five year projection. *J. Libr. Autom.* **10**(1), 5–27.

Artandi, S. (1968). "An Introduction to Computers in Information Science." Scarecrow Press, Metuchen, New Jersey.

Artandi, S. (1972). "An Introduction to Computers in Information Science," 2nd ed. Scarecrow Press, Metuchen, New Jersey.

Artandi, S. (1975). Theories of information. *In* "Essays for Ralph Shaw" (N. D. Stevens, ed.), pp. 157–170. Scarecrow Press, Metuchen, New Jersey.

Association of American Library Schools (1980). Task Force on Implications of the White House Conference on Library and Information Services: Implications of the White House Conference on Library and Information Services for Library Education. *J. Educ. Librarianship* **21**(3), 246–262.

Association of College and Research Libraries (1979). *In* "New Horizons for Academic Libraries" (R. D. Stuart and R. D. Johnson, eds.), Papers presented at the First National Conference of the ACRL, Boston, Massachusetts, November 8–11, 1978. K. G. Saur, New York.

Atherton, P. (1978). "Books Are for Use: Final Report of the Subject Access Project to the Council on Library Resources," ED 156 131. Educational Resources Information Center, Bethesda, Maryland.

Austin, C. J. (1968). "MEDLARS 1963–1967." National Library of Medicine, National Institutes of Health, Public Health Service, U. S. Department of Health, Education and Welfare, Bethesda, Maryland.

Avram, H. D. (1968). "The MARC Pilot Project: Final Report on a Project Sponsored by the Council on Library Resources, Inc." Library of Congress, Washington, D. C.

Avram, H. D. (1970b). The evolving MARC system: The concept of a data utility. *In* "Proceedings of the 1970 Clinic on Library Application of Data Processing" (K. L. Henderson, ed.), pp. 1–26. University of Illinois, Urbana.

Avram, H. D. (1971a). Library automation. *Annu. Rev. Inf. Sci. Technol.* **6**, 171–217.

Avram, H. D. (1971b). The national scene. *In* "Network Concepts: Four Points of View" (R. A. Matzek, ed.), pp. 22–30. Catholic Library Association, Haverford, Pennsylvania.

Avram, H. D. (1972). "RECON Pilot Project: Final Report," ED 082 793. Library of Congress, Washington, D. C.

Avram, H. D. (1975). Machine-readable cataloging (MARC) program. *Encyl. Libr. Inf. Sci.* **16**, 380–413.

Avram, H. D. (1979). The governance of library networks: A call for action. *In* "The Structure and Governance of Library Networks" (A. Kent and T. J. Galvin, eds.), pp. 221–228. Dekker, New York.

Avram, H. D. (1982). Network-level decisions: Basic and key issues. *In* "Information Technology: Critical Choices for Library Decision-makers" (A. Kent and T. J. Galvin, eds.), pp. 157–167. Dekker, New York.

Avram, H. D. (1985). Texas Library Association Annual Meeting, Dallas. Avram was one of the speakers focusing on the problems facing networks and bibliographic utilities as local automated systems emerge. Her reply to a question about whether and when LC expected to change its subject access system.

Avram, H. D., and Markuson, B. E. (1967). Library automation and project MARC: An experiment in the distribution of machine-readable cataloging data. In "The Brasenose Conference on the Automation of Libraries" (J. Harrison and P. Laslett, eds.), pp. 97–127. Mansell Information/Publishing LTD., London.

Avram, H. D., and Maruyama, L. S., eds. (1977). "Toward a National Library and Information Service Network: The Library Bibliographic Component," Prelim. ed. Library of Congress, Washington, D. C.

Avram, H. D., and Pulsifer, J. S. (1971). Bibliographic services for a national network. In "Proceedings of the Conference on Interlibrary Communications and Information Networks" pp. 92–100. American Library Association, Chicago, Illinois.

Avram, H. D., Guiles, K. D., and Meade, G. T. (1967). Fields of information on Library of Congress catalog cards: Analysis of a random sample, 1950–1964. Libr. Q. 37(2), 180–192.

Avram, H. D., Knapp, J. F., and Rather, L. J. (1968). "The MARC II Format: A Communications Format for Bibliographic Data, ED 204 413. Information Systems Office, Library of Congress, Washington, D. C.

Bar-Hillel, Y. (1957). A logician's reaction to theorizing on information search systems. Am. Doc. 8 (2), 103–113.

Baumol, W. J., and Marcus, M. (1973). "Economics of Academic Libraries." American Council on Education, Washington, D. C.

Bean, W. B. (1982). Preface. In "A History of the National Library of Medicine: The Nation's Treasury of Medical Knowledge" (W. D. Miles, ed.), p. iii. National Library of Medicine, Washington, D. C.

Becker, J., ed. (1971). "Proceedings of the Conference on Interlibrary Communications and Information Networks." American Library Association, Chicago, Illinois.

Becker, J. (1973). Library networks: The beacon lights. In "Proceedings of the 1973 Clinic on Library Applications of Data Processing" (F. W. Lancaster, ed.), pp. 171–179. Graduate School of Library Science, University of Illinois, Urbana-Champaign.

Becker, J. (1975). A brief history of online bibliographic systems. In "Information Systems and Networks" (J. Sherrod, ed.), pp. 3–13. Greenwood Press, Westport, Connecticut.

Becker, J. (1976). The rich heritage of information science. Bull. Am. Soc. Inf. Sci. 2(8), 9–13.

Becker, J. (1979). Network functions: Reactions. In "The Structure and Governance of Library Networks" (A. Kent and T. J. Galvin, eds.), pp. 85–91. Dekker, New York.

Becker, J., and Olsen, W. C. (1968). Information networks. Annu. Rev. Inf. Sci. Technol. 3, 289–327.

Becker, J., and Pulsifer, J. S. (1973). "Application of Computer Technology to Library Processes: A Syllabus." Scarecrow Press, Metuchen, New Jersey.

Bell, D. (1973). "The Coming of the Post-Industrial Society: A Venture in Social Forecasting." Basic Books, New York.

Belzer, J. (1969). Charles Babbage. In "Encyclopedia of Library and Information Science" (A. Kent and H. Lancour, eds.), Volume 2, pp. 240–242. Dekker, New York.

Bennett, J. L. (1972). The user interface in interactive systems. Annu. Rev. Inf. Sci. Technol. 7, 159–196.

Benton, D. (1979). Introduction. In "The Structure and Governance of Library Networks" (A. Kent and T. J. Galvin, eds.), pp. xv–xvi. Dekker, New York.

Berry, J. (1965). It's a wise child. Libr. J. 90(19), 4724.

Black, D. V., and Farley, E. A. (1966). Library Automation. Annu. Rev. Inf. Sci. Technol. 1, 273–303.

Black, S. W. (1969). Library economics. In "Libraries at Large: Tradition, Innovation, and the National Interest" (D. M. Knight and E. S. Nourse, eds.), pp. 590–596. Bowker, New York.

Bloomquist, H. (1963). The status and needs of medical school libraries in the United States. J. Med. Educ. 38(3), 145–163.

Bohnert, L. (1977). Nonconventional technical information systems in common use. Encycl. Libr. Inf. Sci. 20, 71–90.

Bookstein, A., and Swanson, D. R. (1974). Probabilistic models for automatic indexing. J. Am. Soc. Inf. Sci. 25(5), 312–318.

Bookstein, A., and Swanson, D. R. (1975). A decision theoretic foundation for indexing. *J. Am. Soc. Inf. Sci.* **26**(1), 45–50.

Booth, B. (1979). A "new" ERIC thesaurus, fine tuned for searching. *Online (Weston, Conn.)* **3**(3), 20–29.

Borgman, C. L. (1982). Mental models: Ways of looking at a system: Training users with mental models can improve performance. *Bull. Am. Soc. Inf. Sci.* **9**(2), 38–39.

Borgman, C. L. (1983). "End User Behavior on the Ohio State University Libraries' Online Catalog: A Computer Monitoring Study," OCLC Res. Proj. Ser. No. OCLC/OPR/RR83/7. Online Computer Library Center (OCLC), Dublin, Ohio.

Borgman, C. L. (1984a). Psychological research in human–computer interaction. *Annu. Rev. Inf. Sci. Technol.* **19**, 33–64.

Borgman, C. L. (1984b). The user's mental model of an information retrieval system: Effects on performance. Ph.D. Dissertation, Stanford University, Stanford, California.

Borgman, C. L. (1985). "Human Factors in the Use of Computer Networks." In LOCAL AREA NETWORKS AND LIBRARIES. PACIFIC INFORMATION. 73–88.

Borgman, C. L., and Kaske, N. K. (1981). Determining the number of terminals required for an on-line catalog through queueing analysis of catalog traffic data. *In* "Proceedings of the 1980 Clinic on Library Applications of Data Processing" (J. L. DeVilbiss, ed.), pp. 20–36. Graduate School of Library and Information Science, University of Illinois, Urbana-Champaign.

Borko, H. (1966). "Utilization of On-Line Interactive Displays," SP2575, AD640652. Santa Monica, California.

Borko, H. (1967). Design of information systems and services. *Annu. Rev. Inf. Sci. Technol.* **2**, 35–61.

Borko, H. (1968a). Information science: What is it? *Am. Doc.* **19**(1), 3–5.

Borko, H. (1968b). National and international information networks in science and technology. *AFIPS Conf. Proc.* **33**, Part 2, 1469–1472.

Borko, H. (1975). Information networks at the university: A description and prediction. *In* "Information Systems and Networks" (J. Sherrod, ed.), pp. 155–162. Greenwood Press, Westport, Connecticut.

Borko, H., and Bernier, C. L. (1975). "Abstracting Concepts and Methods." Academic Press, New York.

Borko, H., and Bernier, C. L. (1978). "Indexing Concepts and Methods." Academic Press, New York.

Borko, H., and Doyle, L. B. (1964). The changing horizon of information retrieval. *Am. Behav. Sci.* **7**(10), 3–8.

Boulding, K. (1956). "General Systems Theory: The Skelton of Science," General Systems: First Yearbook. Society for General Systems Research, Ann Arbor, Michigan.

Bourne, C. P. (1966). Evaluation of indexing systems. *Annu. Rev. Inf. Sci. Technol.* **1**, 171–190.

Bourne, C. P. (1974). "Analysis of ERIC On-Line File Searching Procedures and Guidelines for Searching: Final Report," ED 101 757. University of California, Berkeley Institute of Library Research, Lockheed Research Laboratory, Palo Alto.

Bourne, C. P. (1980). On-line systems: History, technology, and economics. *J. Am. Soc. Inf. Sci.* **31**(3), 155–160.

Bracken, M. C. (1971). An analysis of the evolution of the National Library of Medicine: Implications for the Development of Scientific and Technical Information Networks. Ph.D. Dissertation, The American University, Washington, D. C.

Bradford, S. C. (1948). "Documentation." Crosby Lockwood & Son, London.

Brandhorst, W. T. (1977). ERIC: Reminders of how it can help you. *Phi Delta Kappan* **58**(8), 627–630.

Brandhorst, W. T., and Eckert, P. F. (1972). Document retrieval and dissemination systems. *Annu. Rev. Inf. Sci. Technol.* **7**, 379–437.

Brillouin, L. (1962). "Science and Information Theory," 2nd ed. Academic Press, New York.

Brown, G. W., Miller, J. G., and Kennan, T. A. (1967). "EDUNET: Report of the Summer Study on Information Networks." Wiley, New York.

Brown, R. C. W. (1982). Network-level decisions: Reaction. *In* "Information Technology: Critical Choices for Library Decision-makers" (A. Kent and T. J. Galvin, eds.), pp. 177–189. Dekker, New York.

Buckland, L. F. (1965). "The Recording of Library of Congress Bibliographic Data in Machine Form." Council on Library Resources, Washington, D. C.

Bunch, S. R., and Alsberg, P. A. (1977). Computer communication networks. *Annu. Rev. Inf. Sci. Technol.* **12**, 183–216.

Burchinal, L. G. (1971). ERIC: The national education documentation retrieval system of the United States. ERIC meeting a national need. *Educ. Doc. Inf.* **178**(1), 9–15.

Bush, V. (1945a). As we may think. *Atl. Mon.* **176**(1), 101–108.

Bush, V. (1945b). "Science, the Endless Frontier: A Report to the President on a Program for Postwar Scientific Research, July, 1945." Public Affairs Press, Washington, D. C. (reprinted by the National Science Foundation in 1960).

Bush, V. (1946). "Endless Horizons." Public Affairs Press, Washington, D. C.

Bush, V. (1967). "Science Is Not Enough," pp. 75–101. William Morrow, New York.

Butler, B. (1974). Automatic format recognition (AFR) of MARC bibliographic elements: A review and projection. *J. Libr. Autom.* **7**(1), 27–42.

Butler, B. (1975). State of the nation in networking. *J. Libr. Autom.* **8**(3), 200–220.

Bystrom, J. W. (1979). A proposal for new federal legislation. *In* "The Structure and Governance of Library Networks" (A. Kent and T. J. Galvin, eds.), pp. 251–274. Dekker, New York.

Camp, J. H. (1985). Developments at DIALOG. *Online Rev.* **9**(5), 377–383.

Carnovsky, L., ed. (1969a). "Library Networks: Promise and Performance." Univ. of Chicago Press, Chicago, Illinois.

Carnovsky, L., ed. (1969b). *Libr. Q.* **39**(1), 1–108.

Carter, G. C. (1985a). Numerical databases: Their vital role in information science. Part I. *Bull. Am. Soc. Inf. Sci.* **11**(3), 6–8.

Carter, G. C. (1985b). Numerical databases: Their vital role in information science. Part II. *Bull. Am. Soc. Inf. Sci.* **11**(4), 10–12.

Carterphone (1971). Unanimous FCC vote OKs carriers' entry. C. W. Washington Bureau. *Computerworld* June 2, pp. 1 and 3.

Casey, R. S., and Perry, J. W. (1951). "Punched Cards, Their Applications to Science and Industry." Reinbold, New York.

Cawkell, A. E. (1980). Information technology and communications. *Annu. Rev. Inf. Sci. Technol.* **15**, 37–65.

Cherry, C. (1957). "On Human Communication: A Review, a Survey, and a Criticism." MIT Press, Cambridge, Massachusetts.

Citron, J., Hart, L., and Ohlman, H. (1958). "A Permutation Index to the Preprints of the International Conference on Scientific Information," SP44. Systems Development Corporation, Santa Monica, California.

Clapp, V. W. (1965). Foreword. *In* "Libraries of the Future" (J. C. R. Licklider, ed.), pp. v–ix. MIT Press, Cambridge, Massachusetts.

Clarke, A. C. (1945). Extra-terrestrial relays. *Wireless World: Radio Electron.* October, pp. 305–308.

Clarke, A. C. (1962). The social consequences of the communications satellites. *Horizon* **4**(3), 16–21.

Clarke, A. C. (1967–1977). The second century of the telephone. *In* "The View from Serendip" (A. C. Clarke, ed.), pp. 241–265. New York: Random House.

Cleveland, D. B., and Cleveland, A. D. (1983). "Introduction to Indexing and Abstracting." Libraries Unlimited, Littleton, Colorado.

Cleverdon, C. W. (1960). The ASLIB Cranfield research project on the comparative efficiency of indexing systems. *Aslib Proc.* **12**(12), 421–431.

Cleverdon, C. W. (1965). The Cranfield hypothesis. *Libr. Q.* **35**(2), 121–125.

Cleverdon, C. W. (1967). The Cranfield tests on index language devices. *Aslib Proc.* **19**(6), 173–194.

Cleverdon, C. W. (1970). Review of the origins and development of research. 2. Information and its retrieval. *Aslib Proc.* **22**(11), 538–549.

Cleverdon, C. W. (1971). Design and evaluation of information systems. *Annu. Rev. Inf. Sci. Technol.* **6**, 41–73.

Cochrane, P. A. (1978). "Books Are for Use: Final Report of the Subject Access Project to the Council on Library Resources," ED 156 131. School of Information Studies: Syracuse University, Syracuse, New York.

Cochrane, P. A. (1982a). Friendly catalog forgives user errors. *Am. Libr.* **13**(5), 303–306.

Cochrane, P. A. (1982b). Subject access in the online catalog. *Res. Libr. OCLC, Q.* January, pp. 1–7.

Cochrane, P. A. (1983). A paradigm shift in library science. *Inf. Technol. Libr.* **2**(1), 3–4.

Cochrane, P. A. (1984). Modern subject access in the online age. *Am. Libr.* **15**(2–7), 80–83 (conceived as a continuing education series that was to have continued through July/August).

Cochrane, P. A., and Markey, K. (1983). Catalog use studies—Since the introduction of online catalogs: Impact on design for subject access. *Libr. Inf. Sci. Res.* **5**(4), 337–363.

Combs, B. (1973). TYMNET: A distributed network. *Datamation* **19**(7), 40–43.

Connor, J. H. (1967). Selective dissemination of information: A review of the literature and the issues. *Libr. Q.* **37**(4), 373–391.

Connor, J. H. (1971). *In* "Key Papers in Information Science" (A. W. Elias, ed.), pp. 135–153. American Society for Information Science, Washington, D. C.

Cooper, M. D. (1979). The economics of library size: A preliminary inquiry. *Libr. Trends* **28**(1), 878–879.

Cooper, M. D. (1983). The economies of scale in academic libraries. *Libr. Res.* **5**, 207–219.

Cooper, M. D. (1984). Economies of scale in large academic libraries. *Libr. Inf. Sci. Res.* **6**, 321–333.

Cooper, M. D. (1986). Economic issues and trends in academic libraries. *In* "The Economics of Research Libraries" (M. M. Cummings, ed.), Appendix A, pp. 141–174. Council on Library Resources, Washington, D. C.

Council on Library Resources (1986). "Annual Report, 1986." Council on Library Resources, Washington, D. C.

Cox, K. A. (1971). Federal communications policy and library information networks. *In* "Proceedings of the Conference on Interlibrary Communications and Information Networks" (J. Becker, ed.), pp. 6–10. American Library Association, Chicago, Illinois.

Cox, N. S. M., Dews, J. D., and Dolby, J. L. (1967). "The Computer and the Library." The Role of the Computer in the Organization and Handling of Information in Libraries." Archon Books, Hamden, Connecticut.

Crane, D. (1968). "Social Structure in a Group of Scientists: Test of the 'Invisible College' Hypothesis. Johns Hopkins University, Baltimore, Maryland.

Crystal, M. I., and Jakobson, G. E. (1982). FRED, a front end for databases. *Online (Weston, Conn.)* **6**(5), 27–30.

Cuadra, C. A. (1966). Introduction to the ADI annual review. *Annu. Rev. Inf. Sci. Technol.* **1**, 1–14.

Cuadra, C. A. (1971a). On-line systems: Promise and pitfalls. *J. Am. Soc. Inf. Sci.* **22**(2), 107–114.

Cuadra, C. A. (1971b). Library automation and networks. *In* "Network Concepts: Four Points of View" (R. A. Matzek, ed.), pp. 4–18. Catholic Library Association, Haverford, Pennsylvania.

Cuadra, C. A. (1975). SDC experiences with large databases. *J. Chem. Inf. Comput. Sci.* **15**(1), 48–51.

Cuadra, C. A. (1978). Commercially funded on-line retrieval services—Past, present and future. *ASLIB Proc.* **30**(1), 2–15.

Cuadra, C. A. (1980). The role of the private sector in the development and improvement of library and information services. *Libr. Q.* **50**(1), 94–111.

Cuadra, C. A. (1981). A brief introduction to electronic publishing. *Electron. Publ. Rev.* **1**(1), 29–34.

Cuadra, C. A. (1985). Integrating the personal computer into a multiuser database environment. *In* "National Online Meeting, 6th, New York, 1985?" (M. E. Williams and T. H. Hogan, eds.). Learned Information, Medford, New Jersey.

Cuadra, C. A. (1986). The coming era of local electronic libraries. *In* "Libraries and Information Science in the Electronic Age" (H. Edelman, ed.), pp. 11–22. ISI Press, Philadelphia, Pennsylvania.

Cuadra, C. A. (1987). History offers clues to the future: User control returns. *Online (Weston, Conn.)* **11**(1), 46–48.

Cuadra Calls for Ground-Rules on Downloading. (1983). *Online Rev.* **7**(1), 8.

Cuadra Associates (1979). "Directory of Online Databases: A Quarterly." Cuadra Associates, Santa Monica, California.

Cuadra, N. G. (1981). STAR: A microcomputer system of data entry, retrieval and publication support. *Electron. Publ. Rev.* **1**(2), 131–138.

Cummings, M. M., ed. (1986). "The Economics of Research Libraries." Council on Library Resources, Washington, D. C.

Davis, C., compiler (1980). "Library Science: A Dissertation Bibliography." University of Illinois, Urbana/Champaign.

Davis, R. M. (1965). A history of automated displays. *Datamation* **11**, 24–28.

Davis, R. M. (1966). Man–machine communication. *Annu. Rev. Inf. Sci. Technol.* **1**, 221–254.

Davis, R. M. (1971). The national biomedical communications network as a developing structure. *In* "Proceedings of the Conference on Interlibrary Communications and Information Netoworks" (J. Becker, ed.), pp. 294–309. American Library Association, Chicago, Illinois.

Davis, R. M. (1971). The National Biomedical Communications Network as a Developing Structure. *Bulletin of the Medical Library Association* **59**(1), 1–20.

Davis, R. M. (1987). Where will technology put the library of the 21st century. *Bulletin of the Medical Library Association* **75**(1), 1–6.

Davis, W. S., and McCormack, A. (1979). "The Information Age." Addison-Wesley, Reading, Massachusetts.

Debons, A., and Montgomery, K. L. (1974). Design and evaluation of information systems. *Annu. Rev. Inf. Sci. Technol.* **9**, 25–55.

De Gennaro, R. (1967a). Discussion. In A. H. Chapin et al. "Needs and Aims: The Situation at the British Museum, the Bodleian Library, Oxford, and Cambridge University Library." *In* "The Brasenose Conference on the Automation of Libraries" (J. Harrison and P. Laslett, eds.), pp. 2–22. Information/Publishing Ltd., London.

De Gennaro, R. (1967b). A strategy for conversion of research library catalogs to machine readable form. *Coll. Res. Libr.* **28**(4), 253–257.

De Gennaro, R. (1968). The development and administration of automated systems in academic libraries. *J. Libr. Autom.* **1**(1), 75–91.

De Gennaro, R. (1971a). *In* "Key Papers in Information Science" (A. W. Elias, ed.), pp. 181–197. American Society for Information Science, Washington, D. C.

De Gennaro, R. (1971b). Introduction. *In* "Network Concepts: Four Points of View" (R. A. Matzek, ed.), pp. 19–21. Catholic Library Association, Haverford, Pennsylvania.

De Gennaro, R. (1973). Providing bibliographic services from machine-readable data bases—The library's role. *J. Libr. Autom.* **6**(4), 215–222.

De Gennaro, R. (1975a). Library automation: The second decade. *J. Libr. Autom.* **8**(1), 3–4.

De Gennaro, R. (1975b). Public Notice: We librarians are no longer responsible for the debts of our former suitors. *Am. Libr.* **6**(8), 456–457.

De Gennaro, R. (1976). Library automation: Changing patterns and new directions. *Libr. J.* **101**(1), 175–183.

De Gennaro, R. (1977). Wanted: A minicomputer serials control system. *Libr. J.* **102**(8), 878–879.

De Gennaro, R. (1979a). Research libraries enter the information age. *Libr. J.* **104**(20), 2405–2410. (the Richard Rogers Bowker Memorial Lecture).

De Gennaro, R. (1979b). From monopoly to competition: The changing library network scene. *Libr. J.* **104**(11), 1215–1217.

De Gennaro, R. (1980). The role of the academic library in networking. *In* "Networks for Networkers: Critical Issues in Cooperative Library Development" (B. E. Markuson and B. Woolls, eds.), pp. 304–308. Neal-Schuman, New York.

De Gennaro, R. (1982). Libraries, technology, and the information marketplace. *Libr. J.* **107**, 1045–1054.

De Gennaro, R. (1984a). Will success spoil OCLC? *Libr. J.* **109**(6), 626.

De Gennaro, R. (1984b). Shifting gears: Information technology and the academic library. *Libr. J.* **109**(11), 1204–1209.

de Sola Pool, I. (1974). "A Study of Worldwide Packet-Switched Data Communication and Information Retrieval Systems." Institute of Technology, Center for Policy Alternatives, Cambridge, Massachusetts.

de Sola Pool, I. (1976). International aspects of computer communications. *Telecommun. Policy* **1** (1), 33–51.

de Sola Pool, I. (1979). The problems of WARC [World Administrative Radio Conference]: The U. S. faces WARC. *J. Commun.* **29**(1), 187–196.

de Sola Pool, I. (1983a). "Forecasting the Telephone: A Retrospective Technology Assessment." ABEE Publishers, Norwood, New Jersey.

de Sola Pool, I. (1983b). "Technologies for Freedom." Belknap Press, Cambridge, Massachusetts.

de Solla Price, D. J. (1965a). "Little Science, Big Science." Columbia Univ. Press, New York.

de Solla, Price, D. J. (1965b). Networks of scientific papers. *Science* **149** 510–515.

Dick, R. S. (1984). The integrated library system; A historical overview. *Inf. Technol. Libr.* **3**(2), 144–148.

Dodson, J. T. (1974). OCLC comes to the southwest. *Tex. Libr. J.* **50**(1), 15–16.

Doszkocs, T. E. (1978). An associative interactive dictionary (AID) for online bibliographic searching. *Proc. Am. Soc. Inf. Sci. Annu. Meet.* pp. 105–109.

Drew, D. L., Summit, R. K., Tanaka, R. I., and Whiteley, R. B. (1966). An on-line technical library reference retrieval system. *Am. Doc.* **17**(1), 3–7.

Dreyfus, H. L. (1979). "What Computers Can't Do: The Limits of Artificial Intelligence," Rev. ed. Harper & Row, New York.

Elias, A. W., ed. (1971). "Key Papers in Information Science." American Society for Information Science, Washington, D. C.

Eller, J. L., and Panek, R. L. (1968). Thesaurus development for a decentralized information network. *Am. Doc.* **19**(3), 213–220.

Emling, J. M., Harris, J. R., and McMains, H. H. (1964). Networks of Communications. *In* "Libraries and Automation" (B. E. Markuson, ed.), pp. 203–219. Library of Congress, Washington, D. C.

Enright, B. J. (1985). Review of F. G. Kilgour, "Collected Papers," 2 vols. Online Computer Library Center (OCLC) Dublin, Ohio, 1984. *J. Doc.* **41**(1), 40–43.

Evans, G. T. (1973). Bibliographic data centers in New York State. *In* "Proceedings of the 1973 Clinic on Library Applications of Data Processing" (F. W. Lancaster, ed.), pp. 150–164. Graduate School of Library Science, University of Illinois, Urbana-Champaign.

Evans, G. T. (1979). On-line library networking: A bibliographic essay. *Am. Soc. Inf. Sci. Bull.* **5** (5), 11–13.

Evans, G. T. (1981). Library networks. *Annu. Rev. Inf. Sci. Technol.* **16**, 211–245.

Evans, G. T. (1983). Library networking in the United States, 1982. *In* "The Bowker Annual of Library and Book Trade Information" (J. O'Hare and F. L. Schick, eds.), 28th ed., pp. 70–76. Bowker, New York.

Fairthorne, R. A. (1965). Some basic comments on retrieval testing. *J. Doc.* **21**(4), 267–270.

Fairthorne, R. A. (1969). The scope and aims of the information sciences and technologies. *In* "International Federation for Documentation on Theoretical Problems of Informatics," FID 435, (Skera and Cleveland, eds.) pp. 25–31, Viniti, Moscow.

Fano, R. M., and Corbato, F. J. (1966). Time-sharing on computers. *Sci. Am.* **215**, 128–136, 138, 140.

Farradane, J. (1948). The scientific approach to documentation. *In* "The Royal Society Scientific Information Conference 21 June–2 July, 1948," Pap. No. 22, pp. 422–429. Royal Society, London.

Feigenbaum, E. A., and McCorduck, P. (1983). "The Fifth Generation: Artificial Intelligence and Japan's Computer Challenge to the World." Addison-Wesley, Reading, Massachusetts.

Ferguson, D., Kaske, N. K., Lawrence, G. S., Matthews, J. R., and Zich, B. (1982). The CLR public online catalog study: An overview. *Inf. Technol. Libr.* **1**(2), 84–88.

Fischer, M. (1966). The KWIC index concept: A retrospective view. *Am. Doc.* **17**(2), 57–70.

Foskett, D. J. (1973). Information science as an emergent discipline: Educational implications. *J. Librarianship* **5**(3), 161–174.

Freedman, M. J., and Malinconico, S. M., eds. (1979). "The Nature and Future of the Catalog: Proceedings of the American Library Association's Information Science and Automation Division's 1975 and 1977 Institutes on the Catalog." Oryx Press, Phoenix, Arizona.

Freeman, M. E. (1968). The science information exchange as a source of information. *Spec. Libr.* **59** (2), 86–90.

Frisch, I. T., and Frank, H. (1975). Computer communications: How we got where we are. *AFIPS Conf. Proc.* **44**, 109–117.

Fry, B. M. (1953). "Library Organization and Management of Technical Report Literature." Catholic University of America Press, Washington, D. C.

Fry, B. M. (1972). "Evaluation Study of ERIC Products and Services," Vols. I–IV, ED 060, pp. 923–926; Summ. Vol. ED 060, p. 922. Graduate Library School, Indiana University, Bloomington.

Fry, B. M. (1973). Information storage and retrieval has come of age. *Inf. Storage Retr.* **9**(1), i–ii (editorial).

Fuller, R. B. (1970). General systems theory. *In* Operating Manual for Spaceship Earth," Pocket Books, pp. 51–67. Pocket Books, New York.

Fussler, H. H. (1973). "Research Libraries and Technology: A Report to the Sloan Foundation." Univ. of Chicago Press, Chicago, Illinois.

Gardner, J. W. (1964). "Self Renewal." Harper & Row, New York.

Gardner, J. W. (1965). How to prevent organizational dry rot. *Harper's Mag.* **231**(1385), 20–26.

Garfield, E. (1955). Citation indexes for science. *Science* **122**, 108–111.

Garfield, E. (1959). A unified index to science. *In* "Proceedings of the International Conference on Scientific Information," Vol. 1, pp. 461–474. National Academy of Science, National Research Council, Washington, D. C.

Garfield, E. (1961). An algorithm for translating chemical names to molecular formulas. Ph.D. Dissertation, University of Pennsylvania, Philadelphia.

Garfield, E. (1967). Primordial concepts, citation indexing, and historio-bibliography. *J. Libr. Hist.* **2**(3), 235–249.

Garfield, E. (1975). Citation analysis, mechanical translation of chemical nomenclature, and the macrostructure of science. *J. Chem. Inf. Comput. Sci.* **15**(3), 153–155.

Garfield, E. (1976). The permuterm subject index: An autobiographical review. *J. Am. Soc. Inf. Sci.* **27**(5), 288–291.

Garfield, E. (1977). "Essays of an Information Scientist," 2 vols. ISI Press, Philadelphia, Pennsylvania.

Garfield, E. (1977–1980). "Essays of an Information Scientist," Vol. 3. ISI Press, Philadelphia, Pennsylvania.

Garfield, E. (1978a). Current comments: Information science and technology have come of age— Organizational names should show it. *Curr. Contents* No. 12, p. 6.

Garfield, E. (1978b). Current comments. To remember Ralph Shaw. *Curr. Contents* No. 23, p. 5.

Garfield, E. (1978c). Where is chemical information going? *J. Chem. Inf. Comput. Sci.* **18**(1), 1–4.

Garfield, E. (1979). "Citation Indexing—Its Theory and Application in Science, Technology, and Humanities, Preface, pp. xiii–xv. Wiley, New York.

Garfield, E. (1981–1983). "Essays of an Information Scientist," Vol. 4. ISI Press, Philadelphia, Pennsylvania.

Garfield, E. (1983). "Essays of an Information Scientist," Vol. 5. ISI Press, Philadelphia, Pennsylvania.

Garfield, E. (1984). "Essays of an Information Scientist," Vol. 6. ISI Press, Philadelphia, Pennsylvania.

Gaspen, D. K., and Juergens, B., eds. (1980). "Closing the Catalog: Proceedings of the 1978 and 1979 Library and Information Technology Association Institutes." Oryx Press, Phoenix, Arizona.

Gechman, M. C. (1972). Generation and use of machine-readable bibliographic data bases. *Annu. Rev. Inf. Sci. Technol.* **7**, 323–378.

Gilbert, E. N. (1966). Information theory after 18 years. *Science* **152**, 320–326.

Giuliano, V. E. (1979). A manifesto for librarians. *Libr. J.* **104**(16), 1837–1842.

Giuliano, V. E., Ernst, M., Crooks, S., Dunlop, J., Becker, J., and Oettinger, A. (1978). "Into the Information Age: A Perspective for Federal Action on Information." American Library Association, Chicago, Illinois. (a report prepared by Arthur D. Little, Inc. for the National Science Foundation).

Gorman, M. (1979). A modest proposal for a future national bibliographic system. *Am. Libr.* **10**(3), 147–149.

Gorman, M. (1984). Online access and organization and administration of libraries. *In* "Online Catalogs: Online Reference: Converging Trends" (B. Aveny and B. Butlers, eds.), pp. 153–164. American Library Association, Chicago, Illinois.

Gorn, S. (1967). The computer and information sciences and the community of disciplines. *Behav. Sci.* **12**(6), 433–452.

Gough, C., and Srikantaiah, T. (1978). "Systems Analysis in Libraries." Linnet Books, Hamden, Connecticut.

Gould, J. D., and Lewis, C. (1983). Designing for usability—Key principles and what designers think. *In* "Human Factors in Computing Systems: Proceedings of the Association for Computing Machinery, 1983" (A. Janda, ed.), Special Interest Group on Computer and Human Interaction and the Human Factors Society Conference, 1983, pp. 50–53. ACM, New York.

Gray, P. (1979). "LC Post-coordinate searching" (unpublished typescript). Department of Library and Information Science, East Texas State University, Commerce.

Greenberger, M., ed. (1965). "Computers and the World of the Future." MIT Press, Cambridge, Massachusetts (c. 1962).

Greenberger, M., ed. (1971). "Computers, Communications, and the Public Interest." Johns Hopkins Press, Baltimore, Maryland.

Greenberger, M., Aronofsky, J., McKenney, J. L., and Massey, W. F. (1973). Computer and Information Networks. *Science* **182,** 29–35.

Greenwood, P. W., and Weiler, D. M. (1972). "Alternative Models for the ERIC Clearinghouse Network," ED 058 508. Rand Corporation, Santa Monica, California.

Grosch, A. N. (1976). Library automation. *Annu. Rev. Inf. Sci. Technol.* **11,** 225–266.

Gull, C. D. (1956). Seven years of work on the organization of materials in the special library. *Am. Doc.* **7**(4), 320–329.

Haas, W. J. (1982). Network-level decisions: Open commentary. *In* "Information Technology: Critical Choices for Decision-makers" (A. Kent and T. J. Galvin, eds.), pp. 147–156. Dekker, New York.

Hales, C. (1980). The evolution of the international information system on research in documentation. *J. Am. Soc. Inf. Sci.* **31**(4), 293–297.

Hammer, D. P. (1967). National information networks (under: National information issues and trends). *Annu. Rev. Inf. Sci. Technol.* **2,** 385–417.

Hammer, D. P., ed. (1976). "The Information Age: Its Development, Its Impact." Scarecrow Press, Metuchen, New Jersey.

Harmon, G. (1969). Information science as an integrative discipline. *ASIS Annu. Meet.* **32,** 459–462.

Harmon, G. (1970). Human memory limits as a factor in the formation of disciplinary systems (Library Science). Ph.D. Thesis, Case Western University, Cleveland, Ohio.

Harmon, G. (1971). Opinion paper on the evolution of information science. *J. Am. Soc. Inf. Sci.* **22**(4), 235–241.

Harmon, G. (1973). "Human Memory and Knowledge: A Systems Approach." Greenwood Press, Westport, Connecticut.

Harrison, J., and Laslett, P., eds. (1967). "The Brasenose Conference on the Automation of Libraries," Proceedings of the Anglo-American Conference on the Mechanization of Library Services held at Oxford under the Chairmanship of Sir Frank Francis and Sponsored by the Old Dominion Foundation of New York, 30 June–3 July 1966. Mansell Information/Publishing Ltd., London.

Hawkins, D. T. (1976). Impact of on-line systems on a literature searching service. *Spec. Libr.* **67**(12), 559–567.

Hawkins, D. T. (1978). Bibliometrics of the online information retrieval literature. *Online Rev.* **2**(4), 345–352.

Hawkins, D. T. (1980a). "Online Information Retrieval Bibliography, 1964–1979." Learned Information, Marlton, New Jersey.

Hawkins, D. T. (1980b). Six years of online searching in an industrial library network. *Sci. Technol. Libr.* **1**(1), 57–77.

Hawkins, D. T. (1981). Online information retrieval systems. *Annu. Rev. Inf. Sci. Technol.* **16,** 171–208.

Hawkins, D. T., and Brown, C. P. (1980). What is an online search? *Online (Weston, Conn.)* **4**(1), 12–18.

Hawkins, D. T., and Levy, L. R. (1985). Front end software for online database searching. Part I. Definitions, systems features and evaluation. *Online (Weston, Conn.)* **9**(6), 30–38.

Hawkins, D. T., and Levy, L. R. (1986a). Front end software for online database searching. Part II. The market place. *Online (Weston, Conn.)* **10**(1), 33–40.

Hawkins, D. T., and Levy, L. R. (1986b). Front end software for online database searching. Part III. Product selection chart and bibliography. *Online (Weston, Conn.)* **10**(3), 49–58.

Hawkins, D. T., and Wagers, R. (1982). Online bibliographic search strategy development. *Online (Weston, Conn.)* **6**(3), 12–19.

Hay, G. A. (1981). The next fifty years in libraries. Reprinted from Reed College. *Reed* **59**(10), 11–14 (for inclusion in Kilgour, 1984a, Vol. 2, pp. 463–466).

Hayes, R. M. (1964). Implications for librarianship of computer technology. *In* "Proceedings of the 1964 Clinic on Library Applications of Data Processing" (H. Goldhor, ed.), pp. 1–6. University of Illinois, Urbana.

Hayes, R. M. (1979). The impact of technology on the governance of library networks: Reactions. *In*

"The Structure and Governance of Library Networks" (A. Kent and T. J. Galvin, eds.), pp. 153–158. Dekker, New York.

Hays, D. G. (1968). "A Billion Books for Education in America and the World: A Proposal," Memo. RM 5574–RC. Rand Corporation, Santa Monica, California.

Heart, F. E., Kahn, R. E., Ornstein, S. M., Crowther, W. R., and Walden, D. C. (1970). The interface message processor for the ARPA computer network. *AFIPS Conf. Proc.* **36,** 551–567.

Heilprin, L. B. (1963). Toward a definition of information science. *In* "Automation and Scientific Communication" (H. P. Luhn, ed.), Short Papers, Part 2, pp. 239–241. American Documentation Institute, Washington, D. C.

Heims, S. J. (1980). "John von Neumann and Norbert Wiener: From Mathematics to the Technologies of Life and Death." MIT Press, Cambridge, Massachusetts.

Henderson, M. (1976). *Federal information centers In* "The Federal Sector." *In* "The Information Age: Its Development, Its Impact" (D. P. Hammer, ed.), pp. 95–97. Scarecrow Press, Metuchen, New Jersey.

Hendricks, D. D. (1973). "A Report on Library Networks," Occas. Pap. No. 108. Graduate School of Library Science, University of Illinois, Urbana.

Herner, S. (1984). Brief History of information science. *J. Am. Soc. Inf. Sci.* **35**(3), 157–163.

Hersey, D. F. (1978). Information systems for research in progress. *Annu. Rev. Inf. Sci. Technol.* **13,** 263–295.

Highfill, W. C. (1969). The relationship of indexing depth to subject catalog effectiveness. Ph.D. Dissertation, University of Illinois, Urbana.

Hildreth, C. R. (1982a). What else can you do with a philosophy degree? Meet Charles Hildreth, metaphysician of online public access catalogs. *Am. Libr.* **13**(10), 657.

Hildreth, C. R. (1982b). "Online Public Access Catalogs: The User Interface." Online Computer Library Center (OCLC), Dublin, Ohio.

Hildreth, C. R. (1983). To Boolean or not to Boolean. "*Inf. Technol. Libr.* **2**(3), 235–237.

Hildreth, C. R. (1984). User feedback in the design process. *In* "Online Catalog Design Issue: A Series of Discussions," Report of a Conference Sponsored by the Council on Library Resources: 1983 September 21–23, Baltimore, Maryland, (B. Aveny, ed.), pp. 67–102. Council on Library Resources, Washington, D. C.

Hildreth, C. R. (1985). Online public access catalogs. *Annu. Rev. Inf. Sci. Technol.* **20,** 233–285.

Hines, T. C., and Harris, J. L. (1968). "Book Reviews: Thesaurus of ERIC Descriptors." U. S. Office of Education, Resources Information Center, Bureau of Research, U. S. Gov. Printing Office, Washington, D. C. *Am. Doc.* **19**(4), 418–419.

Hobbs, L. C. (1976). A look at the future. *Computers* December 1, pp. 9–10.

Hollaar, L. A. (1979). Unconventional computer architectures for information retrieval. *Annu. Rev. Inf. Sci. Technol.* **14,** 129–151.

Holmes, E., and Armstrong, A. A. (1982). Whither OCLC? *Bull. Am. Soc. Inf. Sci.* **8**(6), 16–19.

Hopkins, J. (1973). The Ohio College library center. *Libr. Resour. Tech. Serv.* **17**(3), 308–319.

Huffenberger, M. A., and Wigington, R. L. (1979). Database management systems. *Annu. Rev. Inf. Sci. Technol.* **14,** 153–190.

Humphrey, H. H. (1970). Information for peace. *J. Am. Soc. Inf. Sci.* **21**(1), 4–7.

Huskey, H. D. (1970). Computer technology. *Annu. Rev. Inf. Sci. Technol.* **5,** 73–139.

Immroth, J. P. (1971). "Analysis of Vocabulary Control in a Library of Congress Classification and Subject Headings." Libraries Unlimited, Littleton, Colorado.

International Conference on Scientific Information. (1959). "Proceedings of an International Conference on Scientific Information," Washington, D. C., week of November 17, 1958, 2 vols. Academy of Sciences, National Research Council, Washington, D. C.

Jahoda, G. (1960). "Correlative Indexing Systems for the Control of Research Records" (Library Science). D. L. S. School of Library Service, Columbia University, New York.

Journal of Library Automation (1977). *J. Libr. Autom.* **10**(2), 101–180.

Kallenbach, S., and Jacobson, S. (1980). Staff response to changing systems: From manual to OCLC to RLIN. *J. Acad. Librarianship* **6**(5), 264–267.

Kantor, P. B. (1982). Evaluation of feedback in information storage and retrieval systems. *Annu. Rev. Inf. Sci. Technol.* **17,** 99–120.

Kaske, N. K., and Ferguson, D. (1980). "On-line Public Access to Library Bibliographic Data Bases: Developments, Issues and Priorities," Final Report to the Council on Library Resources, ED 195 275, OCLC 800 1575. OCLC, Inc., and the Research Libraries Group, Columbus, Ohio.

Kaske, N. K., and Sanders, N. P. (1983). ''A Comprehensive Study of Online Public Access Catalogs: An Overview and Application of Findings,'' Final Report to the Council on Library Resources, Vol. 3, ED 231 404. Online Computer Library Center, Inc., Dublin, Ohio.

Katter, R. V. (1969). Design and evaluation of information systems. *Annu. Rev. Inf. Sci. Technol.* **4**, 31–70.

Katter, R. V., and McCarn, D. B. (1971). AIM-TWX: An experimental on-line bibliographic retrieval system. *In* ''Interactive Bibliographic Search: The User/Computer Interface'' (D. E. Walker, ed.), pp. 121–141. AFIPS Press, Montvale, New Jersey.

Katter, R. V., and Pearson, K. M., Jr. (1975). MEDLARS II: A third generation bibliographic production system. *J. Libr. Autom.* **8**(2), 87–97.

Katz, W. A., ed. (1982a). ''Introduction to Reference Work: Reference Services and Reference Processes,'' 4th ed., Vol. 2. McGraw-Hill, New York.

Katz, W. A. (1982b). Networks and interlibrary loan. *In* ''Introduction to Reference Work: Reference Services and Reference Processes'' (W. A. Katz, ed.), 4th ed., Vol. 2, pp. 207–254. McGraw-Hill, New York.

Kehl, W. (1973). The UCLA campus computing network: An ARPANET resource. *Educom* **8**(4), 10–17.

Kehoe, C. A. (1985). Interfaces and expert systems for online retrieval. *Online Rev.* **9**(6), 489–505.

Kemeny, J. G. (1965). c. 1962. A library for 2000 A.D. *In* ''Computers and the World of the Future'' (M. Greenberger, ed.), pp. 134–178. MIT Press, Cambridge, Massachusetts.

Kemeny, J. G. (1971). Large time-sharing networks. *In* ''Computers, Communications, and the Public Interest'' (M. Greenberger, ed.), pp. 1–36. Johns Hopkins Press, Baltimore, Maryland.

Kemeny, J. G. (1972). ''Man and the Computer.'' Scribner's, New York.

Kent, A., and Galvin, T. J., eds. (1978). ''The On-Line Revolution in Libraries,'' Proceedings of the 1977 Conference in Pittsburgh, Pennsylvania. Dekker, New York.

Kent, A., and Galvin, T. J., eds. (1979). ''The Structure and Governance of Library Networks,'' Proceedings of the 1978 Conference in Pittsburgh. Dekker, New York.

Kent, A., and Galvin, T. J., eds. (1982). ''Information Technology: Critical Choices for Library Decision-makers.'' Dekker, New York.

Kent, A. *et al.* (1962). ''The Library of Tomorrow—Today and Information Service of Educational Research Materials,'' NDEA - VIIB170, ED 003 251. Western Reserve University, School of Library Science, Cleveland, Ohio.

Kershner, L. M. (1979). Research libraries information network. *Bull. Am. Soc. Inf. Sci.* **5**(5), 20–21.

Kesner, R. M., and Jones, C. H. (1984). ''Microcomputer Applications in Libraries: A Management Tool for the 1980s and Beyond,'' New Directions in Librarianship, No. 5. Greenwood Press, Westport, Connecticut.

Kessler, H. E. (1974). Education, computing and networking: a review and prospect. *Educom* **9**(1), 2–8.

Kessler, M. M. (1965). The MIT technical information project. *Phys. Today* **18**(3), 28–36.

Kiewitt, E. L. (1979). ''Evaluating Information Retrieval Systems: The Probe Program.'' Greenwood Press, Westport, Connecticut.

Kilgour, F. G. (1967). Comprehensive modern library systems. *In* ''The Brasenose Conference on the Automation of Libraries'' (J. Harrison and P. Laslett, eds.), pp. 46–56. Mansell Information/Publishing Ltd., London.

Kilgour, F. G. (1968a). Computers for university libraries. Introduction. *Drexel Libr. Q.* **4**(3), 155–157.

Kilgour, F. G. (1968b). Computers for university libraries. University Libraries and computation. *Drexel Libr. Q.* **4**(3), 156–176.

Kilgour, F. G. (1968c). Retrieval of single entries from a computerized library catalog file. *Proc. Am. Soc. Inf. Sci.* **5**, 133–136.

Kilgour, F. G. (1968d). Initial system design for the Ohio College center: A case history. *In* ''Proceedings of the 1968 Clinic on Library Applications of Data Processing'' (D. E. Carroll, ed.), pp. 79–88. University of Illinois, Urbana.

Kilgour, F. G. (1969). Library automation. *Annu. Rev. Inf. Sci. Technol.* **4**, 305–337.

Kilgour, F. G. (1970). A regional network—Ohio College Library Center. *Datamation* **16**(2), 87–89.

Kilgour, F. G. (1973). Catalog records retrieved by personal author using derived search keys. *J. Libr. Autom.* **6**(2), 103–108.

Kilgour, F. G. (1976). Historical development of library computerization. *In* "The Information Age: Its Development, Its Impact" (D. P. Hammer, ed.), pp. 241–257. Scarecrow Press, Metuchen, New Jersey.

Kilgour, F. G. (1979a). Shared cataloging at OCLC. *Online Rev.* **3**(3), 275–279.

Kilgour, F. G. (1979b). "Description of a Computerized On-Line Interlibrary Loan System," ED 185 989. Educational Resources Information Center, Washington, D. C.

Kilgour, F. G. (1979c). Design of online catalogs. *In* "The Nature and Future of the Catalog: Proceedings of the American Library Association's Information Science and Automation Divisions 1975 and 1977 Institutes on the Catalog," (M. J. Freedman and S. M. Melinconico, eds.), pp. 34–41; discussion with S. Lubetsky and others, pp. 41–45. Oryx Press, Phoenix Arizona.

Kilgour, F. G. (1979d). Interlibrary loans on-line. *Libr. J.* **104**(4), 460–463.

Kilgour, F. G. (1979e). In OCLC's Letter to Users dated August 29.

Kilgour, F. G. (1980). New information systems (acceptance speech upon receiving the 15th Award of Merit from the American Society for Information Science at their 42nd annual meeting, October 17, 1979, at Minneapolis, Minnesota). *Bull. Am. Soc. Inf. Sci.* **6**(3), 13.

Kilgour, F. G. (1983). Public policy and national and international networks. *Inf. Technol. Libr.* **2** (3), 239–245.

Kilgour, F. G. (1984a). "Collected Papers" (compiled by P. A. Becker and A. T. Dodson; edited by L. L. Yoakam), 2 vols. Online Computer Library Center (OCLC), Dublin, Ohio.

Kilgour, F. G. (1986). "Libraries and Information Science in the Electronic Age" pp. 1–10. ISI Press, Philadelphia, Pennsylvania.

Kilgour, F. G., Long, P. L., and Leiderman, E. B. (1970). Retrieval of bibliographic entries from a name–title catalog by use of truncated search keys. *Proc. Am. Soc. Inf. Sci.* **7**, 79–82.

Kilgour, F. G., Long, P. L., Leiderman, E. B., and Landgraf, A. L. (1971). Title-only entries retrieved by use of truncated search keys. *J. Libr. Autom.* **4**(4), 207–210.

King, D. W. (1968). Design and evaluation of information systems. *Annu. Rev. Inf. Sci. Technol.* **3**, 61–103.

King, D. W., and Bryant, E. C. (1971). "The Evaluation of Information Services and Products." Information Resources Press, Washington, D. C.

King, D. W., Edmundson, H. P., Flood, M. M., Kochen, M., Libby, R. L., Swanson, D. R., and Wyley, A. (1963). "Automation and the Library of Congress." Library of Congress, Washington, D. C.

Kitagawa, T. (1968). "Information Science and Its Connection with Statistics." Research Institute of Fundamental Information Science, Kyushu University, Fukuoka, Japan.

Knox, W. T. (1966). Toward national information networks. *Phys. Today* **19**(1), 39–44.

Kochen, M. (1969). Stability in the growth of knowledge. *American Documentation* **20**(3), 186–197.

Kochen, M. (1974). Views on the foundations of information science. *In* "Information Science, Search for Identity" (A. Debons, ed.), pp. 171–187. Dekker, New York.

Kraft, D. H., and McDonald, D. D. (1976). Library operations research, its past and our future. *In* "The Information Age: Its Development, Its Impact" (D. P. Hammer, ed.), pp. 122–144. Scarecrow Press, Metuchen, New Jersey.

Kronick, D. A. (1985). Citation indexing and analysis. *In* "The Literature of the Life Sciences: Reading, Writing, Research," pp. 128–139. ISI Press, Philadelphia, Pennsylvania.

Kruzas, A., and Schmittroth, J., Jr., eds. (1981). "New Information Systems and Services: A Periodic Supplement to Encyclopedia of Information Systems and Services." Gale Research, Detroit, Michigan.

Lacy, D. (1969). The traditional library. *In* "Library Networks: Promise and Performance" (L. Carnovsky, ed.), pp. 13–22. Univ. of Chicago Press, Chicago, Illinois.

Lancaster, F. W. (1968a). "Evaluation of the MEDLARS Demand Search Service." National Library of Medicine, Bethesda, Maryland.

Lancaster, F. W. (1968b). "Information Retrieval Systems: Characteristics, Testing and Evaluation." Wiley, New York.

Lancaster, F. W. (1969). Evaluating the performance of a large computerized information system. *JAMA, Am. Med. Assoc.* **207**(1), 114–120.

Lancaster, F. W. (1972a). "Vocabulary Control for Information Retrieval." Information Resources Press, Washington, D. C.

Lancaster, F. W. (1972b). "Evaluation of On-Line Searching in MEDLARS (AIM-TWX) by Biomedical Practitioners,'' Occas. Pap. No. 101. Graduate School of Library Service, University of Illinois, Urbana-Champaign.

Lancaster, F. W. (1978a). Whither libraries or wither libraries. *Coll. Res. Libr.* **39**(5), 345–357.

Lancaster, F. W. (1978b). ''Toward Paperless Information Systems.'' Academic Press, New York.

Lancaster, F. W. (1979). ''Information Retrieval Systems: Characteristics, Testing and Evaluation,'' 2nd ed. Wiley, New York.

Lancaster, F. W., and Fayen, E. G. (1973). ''Information Retrieval On-Line.'' Melville Publ. Co., Los Angeles, California.

Lancaster, F. W., and Gillespie, C. J. (1970). Design and evaluation of information systems. *Annu. Rev. Inf. Sci. Technol.* **5**, 33–70.

Lancaster, F. W., and Jenkins, G. T. (1970). Quality control ''applied'' to the operations of a large information system. *J. Am. Soc. Inf. Sci.* **21**(5), 370–371.

Lazerow, S. (1974). Institute for scientific information. *Encycl. Libr. Inf. Sci.* **12**, 89–97. (reprinted in *Curr. Contents* No. 1, pp. R-1–R-8).

Lee, J. M., ed. (1982). ''Who's Who in Library and Information Services.'' American Library Association, Chicago, Illinois.

Lewis, P., Pearse, L., and Schieber, P. (1986). Highlights of users council meeting, September 21–23, 1986. *OCLC Newsl.* November pp. 15–18.

Library of Congress, chief (1978). Processing Department and Subject Cataloging Division. Letter to Dorothy B. Lilley, dated November 27.

Licklider, J. C. R. (1960). Man–computer symbiosis. *IRE Trans. Hum. Factors Electron.* **HFE-1**, 4–11.

Licklider, J. C. R., ed. (1965). ''Libraries of the Future,'' Report of a study sponsored by the Council on Library Resources, Inc. MIT Press, Cambridge, Massachusetts.

Licklider, J. C. R. (1968). Man–computer communication. *Annu. Rev. Inf. Sci. Technol.* **3**, 201–240.

Licklider, J. C. R. (1971). A hypothetical plan for a library-information network. *In* ''Proceedings of the Conference on Interlibrary Communications and Information Networks'' (J. Becker, ed.), pp. 310–316. American Library Association, Chicago, Illinois.

Little, A. D., Inc. (1978). ''A New Governance Structure for OCLC: Principles and Recommendations.'' Scarecrow Press, Metuchen, New Jersey.

Long, P. L. (1973). OCLC: From concept to functioning network. *In* ''Proceedings of the 1973 Clinic on Library Applications of Data Processing'' (F. W. Lancaster, ed.), pp. 165–170. Graduate School of Library Science, University of Illinois, Urbana/Champaign.

Long, P. L. (1976). Computer technology—An update. *Annu. Rev. Inf. Sci. Technol.* **11**, 211–222.

Lorenz, J. G. (1977). The national bibliographic network: The view from the research library. *J. Libr. Autom.* **10**(2), 114–119.

Luhn, H. P. (1953). A new method of recording and searching information. *Am. Doc.* **4**(1), 14–16.

Luhn, H. P. (1957). A statistical approach to mechanized encoding and searching library information. *IBM J. Res. Dev.* **1**(4), 309–317.

Luhn, H. P. (1958a). The automatic creation of literature abstracts. *IBM J. Res. Dev.* **2**(2), 159–165 and 317.

Luhn, H. P. (1958b). A business intelligence system. *IBM J. Res. Dev.* **2**, 314–319.

Luhn, H. P. (1959a). ''Keyword-in-Context Index for Technical Literature (KWIC Index),'' Rep. RC-127. IBM Corporation, Advanced System Development Division, Yorktown Heights, New York.

Luhn, H. P. (1959b). ''Selective Dissemination of New Scientific Information with the Aid of Electronic Processing Equipment.'' IBM Corporation, Advanced System Development, Yorktown Heights, New York.

Luhn, H. P. (1960). *Am. Doc.* **11**(4), 288–295.

Luhn, H. P. (1959c). The IBM Universal Card Scanner for Punched Card Information Searching Systems. *In* ''Studies in Coordinate Indexes'' (Taube, ed.), Volume 5, pp. 112–139. Documentation, Inc., Washington, D. C.

Luhn, H. P. (1968a). *In* ''H. P. Luhn: Pioneer of Information Science'' (C. K. Schultz, ed.), p. 26. Spartan Books, New York.

Luhn, H. P. (1968b). *In* ''H. P. Luhn: Pioneer of Information Science'' (C. K. Schultz, ed.), pp. 118–125. Spartan Books, New York.

Luhn, H. P. (1968c). *In* "H. P. Luhn: Pioneer of Information Science" (C. K. Schultz, ed.), pp. 227–235. Spartan Books, New York.

Luhn, H. P. (1968d). *In* "H. P. Luhn: Pioneer of Information Science" (C. K. Schultz, ed.), pp. 246–254. Spartan Books, New York.

McCarn, D. B. (1978). Online systems—Techniques and services. *Annu. Rev. Inf. Sci. Technol.* **13**, 85–124.

McCarthy, J. (1965). Time-sharing computer systems. *In* "Computers and the World of the Future" (M. Greenberger, ed.), pp. 220–248. MIT Press, Cambridge, Massachusetts.

McGill, M. J., and Huitfeldt, J. (1979). Experimental techniques of information retrieval. *Annu. Rev. Inf. Sci. Technol.* **14**, 93–127.

Machlup, F. (1962). "The Production and Distribution of Knowledge in the United States." Princeton Univ. Press, Princeton, New Jersey.

McLuhan, M. (1964). "Understanding Media: The Extensions of Man." McGraw-Hill, New York.

Malinconico, S. M. (1977). Introduction. *J. Libr. Autom.* **10**(2), 101–102.

Malinconico, S. M. (1982). Frederick Gridley Kilgour: ALA life membership award. *Inf. Technol. Libr.* **1**(3), 295–296.

Malinconico, S. M., and Rizzolo, J. A. (1973). The New York Public Library automated book catalog subsystem. *J. Libr. Autom.* **6**(1), 3–36.

Mandel, C. A., and Herschman, J. (1983). Online subject access—Enhancing the library catalog. *J. Acad. Librarianship* **9**(3), 148–155.

Markuson, B. E., ed. (1964). "Libraries and Automation," Proceedings of the Conference on Libraries and Automation held at Airlie Foundation, Warrenton, Virginia, May 26–30, 1963, under the sponsorship of the Library of Congress, The National Science Foundation and the Council on Library Resources. Library of Congress, Washington, D. C.

Markuson, B. E. (1966). A system development study for the Library of Congress automation program. *Libr. Q.* **36**(3), 197–233.

Markuson, B. E. (1967). Automation in libraries and information centers. *Annu. Rev. Inf. Sci. Technol.* **2**, 255–284.

Markuson, B. E. (1976). Library networks: Progress and problems. *In* "The Information Age: Its Development, Its Impact" (D. P. Hammer, ed.), pp. 34–59. Scarecrow Press, Metuchen, New Jersey.

Markuson, B. E. (1980). Revolution and evolution: Critical issues in library network development. *In* "Networks for Networkers: Critical Issues in Cooperative Library Development" (B. E. Markuson and B. Woolls, eds.), pp. 3–28. Neal-Schuman, New York.

Markuson, B. E., and Woolls, B., eds. (1980). "Networks for Networkers: Critical Issues in Cooperative Library Development." Neal-Schuman, New York.

Maron, M. E. (1961). Automatic indexing: An experimental inquiry. *J. Assoc. Comput. Mach.* **8**, 404–417.

Maron, M. E. (1971). *In* "Key Papers in Information Science" (A. W. Elias, ed.), pp. 94–107. American Society for Information Science, Washington, D. C.

Maron, M. E., and Kuhns, J. L. (1960). On relevance, probabilistic indexing and information retrieval. *J. Assoc. Comput. Mach.* **7**, 216–244.

Marron, B., and Fife, D. (1976). Online systems—Techniques and services. *Annu. Rev. Inf. Sci. Technol.* **11**, 163–210.

Martin, S. K. (1983). Governance issues for automated library networks: The impact of and implications for large research libraries. Ph.D. Dissertation. Library and Information Studies, Graduate Division of the University of California at Berkeley.

Martin, T. H. (1973). The user interface in interactive systems. *Annu. Rev. Inf. Sci. Technol.* **8**, 203–219.

Mathews, W. D. (1979). The impact of technology on the governance of library networks. *In* "The Structure and Governance of Library Networks" (A. Kent and T. J. Galvin, eds.), pp. 121–140. Dekker, New York.

Matzek, R. A., ed. (1971). "Network Concepts: Four Points of View." Catholic Library Association, Haverford, Pennsylvania.

Mauchley, J. W. (1965). Panel discussion. *In* "Computers and the World of the Future" (M. Greenberger, ed.), p. 238. MIT Press, Cambridge, Massachusetts.

Meadow, C. T. (1970). "Man–Machine Communication." Wiley (Interscience), New York.

Meise, N. R. (1969). "Conceptual Design of an Automated National Library System." Scarecrow Press, Metuchen, New Jersey.

Miles, W. D., ed. (1982). "A History of the National Library of Medicine." U. S. Department of Health and Human Services, Public Health Services, National Institutes of Health, National Library of Medicine, Washington, D. C.

Miller, R. F., and Tighe, R. L. (1974). Library and information networks. *Annu. Rev. Inf. Sci. Technol.* **9**, 173–219.

Mills, R. G. (1967). Man–machine communication and problem solving. *Annu. Rev. Inf. Sci. Technol.* **2**, 223–254.

Milstead, J. L. (1984). "Subject Access Systems: Alternatives in Design." Academic Press, Orlando, Florida.

Moffett, W. A. (1979). College libraries and a national information policy: Whistling in the grave yard. *Coll. Res. Libr.* **40**(1), 22–25.

Mohrhardt, F. E. (1964). Documentation: A synthetic science. *Wilson Libr. Bull.* **38**(9), 743–749.

Molz, R. K. (1984). The establishment of NCLIS. *In* "National Planning for Library Service 1935–1975," pp. 110–120. American Library Association, Chicago, Illinois.

Mooers, C. N. (1960). The next twenty years in information retrieval—some goals and predictions. *American Documentation* **11**(3), 229–236.

Moore, B. B., and Young, C. C. (1985). Library/information services and the nation's elderly. *J. Am. Soc. Inf. Sci.* **36**(6), 364–368.

Moore, H. (1968). H. P. Luhn, engineer. *In* "H. P. Luhn: Pioneer of Information Science" (C. K. Schultz, ed.), pp. 16–20. Spartan Books, New York.

Moran, L. P. (1976). National agricultural library. *Encycl. Libr. Inf. Sci.* **19**, 27–45.

Mumford, L. Q. (1964). Welcoming address. *In* "Libraries and Automation" (B. E. Markuson, ed.), pp. 7–8. Library of Congress, Washington, D. C.

Naisbitt, J. (1982). "Megatrends: Ten New Directions Transforming our Lives." Warner Books, New York.

National Agricultural Library (1983). NAL Overhaul urged by blue ribbon federal panel. *Libr. J.* **108**(6), 536.

National Commission on Library and Information Science (NCLIS) (1975). "Toward a National Program for Library and Information Services: Goals for Action." NCLIS, Washington, D. C.

National Commission on Library and Information Science (NCLIS) (1977). "Effective Access to the Periodical Literature: A National Program." NCLIS, Washington, D. C.

National Commission on Library and Information Science (NCLIS) (1983). NCLIS task force on cultural minorities reports. *Libr. J.* **108**(21), 2190–2192.

National Commission on Libraries and Information Science (NCLIS). 1983–1984. Annual Report. Washington, D.C.: NCLIS.

National Commission on Libraries and Information Science (NCLIS) (1983–1984). "Response to 'A Nation at Risk,'" Annual Report, pp. 13–15. NCLIS, Washington, D. C.

National Commission on Library and Information Science (NCLIS) (1984). NCLIS statement urges strong school libraries. *Sch. Libr. J.* **30**, 80–81.

Neufeld, M. L., and Cornog, M. (1986). Database history: From dinosaurs to compact discs. *J. Am. Soc. Inf. Sci.* **37**(4), 183–190.

Nilles, J. M. (1984). Computer. *Colliers Encycl.* **7**, 113–132.

Noyce, R. N. (1977). Microelectronics. *Sci. Am.* **237**(3), 63–69. September.

OCLC, Inc. (1978). OCLC becomes democratized, nationwide corporation. *Am. Libr.* **9**(1), 4.

OCLC, Inc. (1980). OCLC creator to return to creative activities. *Am. Libr.* **11**, 186.

O'Connor, J. (1973). Text searching retrieval of answer-sentences and other answer passages. *J. Am. Soc. Inf. Sci.* **24**(6), 445–460.

O'Connor, J. (1975). Retrieval of answer sentences and answer-figures from papers by text searching. *Inf. Process. Manage.* **11**(5–7), 155–164.

Oettinger, A. G. (1969). "Run, Computer, Run: The Mythology of Educational Innovation: An Essay by Anthony G. Oettinger with the Collaboration of Sema Marks." Harvard Univ. Press, Cambridge, Massachusetts.

Ohio College Library Center (OCLC) (1973). Ivy libraries to use OCLC. *Coll. Res. Libr. News* **34**(5), 101–102.

O'Leary, M. (1986). Wilsonline: Online power for every library. *Database* **9**(2), 102–107.

Olson, E. E., Shank, R., and Olsen, H. A. (1972). Library and information networks. *Annu. Rev. Inf. Sci. Technol.* **7**, 279–321.

O'Neill, E. T., and Aluri, R. (1979). "Research Report on Subject Heading Patterns in OCLC Monographic Records." OCLC, Inc., Columbus, Ohio.

Otten, K., and Debons, A. (1970). Towards a metascience of information: Informatology. *J. Am. Soc. Inf. Sci.* **21**(1), 89–94.

Overhage, C. F. J. (1969). Information networks. *Annu. Rev. Inf. Sci. Technol.* **4**, 339–377.

Overhage, C. F. J., and Harmon, R. J. (1965). "Planning Conference on Information Transfer Experiments (INTREX)." MIT Press, Cambridge, Massachusetts.

Paisley, W. J. (1965a). Extent of information-seeking as a function of subjective certainty and the utility of information. Ph.D. Dissertation, Stanford University, Stanford, California.

Paisley, W. J. (1965b). "The Flow of (Behavioral) Science Information: A Review of the Research Literature." Institute for Communications Research, Stanford, California.

Paisley, W. J. (1986). The convergence of communication and information science. *In* "Libraries and Information Science in the Electronic Age" (H. Edelman, ed.), pp. 122–153. ISI Press, Philadelphia, Pennsylvania.

Palmour, V. E., and Roderer, N. K. (1978). Library resource sharing through networks. *Annu. Rev. Inf. Sci. Technol.* **13**, 147–177.

Palmour, V. E., Bryant, E. C., Caldwell, N. W., and Gray, L. M. (1972). "A Study of the Characteristics, Costs and Magnitude of Interlibrary Loans in Academic Libraries." Greenwood Publ. Co., Westport, Connecticut [study conducted for Association of Research Libraries ARL].

Palmour, V. E., Bellassi, M. C., and Gray, L. M. (1974a). "Access to Periodical Resources: A National Plan." Association of Research Libraries (ARL), Washington, D. C.

Palmour, V. E., Bellassi, M. C., and Roderer, N. K. (1974b). "Resource and Bibliographic Support for a Nationwide Library Program." National Commission on Libraries and Information Science (NCLIS), Washington, D. C.

Parker, E. B., and Paisley, W. J. (1966). Research for psychologists at the interface of the scientist and his information system. *Am. Psychol.* **21**(11), 1061–1071.

Parker, E. B., and Paisley, W. J. (1971). *In* "Key Papers in Information Science" (A. W. Elias, ed.), pp. 56–66. American Society for Information Science, Washington, D. C.

Parker, R. W. (1965). The SABRE system. *Datamation* **11**, 49–52.

Penniman, W. D., Krohn, R. E., and Kovacs, G. J. (1974). A framework for the study of emerging network technology. *J. Am. Soc. Inf. Sci.* **25**(6), 378–380.

Peters, J. R. (1981). AGRICOLA. *Database* **4**(1), 13–27.

Plotnik, A., Jacobs, B., McKinnen, M. J., Mitchell, E., McCormick, E., and Wilkins, J., eds. (1975). Washington library power: Who has it, and how it works for you. *Am. Libr.* **6**(11), 647–674.

Power, D. L., Woody, C. A., Scott, F., and Fitzgerald, M. P. (1976). SCORPIO, a subject content oriented retriever for processing information on-line. *Spec. Libr.* **67**, 285–288.

Pratt, A. D. (1975). Libraries, economics and information: Recent trends in information science literature. *Coll. Res. Libr.* **36** (1), 33–38.

Pratt, A. D. (1984). Microcomputers in libraries. *Annu. Rev. Inf. Sci. Technol.* **19**, 247–269.

Preston, G. A. (1982). A foot in both camps: Using RLIN and OCLC. *Libr. J.* **107**, 1948–1951.

Pritchard, S. M. (1981). "Scorpio: A Study of Public Users of the LC Information System" ED 198 801. Library of Congress, Washington, D. C.

Ramsey, H. R., and Grimes, J. D. (1983). Human factors in interactive computer dialog. *Annu. Rev. Inf. Sci. Technol.* **18**, 29–59.

Reader's Digest (1986). Reader's Digest exec editor named to head NCLIS. *Am. Libr.* **17**(8), 576–578.

Reed, M. J. P., and Vrooman, H. T. (1979). Library automation. *Annu. Rev. Inf. Sci. Technol.* **14**, 193–216.

Rees, A. M. (1963). Semantic factors, role indicators *et alia;* eight years of information retrieval at Western Reserve University. *Aslib Proc.* **15**(12), 350–363.

Rees, A. M. (1967). Evaluation of information systems and services. *Annu. Rev. Inf. Sci. Technol.* **2**, 63–86.

Renmore, C. D. (1980). "Silicon Chips and You." Beaufort Books, New York.

Reynolds, D. (1985). "Library Automation: Issues and Applications." Bowker, New York.

Rider, F. (1944). "The Scholar and the Future of the Research Library: A Problem and Its Solution." Hadham Press, New York.

Roberts, L. G. (1976). Development of packet switching networks worldwide. *Telecommunications* **10**(10), 28–32.

Roberts, L. G., and Wessler, B. D. (1970). Computer network development to achieve resource sharing. *In* "American Federation of Information Processing Society (AFIPS), Spring Joint

Computer Conference, Atlantic City, New Jersey," Proc. 36, pp. 543–549. Thompson, Washington, D. C.

Robinson, B. M. (1980). Cooperation and competition among library networks. *J. Am. Soc. Inf. Sci.* **31**(6), 413–424.

Rogers, F. B. (1960a). Review articles: Storing and retrieving information. *In* "Emerging Solutions for Mechanizing the Storage and Retrieval of Information" (compiled by M. Taube), Stud. Coord. Index., Vol. 5. Documentation Inc., Washington, D. C.

Rogers, F. B. (1960b). *Coll. Res. Libr.* **21**(6), 489–492.

Rohrbach, P. T. (1985). "Find: Automation at the Library of Congress: The First Twenty-Five Years and Beyond." Library of Congress, Washington, D. C.

Royal Society (1948). "Royal Society Scientific Information Conference 21 June–2 July, 1948." Royal Society, London.

Salton, G. (1970). Automatic text analysis. *Science* **168**, 335–343.

Salton, G. (1971a). Automatic indexing using bibliographic citations. *J. Doc.* **27**(2), 98–110.

Salton, G., compiler (1971b). "The SMART Retrieval System: Experiments in Automatic Document Processing." Prentice-Hall, Englewood Cliffs, New Jersey.

Samuel, A. L. (1965). "Time-sharing on a Multiconsole Computer," Proj. MAC-TR-16. Massachusetts Institute of Technology, Cambridge, Massachusetts.

Samuelson, K. (1971a). Worldwide information networks. *In* "Proceedings of the Conference on Interlibrary Communications and Information Networks" (J. Becker, ed.), pp. 317–328. American Library Association, Chicago, Illinois.

Samuelson, K. (1971b). International information transfer and network communication. *Annu. Rev. Inf. Sci. Technol.* **6**, 277–324.

Saracevic, T. (1969). Comparative effects of titles, abstracts, and full texts on relevance judgments. *Proc. Am. Soc. Inf. Sci.* **6**, 293–299.

Saracevic, T. (1970a). On the concept of relevance in information science (computer science). Ph.D. Thesis, Case Western Reserve University, Cleveland, Ohio.

Saracevic, T. (1970b). Ten years of relevance experimentation; a summary and synthesis of conclusions. *Proc. Am. Soc. Inf. Sci.* **7**, 33–36.

Saracevic, T. (1976). Relevance: A review of the literature and a framework for thinking on the notion in information science. *In* "Advances in Librarianship" (M. J. Voigt, ed.), Vol. 6, pp. 79–138. Academic Press, New York.

Schiller, H. (1963). What is MEDLARS? *Libr. J.* **88**(5), 949–953.

Schipma, P. B. (1975). Generation and use of machine-readable data bases. *Annu. Rev. Inf. Sci. Technol.* **10**, 237–271.

Schmittroth, J., Jr., ed. (1971). "Encyclopedia of Information Systems."

Schmittroth, J., Jr., ed. (1983). "Encyclopedia of Information Systems and Services," 5th ed. Gale Research, Detroit, Michigan (previously edited by A. Kruzas).

Schramm, W. (1955). Information theory and mass communication. *Journalism Q.* **32**(2), 131–146.

Schultz, C. K., ed. (1968). "H. P. Luhn: Pioneer of Information Science." Spartan Books, New York.

Segal, J. A. S. (1985). Networking and decentralization. *Annu. Rev. Inf. Sci. Technol.* **20**, 203–231.

Sewell, W. (1964). Medical subject headings in MEDLARS. *Bull. Med. Libr. Assoc.* **52**(1), 164–170.

Shannon, C. E., and Weaver, W. (1949). "The Mathematical Theory of Communication." Univ. of Illinois Press, Urbana.

Shaw, R. R. (1951). Machines and the bibliographical problems of the twentieth century. *In* "Bibliography in an Age of Science" (L. N. Ridenour, R. R. Shaw, and A. G. Hill, eds.), pp. 37–71. Univ. of Illinois Press, Urbana.

Sher, M. S. (1974). A case study in networking. *Datamation* **20**(3), 56–59.

Shera, J. H. (1966). "Documentation and the Organization of Knowledge." Archon Books, Hamden, Connecticut.

Shera, J. H. (1972). Documentation into information science. *Am. Libr.* **3**(7), 785–790.

Shera, J. H. (1978). Taube, Mortimer—(1910–1969). *In* "Dictionary of American Library Biography" (G. S. Bobinski *et al.*, eds.), pp. 512–513. Libraries Unlimited, Littleton, Colorado.

Shera, J. H., and Cleveland, D. B. (1977). History and foundations of information science. *Annu. Rev. Inf. Sci. Technol.* **12**, 249–275.

Simms, R. L., and Fuchs, E. (1970). Communications technology. *Annu. Rev. Inf. Sci. Technol.* **5**, 113–139.

Skipper, J. E. (1967). Discussion. *In* "The Brasenose Conference on the Automation of Libraries" (J. Harrison and P. Laslett, eds.), p. 126. Mansell Information/Publishing Ltd., London.

Skolnik, H. (1976). Milestones in chemical information science. *J. Chem. Inf. Comput. Sci.* **16**(4), 187–193.

Slamecka, V. (1968). Graduate programs in information science at the Georgia Institute of Technology. *Spec. Libr.* **59**(4), 246–250.

Smith, L. C. (1979). Selected artificial intelligence techniques in information retrieval systems research. Ph.D. Dissertation, Syracuse University, School of Information Studies, Syracuse, New York.

Smith, L. C. (1980). Artificial intelligence applications in information systems. *Annu. Rev. Inf. Sci. Technol.* **15**, 67–105.

Sproull, L., Weiner, S., and Wolf, D. (1978). "Organizing an Anarchy: Belief, Bureaucracy, and Politics in the National Institute of Education," Univ. of Chicago Press, Chicago, Illinois.

Stanford University (1975). Stanford University's BALLOTS system: Project BALLOTS and the Stanford University libraries. *J. Libr. Autom.* **8**(1), 31–50.

Stern, B. T. (1977). Evaluation and design of bibliographic data bases. *Annu. Rev. Inf. Sci. Technol.* **12**, 3–30.

Stevens, C. H. (1977). Governance of library networks. *Libr. Trends* **26**(2), 219–240.

Stevens, C. H. (1979). Emerging network services. *Am. Soc. Inf. Sci. Bull.* **5**(5), 26.

Stevens, N. D. (1977). Modernizing OCLC's governance. *Libr. J.* **102**(19), 2216–2219.

Stevens, N. D. (1980). An historical perspective on the concept of networks; some preliminary considerations. *In* "Networks for Networkers: Critical Issues in Cooperative Library Development" (B. E. Markuson and B. Woolls, eds.), pp. 29–48. Neal-Schuman, New York.

Stibitz, G. R., and Larrivee, J. A. (1957). "Mathematics and Computers." McGraw-Hill, New York.

Strachey, C. (1960). Time-sharing in large fast computers. *In* "Information Processing," Proc. Int. Conf. Inf. Process., UNESCO, Paris 15–20 June, 1959, pp. 336–341. UNESCO, Paris (cited in Greenberger, 1965, p. 222).

Stratford, J. S. (1984). "OCLC and RLIN: The comparisons studied. *Coll. Res. Libr.* **45**, 123–127.

Summary of a debate between Roderick G. Schwartz and Glyn T. Evans (1980). *In* "Networks for Networkers: Critical Issues in Cooperative Library Development" (B. E. Markuson and B. Woolls, eds.), Appendix A, Part 2, pp. 342–344. Neal-Schuman, New York.

Summit, R. K. (1975a). Information retrieval—Make vs. buy. *In* "Information Systems and Networks" (J. Sherrod, ed.), pp. 101–103. Greenwood Press, Westport, Connecticut.

Summit, R. K. (1975b). Lockheed experience in processing large data bases for its commercial information retrieval service. *J. Chem. Inf. Comput. Sci.* **15**(1), 40–42.

Summit, R. K. (1979). The impact of technology on the governance of library networks—response. *In* "The Structure and Governance of Library Networks" (A. Kent and T. J. Galvin, eds.), pp. 149–151. Dekker, New York.

Summit, R. K. (1987). Online information: A ten-year perspective and outlook. *Online (Westport, Conn.)* **11**(1), 61–64.

Summit, R. K., and Drew, S. J. (1976). The public library as an information center: An experiment in information retrieval services for the general public. *In* "Proceedings of the 1975 Clinic on Library Applications of Data Processing" (F. W. Lancaster, ed.), pp. 91–102. University of Illinois, Urbana/Champaign.

Summit, R. K., and Firschein, O. (1974). Document retrieval systems and techniques. *Annu. Rev. Inf. Sci. Technol.* **9**, 285–331.

Summit, R. K., and Firschein, O. (1977). Public library use of online bibliographic retrieval services: Experience in four public libraries in northern California. *Online (Weston, Conn.)* **1**(4), 58–64.

Svenonius, E. (1971). The effect of specificity on retrieval performance. Ph.D. Dissertation, ED 051 863. University of Chicago, Chicago, Illinois.

Swanson, D. R. (1965). Evidence underlying the Cranfield results. *Libr. Q.* **35**(1), 1–20.

Swanson, D. R. (1980). Evolution, libraries, and the national information policy. *In* "Networks for Networkers: Critical Issues in Cooperative Library Development" (B. E. Markuson and B. Woolls, eds.), pp. 80–99. Neal-Schuman, New York.

Swanson, R. W. (1975). Design and evaluation of information systems. *Annu. Rev. Inf. Sci. Technol.* **10**, 43–101.

Taine, S. I. (1961). The National Library of Medicine Index Mechanization Project. *Bull. Med. Libr. Assoc.* **49**(1), Part 2, 1–96.

Taine, S. I. (1963). Bibliographic data processing at the National Library of Medicine. *Proc. Clin. Libr. Process. Libra., 1963* pp. 109–132.

Taube, M. (1951). Functional approach to bibliographic organization: A critique and a proposal. *In* "Bibliographic Organization" (J. H. Shera and M. E. Egan, eds.), pp. 57–71. Univ. of Chicago Press, Chicago, Illinois.

Taube, M. (1959). The Comac: An Efficient Punched Card Collecting System for Storage and Retrieval of Information. *In* "Studies in Coordinate Indexes" (M. Taube, ed.), Volume 5, pp. 72–85. Documentation, Inc., Washington, D. C.

Taube, M. (1961). "Computers and Common Sense." Columbia Univ. Press, New York.

Taube, M. (1964). The coming of age of information technology. *Bull. Med. Libr. Assoc.* **52**(1), 120–127.

Taube, M., and Wooster, H., eds. (1958). "Information Storage and Retrieval: Theory, Systems, and Devices." Columbia Univ. Press, New York.

Taube, M. (1953–1959). "Studies in Coordinate Indexing," Vols. 1–5. Documentation, Inc., Bethesda, Maryland.

Tauber, M. F., and Lilley, O. L. (1960). "Feasibility Study Regarding the Establishment of an Educational Media Research Information Service." Columbia University, School of Library Service, New York.

Tenopir, C. (1983). Full text, downloading and other issues. *Libr. J.* **108**(11), 1111–1113.

Tenopir, C. (1984a). Full-text databases. *Annu. Rev. Inf. Sci. Technol.* **19**, 215–246.

Tenopir, C. (1984b). Retrieval performance in a full text journal article database. Ph.D. Dissertation. University of Illinois, Urbana.

Tenopir, C. (1984c). Newspapers online. *Libr. J.* **109**(4), 452–453.

Tenopir, C. (1985). Searching Harvard Business Review online. . . . Lessons in searching a full text database. *Online (Westport, Conn.)* **9**(1), 71–75.

Tenopir, C. (1986a). Online searching in schools. *Libr. J.* **111**(2), 60–61.

Tenopir, C. (1986b). Databases on CD-ROM. *Libr. J.* **111**(4), 68–69.

Tenopir, C. (1986c). Change or crisis in the database industry. *Libr. J.* **111**(6), 46–47.

Tenopir, C. (1986e). *InfoTrac:* A laser disc system. *Libr. J.* **111**(14), 168–169.

Tenopir, C. (1987). Online education: Planning for the future. *Online (Westport, Conn.)* **11**(1), 65–66.

Three new NCLIS members; three NCLIS activities. (1985). *Libr. J.* **110**(18), 13–14.

Tighe, R. (1974). Hoist by their own petard. *J. Libr. Autom.* **7**(1), 3–4.

Tocatlian, J. (1973). UNISIST implementation plans. *Proc. Am. Soc. Inf. Sci.* **9**, 9–14.

Toffler, A. (1980). "The Third Wave." Morrow, New York.

Tomberg, A. (1977). European information networks. *Annu. Rev. Inf. Sci. Technol.* **12**, 219–246.

Travis, I. L., and Fidel, R. (1982). Subject analysis. *Annu. Rev. Inf. Sci. Technol.* **17**, 123–157.

Trester, D. J. (1981). "ERIC—The First Fifteen Years, 1964–1979: A History of the Educational Resources Information Center." ERIC Processing and Reference Facility, Bethesda, Maryland.

Trezza, A. F. (1977a). The NCLIS view—A full-service network. *J. Libr. Autom.* **10**(2), 170–176.

Trezza, A. F. (1979). Closing summary. *In* "The Structure and Governance of Library Networks" (A. Kent and T. J. Galvin, eds.), pp. 339–346. Dekker, New York.

Trezza, A. F. (1981). How information networks may develop and accommodate to future trends. *In* "Strategies for Meeting the Information Needs of Society in the Year 2000" (M. Boaz, ed.), pp. 101–116. Libraries Unlimited, Littleton, Colorado.

Trezza, A. F. (1982). "Toward a Federal Library and Information Services Network: A Proposal." Library of Congress, Washington, D. C.

Troan, J. (1963). "An Adventure in Knowledge: The Story of Chemical Abstracts Service." American Chemical Society, Washington, D. C.

Turing, A. M. (1947). "Intelligent Machinery." Written in Cambridge University in 1947—not published for thirty years. Reference to this paper in Feigenbaum and McCorduck (1983, pp. 155–156).

Turing, A. M. (1950). Computing machinery and intelligence. *In* "Perspectives on the Computer Revolution" (Z. W. Pylyshyn, ed.), pp. 224–245. Prentice-Hall, Englewood Cliffs, New Jersey.

Turtle, H., Penniman, W. D., and Hickey, T. (1981). Data entry/display devices for interactive information retrieval. *Annu. Rev. Inf. Sci. Technol.* **16**, 55–83.

University of Chicago Library (1968). "Development of an Integrated Computer-Based Bibliographical Data System for a Large University Library," PB-179426. University of Chicago, Chicago, Illinois.

University of Maryland (1966). Maryland Library School gets $85,936. USOE grant to train ERIC indexers. *Libr. J.* **91**(14), 3674.

U. S. National Science Foundation, Office of Scientific Information (1969). "Current Research and Development in Scientific Documentation 1957–1969." U. S. Govt. Printing Office, Washington, D. C.

U. S. National Science Foundation, Office of Scientific Information (1957). "Current Research and Development in Scientific Documentation 1957," No. 1. U. S. Govt. Printing Office, Washington, D. C.

U. S. National Science Foundation. Office of Scientific Information (1959). "Current Research and Development in Scientific Documentation 1959," No. 3. U. S. Govt. Printing Office, Washington, D. C.

U. S. National Science Foundation. Office of Scientific Information (1966). "Current Research Development in Scientific Documentation" No. 14. U. S. Govt. Printing Office, Washington, D. C.

U. S. White House Conference on Library and Information Services (1980). "Summary, 1980." U. S. Govt. Printing Office, Washington, D. C.

Verhoeff, J., Goffman, W., and Belzer, J. (1961). Inefficiency of the use of Boolean functions for information retrieval systems. *Commun. ACM* **4**(12), 557–558 and 594.

Vickery, B. C. (1961). "On Retrieval System Theory." Butterworth, London.

Vickery, B. C. (1973). The nature of information science. *In* "Toward a Theory of Librarianship. Papers in Honor of Jesse Hauk Shera" (C. H. Rawski, ed.), pp. 147–168. Scarecrow Press, Metuchen, New Jersey.

Voight, M. J. (1976). Europe's plan for a coordinated information system: EURONET. *Libr. J.* **101** (10), 1183–1185.

von Bertalanffy, L. (1968). "General Systems Theory: Foundations, Development, Applications." Braziller, New York.

Walker, D. E., ed. (1971). "Interactive Bibliographic Search. The User/Computer Interface." AFIPS Press, Montvale, New Jersey.

Wanger, J. (1979). Education and training for online systems. *Annu. Rev. Inf. Sci. Technol.* **14**, 219–245.

Wanger, J., and Landau, R. N. (1980). Nonbibliographic on-line data base services. *J. Am. Soc. Inf. Sci.* **31**(3), 171–180.

Wanger, J., Cuadra, C. A., and Fishburn, M. (1976). "Impact of Online Retrieval Services: A Survey of Users, 1974–75." Systems Development Corporation, Santa Monica, California.

Warheit, I. A. (1972). On-line interactive systems in libraries, now and in the future. *In* "Proceedings of the 1972 Clinic on Library Application of Data Processing" (F. W. Lancaster, ed.), pp. 3–21. University of Illinois, Urbana.

Wasserman, A. I. (1974). Psychological factors in information system design. *Proc. Annu. Conf., Assoc. Comput. Mach., 29th, 1974* Vol. 2, p. 743.

Wedgeworth, R. (1980). Coordinating national library programs. *In* "Networks for Networkers: Critical Issues in Cooperative Library Development" (B. E. Markuson and B. Woolls, eds.), pp. 100–108. Neal-Schuman, New York.

Weinberg, A. M. (1963). "Science, Government and Information: The Responsibilities of the Technical Community and the Government in Transfer of Information," Report of the President's Advisory Committee. U. S. Govt. Printing Office, Washington, D. C.

Weinstock, M. (1967). Network concepts in scientific and technical libraries. *Spec. Libr.* **58**(5), 328–334.

Weisbrod, D. L. (1974). Frederick G. Kilgour. *Libr. Resour. Tech. Serv.* **18**(4), 402–405.

Weisman, H. (1967). Information and the discipline of communication sciences. *In* "Levels of Interaction between Man and Information" (P. J. Fasana, ed.), Vol. 4, pp. 8–12. American Documentation Institute, Washington, D. C.

Wellisch, H. (1972). From information science to informatics: A terminological investigation. *J. Librarianship* **4**(3), 157–187.

Welsh, W. J. (1966). Compatibility of systems. *In* "Data Processing in Public and University Libraries" (J. Harvey, ed.), pp. 79–93. Spartan Books, Washington, D. C.

Welsh, W. J. (1979). Welch [*sic*] defines LC's mission. *Am. Libr.* **10**(6), 293 (reply to Gorman's article in Am/Lib. March, 1979, pp. 147–149).

Welsh, W. J. (1985). Foreword. *In* "Find: Automation at the Library of Congress. The First Twenty-Five Years and Beyond" (R. T. Rohrback, ed.), Library of Congress, Washington, D. C. (FIND is a computer search command that the researcher can enter on the computer keyboard to gain access to data from the automated cataloging system at the Library of Congress).

Wente, V. A. (1971). NASA/RECON and user interface considerations. *In* "Interactive Bibliographic Search: The User–Computer Interface" (D. E. Walker, ed.), pp. 95–104. AFIPS Press, Montvale, New Jersey.

Werdel, J. A., and Steele, R. A. (1979). International activities in information science and technology R & D. *Bull. Am. Soc. Inf. Sci.* **5**(3), 12–13.

Wertz, J. A. (1964). Possible applications of data processing equipment in libraries. *In* "Proceedings of the 1964 Clinic on Library Applications of Data Processing" (H. Goldhor, ed.), pp. 112–117. University of Illinois, Urbana.

White, H. S. (1965). In memorium: Dr. Mortimer Taube. *Spec. Libr.* **56**(8), 603.

Wiener, N. (1948). 1961. "Cybernetics: Or Control and Communication in the Animal and the Machine," 2nd ed. Wiley, New York.

Wiener, N. (1950). "The Human Use of Human Beings: Cybernetics and Society." Houghton Mifflin, Boston, Massachusetts.

Wiener, N. (1956). "I Am a Mathematician." Doubleday, New York.

Wilde, D. U. (1976). Generation and use of machine-readable data bases. *Annu. Rev. Inf. Sci. Technol.* **11**, 267–298.

Williams, J. G. (1977). Performance criteria and evaluation for a library resource sharing network. *In* "Library Resource Sharing" (A. Kent and T. J. Galvin, eds.), pp. 225–277. Dekker, New York.

Williams, M. E. (1974). Use of machine-readable data bases. *Annu. Rev. Inf. Sci. Technol.* **9**, 221–284.

Williams, M. E. (1975a). Progress and problems of the data base community. *J. Am. Soc. Inf. Sci.* **26**(5), 305–306.

Williams, M. E. (1975b). Criteria for evaluation and selection of data bases and data base services. *Spec. Libr.* **66**(12), 561–569.

Williams, M. E., editor-in-chief (1976). "Computer-Readable Bibliographic Data Bases: A Directory and Data Source Book," 1st ed. American Society for Information Sciences, Washington, D. C. (loose leaf, subscription basis, describes 301 data bases. Three updates from April 1977 to December 1978).

Williams, M. E. (1977a). Data bases—A history of developments and trends from 1966 through 1975. *J. Am. Soc. Inf. Sci.* **28**(2), 71–78.

Williams, M. E. (1977b). Networks for on-line data base access. *J. Am. Soc. Inf. Sci. Technol.* **28** (5), 247–253.

Williams, M. E. (1977c). The impact of machine-readable data bases on library and information services. *Inf. Process. Manage.* **13**(2), 95–107.

Williams, M. E. (1977d). On-line problems: Research today, solutions tomorrow. *Bull. Am. Soc. Inf. Sci. Technol.* **3**(4), 14–16.

Williams, M. E., editor-in-chief (1979). "Computer-Readable Bibliographic Data Bases: A Directory and Data Source Book," 2nd ed. American Society for Information Sciences, Washington, D. C. (describes 528 databases).

Williams, M. E., editor-in-chief (1982). "Computer-Readable Data Bases: A Directory and Data Source Book," 3rd ed. Knowledge Industries Publications, White Plains, New York (describes 773 databases).

Williams, M. E. (1984). Highlights of the online database field—Statistics, pricing and new delivery mechanisms. *In* "National Online Meeting" (M. E. Williams, and T. H. Hogan, compilers), pp. 1–4. Learned Information, Medford, New Jersey.

Williams, M. E. (1985a). Information science and transparent systems. *Bull. Am. Soc. Inf. Sci.* **11** (4), 5–7, 24.

Williams, M. E. (1985b). Electronic databases. *Science* **228**, 445–456.

Williams, M. E., editor-in-chief (1985c). "Computer-Readable Data Bases: A Directory and Data Source Book," 4th ed. American Library Association, Chicago, Illinois (describes 2,805 databases).

Williams, M. E. (1986). Transparent information systems through gateways, front ends, intermediaries and interfaces. *J. Am. Soc. Inf. Sci.* **37**(4), 204–214.

Williams, M. E. (1988). Defining information science and the role of ASIS. *Bull. Am. Soc. Inf. Sci.* **14**(2), 17–19.

Williams, P. W., and Goldsmith, G. (1981). Information retrieval on mini- and microcomputers. *Annu. Rev. Inf. Sci. Technol.* **16**, 85–111.

Wooster, H. (1971). Current research and development in scientific documentation. *Encycl. Libr. Inf. Sci.* **6**, 336–365.

Wyatt, J. B. (1973). Computing resource networks: A buyer's perspective. *Proc. Educom Spring Conf.* See *Educom* pp. 30ff. (quoted by Kessler, 1974).

Yang, C.-S. (1978). Design and evaluation of file structures. *Annu. Rev. Inf. Sci. Technol.* **13**, 125–143.

Zunde, P., and Gehl, J. (1979). Empirical foundations of information science. *Annu. Rev. Inf. Sci. Technol.* **14**, 67–93.

Index